THE BIG BOOK OF THE DOLLS' HOUSE

THE BIG BOOK OF THE DOLLS' HOUSE

GUILD OF MASTER
CRAFTSMAN PUBLICATIONS

First published 2005 by
Guild of Master Craftsman Publications Ltd
166 High Street, Lewes
East Sussex, BN7 1XU

Main front and back cover photographs show the Stratford Place house and bakery, from The Dolls' House Emporium. Photograph on back cover (by Alec Nisbett) shows the Gothic Gatehouse by Anglesea Dolls' Houses.

Principal photography by Alec Nisbett ©. For other photographic acknowledgements see page 316.

ISBN 1 86108 485 4

British Cataloguing in Publication Data

A catalogue record of this book is available from the British Library.

Managing Editor Gerrie Purcell
Production Manager Hilary MacCallum
Editor Clare Miller
Art Editor Gilda Pacitti

Colour reproduction by Altaimage Ltd.
Printed and bound in Singapore by Kyodo

This book is for Caroline and Sarah

Imperial and metric
The standard dolls' house scales are 1/12 and 1/24, which were originally based on imperial measures: one inch representing one foot. Many dolls' house hobbyists in Britain and especially in America still use feet and inches. In this book imperial measures are given first, followed by the metric equivalent. Accuracy to the millimetre is generally inappropriate, and metric measurements may be rounded up or down a little.

Contents

INTRODUCTION 8

BASIC TOOLS AND MATERIALS 10

Makeovers

The Modern Dolls' House

1/24 Scale

Introduction

When my first book, *The Complete Dolls' House*, was published twelve years ago, the hobby in Britain was still relatively small. I remember wondering if the book would be well received. I need not have worried! The enthusiasm for dolls' houses and miniatures simply grew and grew, and now, with my seventh book, *Dolls' House Shops, Cafés and Restaurants*, recently published (also by GMC Publications Ltd), I realise that miniaturists are keen to read about their hobby.

They are eager to learn how to tackle a wide range of periods and styles, how to decorate appropriately and with the minimum of problems, how to understand the implications of differences of scale, and how to customise inexpensive furniture so that it looks really special.

The outside of the house can also be made to look welcoming, perhaps with the addition of climbing plants, a flower border or shrubs, and some of the ideas on how to create patios, terraces or gardens may be useful.

Just like real homes, dolls' houses can be furnished with a mixture of 'antiques' and accessories chosen simply because they appeal to us, but unlike the real world, we can do exactly as we like. Even a 21st century dolls' house with a modern kitchen and bathroom may contain 'inherited' items of any period. For such special pieces, like those featured throughout this book, we turn to the professionals.

One way in which the hobby has changed in recent years is the increased interest

▼ An outdoor space provides opportunities to create a busy scene.

▼ The many interesting details in every corner of this Tudor house and bakery make it come alive.

in 1/24 scale, which began in America but took much longer to be accepted in Britain where the standard 1/12 scale was already immensely popular. 1/24 has now also been adopted with enthusiasm by countless makers and hobbyists, so much so, that in 1999 I devoted an entire book to this scale, which has a fascination and charm all of its own.

Decorating and furnishing a house in this smaller size needs a different approach and can be quite a challenge. My book on 1/24 scale is included in this compilation edition, to give you all the information and advice you need, whether you are a beginner or already an experienced miniaturist.

The other big change in the hobby is the enthusiasm for reproducing modern-day homes as well as those from earlier periods. Decorative styles from 1900 to the present-day are all popular, and many professional miniaturists have diversified to make 20th century and even ultra-modern furniture and accessories to complement their established period-style designs.

The modern home offers many exciting possibilities to the hobbyist who wants to tackle something up-to-date. Extracts from my book on *The Modern Dolls' House* are also included here, with many ideas on ways to use economical materials to create new decorative schemes, and also on how to adapt easily-obtainable and inexpensive objects.

I am pleased to have the opportunity to include a selection from some of my earlier books in this one, much bigger, volume. The result is the most comprehensive guide yet to the dolls' house hobby, which will be helpful both to beginners and the more experienced. I hope that you will find everything here that you need to inspire you to try new projects, to refine your skills at decoration, and to complete unusual and attractive schemes in your own special way.

Basic tools and materials

Sharp Tools

Blades on craft knives must be changed frequently. They are inexpensive, and they work effectively only when they are sharp.

A good pair of scissors will be adequate for some purposes, but it is far more difficult to cut perfectly straight lines on paper or card. Using the grid on a cutting mat will save a great deal of time and trouble when cutting parallel edges on wallpaper, etc.

Sharpen pencils often, because the width of the line made by a blunt pencil will make measurements inaccurate.

▼ These tools are essential if you plan to add fixtures and fittings. From the top: plastic and raised edge metal rulers, craft knife, pencil, small screwdriver, bradawl, bulldog clip, small saw.

TOOLS REQUIRED FOR FITTING OUT ROOMS

- Small screwdrivers in a selection of sizes.

- Bradawl (a pointed tool for starting a hole in wood to insert screws).

- Craft knife with replaceable blades.

- Transparent plastic ruler (useful for checking detail when marking out patterns).

- Metal ruler with a raised edge for use as a cutting guide.

- Self-healing cutting mat marked out with a squared grid.

- Metal mitre box and saw (eg X-Acto mitre box no. 7533 and knife handle no. 5 fitted with saw blade no.239). Other makes are available, all of them of a fairly standard size, from suppliers of miniature tools.

- Small saw approximately 7in (180mm) long.

- Pencils (well-sharpened).

- Bulldog clips for holding parts together while glue sets.

- Masking tape.

- Magnifier for checking fine detail.

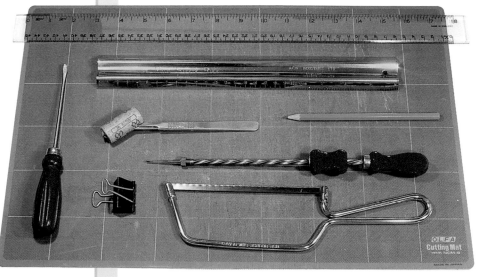

► Tools and glues can be stored away neatly inside the dolls' house while work is in progress. An egg cup makes a useful container for screws.

Safety First

Treat all cutting tools with respect:

Rule 1 To avoid accidents, always check before you cut that your free hand is behind the blade, not in front of it.

Rule 2 Never use cutting tools if you are tired, when it becomes too easy to make a mistake. There is always another day.

Rule 3 Always put a craft knife down while you check or adjust the position of the work. It is easy to forget that you are holding it and to nick yourself.

Glue fumes

Most glues produce fumes to some extent and it is essential to work in a well-ventilated room, preferably with the window open.

Adhesives

Modern adhesives are not interchangeable and work best on the materials for which they are intended. This check list is a brief guide to what is suitable for different materials.

All-purpose clear adhesive For card, paper, wood, ceramics (eg Uhu and Bostik).

PVA whitewood adhesive For permanent fixing of wood: once set, the bond cannot be undone. Evo-Stik Resin 'W' is widely available.

Rubber-based adhesive To attach ceramic tiles to card or wood. Do not use on fabric as this type of glue (eg Copydex) yellows with age.

Superglue To attach ceiling roses, etc. Also use for fixing metal to wood (metal feet, for example, attached to wooden legs on furniture) and to fix together very small parts.

Solid gluestick Generally preferable to paper glue, because it will not crinkle paper by over-wetting.

Suitable paints for interiors

Water-based emulsion paint Interior walls and ceilings and as an undercoat on thinner wooden mouldings.

Gloss paint Do not use.

Semi-matt paint (Satin finish or eggshell finish) Doors, door and window frames, painted panelling.

Model Enamel (Gloss, matt and satin finish) Ornaments and accessories, doorsteps, fireplaces. A few drops can be used as a mixer with emulsion paint.

Gouache (from suppliers of artists' materials) A small amount mixed with emulsion paint and then diluted with a splash of water will produce glowing colours for walls.

Acrylic Can be used as gouache.

Varnish Clear (gloss), matt, semi-matt or coloured. Use varnish formulated for art or craft.

Woodstain Woodstains are useful for fittings and furniture. Wipe on with a dry cloth and use a brush in corners. Can be varnished if shine is wanted.

Makeovers

CHAPTER 1

DECORATION & DISPLAY

There are two main kinds of dolls' house hobbyist: those for whom decorating and making miniatures is an end in itself, and those who prefer to concentrate on collecting. Inevitably, these interests overlap.

Most dolls' house hobbyists, however addicted to making, like to include some professionally made miniatures in their rooms and many like to display attractive miniatures in an appropriate setting.

In a period room the architectural details should be correct and the colour schemes appropriate. In a modern room innovative schemes can include up-to-date designs and simulate new materials.

Adding to your collection

As you buy or make additional miniatures, you may find that some reorganization is necessary. If the decorations already seem perfect it would be a pity to replace them: a simple rearrangement of contents may suffice. Our tastes change, often influenced by current styles of interior decoration, and (as with a real home) renewing the wallpaper or paint colours will sometimes be quite enough to give the room a refreshingly new look.

You may, however, choose to transform the room completely, and there are many ways in which you can achieve this. I here give some examples of changes which will create a different appearance and atmosphere in otherwise similar rooms.

◄ The sumptuously furnished drawing room of this country house is clearly owned by an affluent Georgian family. Despite the grand surroundings it still looks inviting and homely.

Choosing a style

How to arrange your miniatures will depend on whether you want a homely interior or one that will show off a collection as a formal display. An art gallery or antique shop are more formal settings which can work well.

Consider the effect you wish to achieve, but also imagine how this will complement the miniatures you intend to include. Take time to plan the room, and also think about the period.

Collect materials whenever you see them: build up a stock of useful papers, fabrics and other materials for future use. Don't limit yourself to scaled-down versions of the real thing, although these may be best for a period room. After a while the magpie habit will become second nature.

It is worth saving braids and ribbons, lace edgings and gift ties, buttons and jewellery bits and pieces, wallpaper and fabric samples. Giftwrap and pictures from greetings cards are especially useful for modern rooms. The more oddments you have to choose from, the more likely – and the more easily — you are to arrive at an unusual and interesting scheme.

▶ In this comfortable, early nineteenth-century room all the furnishings have been carefully selected for the use and pleasure of the supposed occupants. The wallpaper has been cut and pieced from leftovers of a full-size pattern.

▲ (Top) A spacious hall in an early Victorian house, presented as part of a lived-in home, with evidence of family activities and hobbies.

▲ A later version of the hall now appears as a formal reception area. The major decorative change is to the flooring. Wallpaper and festoon blind remain the same.

◄ This first version of my interior design shop could almost be used as a sitting room. In time, however, the collection of miniatures increased until it warranted a complete rearrangement.

◄ In this later shop layout the decorations are unchanged, but the arrangement gives a very different impression. Which of the two versions do you prefer?

► This small shop measures only 9 in (230 mm) deep, 10$\frac{1}{4}$ in (260 mm) wide and 8 in (200 mm) high. The display space is devoted to dolls' houses which are in 1/144th scale, the right size to suit a 1/12 room.

► The same display space is again used to the full in this second version, where it has been transformed into a modern, upmarket kitchen shop. There are 120 miniatures in this room without it looking overcrowded.

Choose a colour scheme

Start with a basic premise and a selection of colours to choose from. Try out colours using paint sample pots, which are inexpensive and available in most modern paint ranges. For the period room, look at a shade card of authentic historic colours.

If you want to create your own colours do some trial mixes with acrylic paint or artist's gouache and water-based emulsion paint. You will need only a few drops in a neutral base to achieve vivid effects.

As you will know from decorating your own home, a shade can look different in daylight from how it appears in artificial light. Colours also change according to what is placed next to them, and this will be particularly noticeable in the small space of a dolls' house room.

Paint a sample on card and fix papers or fabrics with Blu-tack or double-sided Scotch tape to judge the effect before making a decision. The results may surprise you, and it is worth taking a look at several combinations before you finalize the scheme. It is also worth building up a collection of cuttings from magazines as reference if you plan a modern room or one from a country other than your own. Do not follow ideas slavishly: rather, use them as a starting point.

▲ The painted decoration simulating marbled panels and floor in this stunning room was based on schemes shown in paintings from the early Renaissance. The floor is painted on a resin base, which gives an exceptionally smooth surface. The door is heavily gilded.

▼ A room setting based on the Parrot Room in Sturehov, near Stockholm, elegantly furnished with Gustavian-style furniture. The colour scheme and painted panels look their best in clear Swedish light.

Fireplaces

Most rooms benefit from a focal point and, even where there is central heating this may well be a fireplace. Choose it carefully, as it will set the tone of the room.

◀ In a continental room a tall, woodburning stove, may be used to provide heat.

Some very fine miniature fireplace surrounds are made in cast resin to reproduce the elaborate detail, and they may be a good choice for a period room. Plainer ones, ready to paint, are inexpensive, while fully finished versions with marble or painted surrounds and fitted with grates are available to suit most periods.

ADAPT A PICTURE FRAME

■ A simple way to make two fireplaces is to remove the glass and backing from a small picture frame and cut the frame in two. It may be of wood, leather or resin, any of which can be painted satisfactorily.

▲ The fireplace in an early Tudor home was used both to provide heat and for cooking. A spit to roast meat and a variety of blackened metal pots and griddle plates add realism.

▲ A pretty chimneypiece with carved decoration which would suit a late Georgian, Regency or early Victorian room.

◀ A heavily carved 'stone' fireplace from the sixteenth century features heraldic shields to emphasize the importance of the house owner.

► A simple fireplace which was assembled from cornice moulding left over from another project.

▼ Planning a fireplace design on card before assembly.

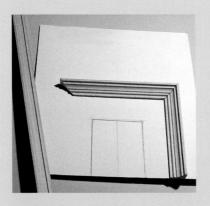

▲ Experimenting with different design ideas. Some mouldings have been painted to show the different styles used, and the pieces are temporarily Blu-tacked to card.

Make a basic fireplace

A plain fireplace can be made from three pieces of wood moulding mitred at the corners, as shown on page 88. Mouldings designed specially for fireplaces are available, but many architrave mouldings are suitable, too. The height of the finished fireplace should relate to the height of the room: experiment with a cardboard cut-out before you decide what will look best.

1 A basic fireplace made from plain stripwood can be built up with additional plain or fancy mouldings to make a more elaborate design, and a mantelshelf can be added.

2 To complete the fireplace, mount on card backing with an aperture cut out for the grate. Glue on ceramic tiles or marbled card to make a surround. Back the aperture with matt black card and glue the entire fireplace to the wall.

▲ An unglazed window on a timber-framed house looks on to a storeroom. Cool air would have helped to keep the food fresh.

Window dressing

Think about the period you wish to replicate. Tudor houses did not at first have glazing in the windows (rudimentary wooden shutters could be closed in order to keep out the wind and rain), whereas late Tudor windows had leaded glazing, supplemented by heavy curtains or tapestries.

Eighteenth-century curtain arrangements helped to define the style of the room and could be either plain white muslin or extravagant drapes. The Victorians added blinds, which were lowered to keep out strong sunlight or to provide privacy. For the dolls' house, such minute quantities of fabric and trimmings are needed that you can afford to use real silk, which will hang well at small windows. Synthetic fabrics have a tendency to stick out, and will not drape well in short lengths.

▲ In this room the two
many-paned windows have
floor-length curtains made from
acid yellow Indian silk trimmed with
thin gold braid. The draping is based
on a Regency example.

▼ Shorter windows in an early
nineteenth-century room are fitted
with lace fixed blinds and ruched
pink silk festoon blinds. This
arrangement neatly solves the
problem of deciding on curtain length.

Use display space to the full

Make sure that all your miniatures can be clearly seen. Any flat surface will serve to display accessories, ornaments and domestic equipment.

A place for everything

Mantelshelves and tables are obvious places for display, but cupboards can be left open to show their contents. Alternatively, you may want to keep tiny items in a drawer – both to stop them rolling away and to create an additional surprise when the drawer is opened.

Dressers through the ages

Dresser shelves can hold a matching dinner or tea service, or a mixture of pottery. The earliest dressers combined a low side table with shelves fitted to the wall above, but before very long this arrangement was amalgamated into a single piece of furniture.

A dresser will fit into most period or modern rooms, as it has never gone out of fashion: today's upmarket country kitchen often boasts a pine dresser filled to overflowing with modern or antique spongeware.

▲ A painted country dresser is filled with kitchen crockery including cheese dishes, spongeware and a Devon 'guggle jug' in the shape of a fish.

▶ The same dresser is now filled with a collection of Staffordshire figures and cookware. Even the top is put to use, showing off lidded jars and vases.

▲ A willow pattern dinner service and a set of mugs in a different design but also in blue-and-white, arranged on a traditional Cotswold-style oak dresser.

▲ A collection of pewter miniatures shows to advantage against darker oak. You can cram on as many pieces as possible without spoiling the effect.

▶ The elegant Regency chiffonier has a similar function to the dresser. The tea service is pewter, handpainted in vivid yellow, while the pleated green silk on the cupboard fronts conceals some of the contents.

Making food

The food shown on the following pages was made by professional miniaturists, but you can make plain food yourself, using one of the modelling compounds which is hardened in the oven. Start with apples, oranges and potatoes to practise the technique before you try something a little more ambitious, such as a cake, chicken or pineapple.

To achieve the most realistic effect, use neutral-coloured modelling compound (instructions for use are provided with the pack). After baking, paint the food with model enamels. Mix colours to achieve the exact shades you want.

◀ Bread, fish and vegetables were staples of the medieval diet, with meat as a rare treat. The fish and bread on this plain table are made of wood and handpainted.

▼ A Tudor banquet may include oysters, a gilded pie, wooden bowls of potage, roast peacock and a boar's head centrepiece. The oranges have been added for effect, not authenticity.

COLOUR MIXES FOR MINIATURE FOOD

■ Apples can be made to look edible by painting in green, yellow or orange shades to give a russet effect. Add a dot with a black fineline pen at the centre top.

■ Oranges are easy too. Use a wooden cocktail stick to rough up the surface of the paint a little before it dries, to create the peel effect.

■ Potatoes for the kitchen or storeroom look realistic if, once the paint is dry, they are dabbed with glue and rolled in instant coffee powder to simulate earth.

▼ Simple food: whole cheeses mature on a plain wooden table.

▼ A well-scrubbed pine table shows food being prepared in a Victorian kitchen. A wooden spice tower and a brass sugar sifter are ready for use.

▲ A Regency supper of fruit, syllabubs, nuts and wine could have been served as a light repast during an evening's entertainment. A glass epergne, fruit stand and decanter add sparkle to the table while the wine is kept cool in a brass-banded mahogany wine cooler.

◄ Dessert could be laid on separate small tables, always (in Victorian times) with a floral centrepiece.

▲ The Victorians paid great attention to the presentation of their food. The table was covered with either white damask or a lacy cloth, while an elaborate floral arrangement or individual nosegays in front of each place setting added to the effect. The centrepiece on this supper table combines flowers with a moulded jelly 'shape'.

▼ Picnic food! A Japanese lunch box or sushi laid on a board is an unusual miniature, and would work well in a modern interior.

Open plan food storage

Before the advent of the refrigerator, even modest homes had a walk-in larder. This was used to store crockery, pans and preserves, and sometimes wine and cider, as well as perishables which needed to be kept cool.

A separate larder in a small room next to the kitchen will allow you to show off a quantity of food and crockery, not only on shelves but perhaps also by using the floor. Should your house have no convenient room adjacent to the kitchen, consider partitioning off a section to use as a larder. A door frame and a non-opening door can be fitted on to the partition wall to suggest access.

▲ A corner for flower-arranging is a useful feature in a country larder: an old cupboard is often used so that vases can be stored below the work surface. This inexpensive cupboard has been stripped and repainted to simulate a distressed finish.

◄ This larder has a floor of 'Welsh slate' cut from a magazine picture. For more realism, use miniature roofing slates, cut into squares, or ceramic flagstones.

Make a walk-in larder

Plan your larder carefully, working out the position and depth of the shelves to suit the miniatures you want to put on them. Provide a wide shelf at the back and at one or both sides for dairy produce, meat and fish, then narrower shelves above for pots, pans and preserves.

There is no need for fancy joinery in a utility room, so keep it simple. The side shelves can be butted up against the ones at the back, and the wood left unpainted to give a clean and well-scrubbed look. The bottom, wider shelf can be about 3in (75mm) from the floor to allow space below for bottles, flagons and wine-making equipment, vegetables and bulk stores in baskets, sacks or tubs. Oddments of woodstrip can be used for the shelves, and shaped or angled pieces will provide shelf-supports.

1 Decide on the width of the lower shelf and cut from stripwood. At the back of a typical larder in 1/12 this might be $1^3/4$in (45mm) deep, and the shelf at the side might be narrower. Adjust the measurements in order to suit your own particular requirements.

2 Cut supports for the back shelf from $^1/_2$in (12mm) square dowelling and glue in position. Glue the shelf onto the supports and to the wall.

3 Cut a support for the side shelf and glue to the wall and floor at the front of the larder. An extra $^1/_2$in (12mm) thick support can be added to the wall under the centre of the shelf. Glue the shelf on top of the support and to the wall.

4 The upper, narrower shelves can be glued to right-angled triangular or plain woodstrip supports and then glued to the wall.

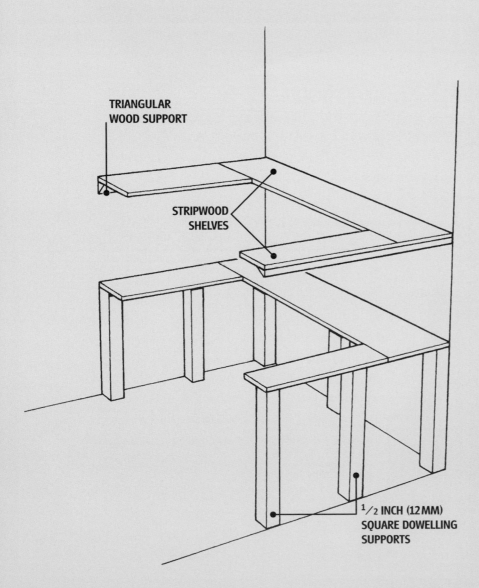

TRIANGULAR
WOOD SUPPORT

STRIPWOOD
SHELVES

$^1/_2$ INCH (12 MM)
SQUARE DOWELLING
SUPPORTS

FURTHER IDEAS FOR OPEN STORAGE

■ Provide a linen cupboard in a bedroom, bathroom or on a landing. For a country effect, arrange piles of neatly folded linen on the shelves. Cut cotton fabric to the exact width of the shelf to be filled and long enough to fold over several times. Crease and press lightly before tying with very thin ribbon.

▶ Make use of luggage. Maximize the potential of a trunk or suitcase by showing what is inside: it would be a waste of space to keep the lid fully closed. The contents can be arranged neatly or left to spill out. You might like to put some folded clothing nearby to suggest packing in progress.

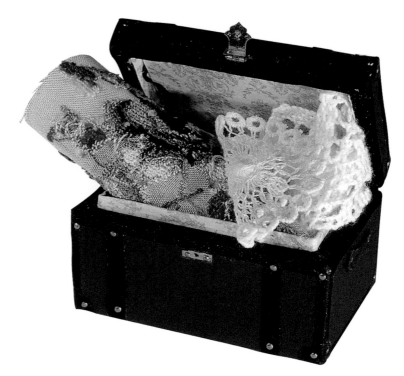

▲ A red leather trunk with removable shelf and the traditional fitted lining of thick flowered paper. The contents include a piece of tiny handworked flower embroidery which was originally part of a fine Swiss handkerchief.

◀ An example of early furniture designed for storage, this Tudor highbacked settle has a hinged seat. It has been left open to reveal folded coarse linen in shades of ochre, which could be produced by using natural plant dyes. Before the invention of the hanging wardrobe, clothing was also folded and stored in this way, and herbs were strewn in the folds.

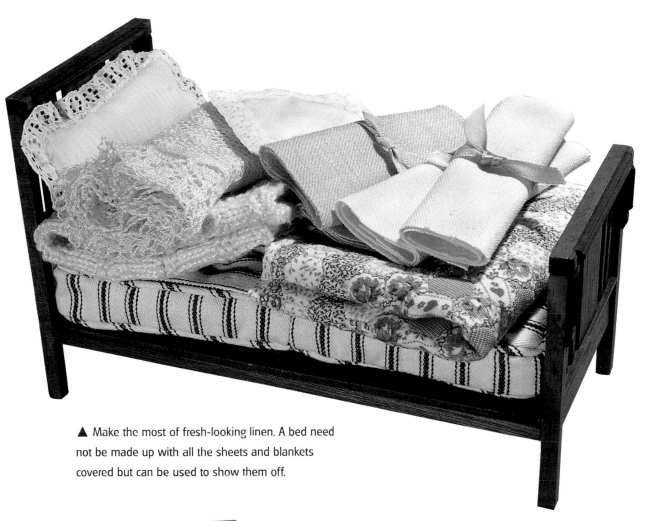

▲ Make the most of fresh-looking linen. A bed need not be made up with all the sheets and blankets covered but can be used to show them off.

◄ A nicely made wardrobe can be used to store linen, and a drawer provides additional space to be filled. Leave the door open to show off your textile collection.

► The Japanese have learned how to use limited storage space to the full. Stepped shelves are used for this scaled-down version of a Girls' Festival Display with a traditional arrangement of dolls and miniatures in a strict hierarchy. The Emperor and Empress are at the top, with court ladies and ministers below and, at the bottom, tiny representations of furniture and food.

First impressions

The first glimpse into a dolls' house before it is opened up is through the windows or a doorway. Even a small window will reveal some of the delights inside. Try to arrange the contents so that there is something interesting to see when you look in.

▲ A pair of 'stone' lions to guard the entrance establishes that this is a wealthy household, so we know that the rooms inside will be well furnished.

A sneak preview

An open doorway or a passage into a building can be visually enticing. A through-passage separating the hall from kitchen and buttery was a common feature of early Tudor houses. Placing a garden feature at the far end will enhance the period atmosphere.

▼ A window opening from the balcony of a Venetian palazzo is heavily latticed but allows a glimpse of the room inside: the feeling of anticipation is immediate.

▼ This striking hall was copied from Powerscourt, an Irish country house. The unusual design of the plasterwork ceiling features shells, which were cast in resin from a hand-carved original. The deer heads feature branching antlers which were all carved individually so that no two are alike.

Making an entrance

An entrance hall or porch needs as much attention as the main rooms. It sets the scene for the style of the house, whether simple or grand.

The hall should reinforce the impression you wish to create, just as it would in real life for a visitor entering the house. Carry through whichever theme you choose. A Georgian hallway, for example, would have a side table. In a Victorian house, you might install an umbrella stand beyond the door for authenticity, while an Edwardian home should perhaps be given a hallstand for coats, hats and umbrellas, and a small modern home might include a bicycle or a pushchair in the hall.

► (Top and right) The theme of this house is sunlight, with the entrance hall (pictured, top), panelled in mahogany and spruce, where the sun's rays appear over a doorway. The gilded metal balusters on the staircase typify the Art Nouveau influence. The sunlight theme is continued outside (pictured, right) with the representation of the sun over the porch, carved in wood by the maker but painted as stone. The stained glass window with its echoing rays provides both light and reflected colour.

◀ Windows let in light and help to illuminate the richly painted and gilded stucco decorations of this miniature of the Ante-Collegio from the Doge's Palace in Venice.

▲ A stone mullioned window offers a view through into a Tudor kitchen with wooden tubs and baskets of vegetables. Strong iron bars keep out potential intruders.

Raising the roof

A typical cottage interior is small, and a traditional cottage will have a thatched roof and tiny windows, making it difficult to see inside. One option (see below) is to have a lift-up roof which will give a good view into the upper rooms. This works well and is just as exciting as opening the front.

▼ The entire thatched roof of this flint and brick Oxfordshire cottage is hinged at the back so that it can be lifted up to give good access to the upper rooms. The main lower front opens in the centre.

CHAPTER 2

PERIOD ROOMS

We all have our favourite historical period and can imagine the type of room we would like to re-create in miniature, whether it is oak-panelled from the age of Henry VIII, a Regency room which might have been lived in by Jane Austen or a Victorian room filled with ornaments.

Many hobbyists prefer to concentrate on grand rooms, partly because a peasant room with an earth floor seems to offer little scope for decoration and cannot be filled with a collection of fine miniatures. Well-filled rooms are a legitimate objective, but even an empty room can give a great deal of pleasure.

If you love ancient buildings, you might find it equally enjoyable to create the impression of age and history by trying out distressed paint finishes and including the bare minimum of furniture in your room.

▶ During the reign of King Charles II, interior decoration became increasingly magnificent as a reaction to the sombre Cromwellian period that had just ended. The panelling in this magnificent Restoration drawing room is richly carved with swags of fruit and flowers below an ornately plastered ceiling. Light is provided by chandeliers and the velvet curtains are trimmed with gold bullion fringing.

◀ ▼ The Pompeiian red walls of this Georgian dining room set off the pictures and mirrors in their gilded frames. The fine mahogany table with a set of matching chairs, is laid for a celebration dinner, with a service of monogrammed fine bone-china, hall-marked silverware and lead crystal glass. On the console tables, Meissen and Ming porcelain are reflected in the mirrors.

▶ This beautiful Islamic room is both exotic and inspirational. The window frames are panelled in limewood, stained and handpainted like the originals from which they were copied. The floor is a combination of individual tiles and painted panels, assembled to create the design.

Research your chosen period

If you plan a period setting, it is best to be authentic. Unless you are already an expert on your chosen period, it is essential to do some research to avoid anachronisms. You may also like to suggest the way in which a room has been used over the generations, by decorating in a style to suit the architecture but including furniture and accessories of a more recent time, just as we do in real life.

Begin, if you can, by visiting a preserved historic house to look at the details at first hand. In Britain it is possible to tour houses from most periods, and European countries are generally rich in buildings which reflect regional vernacular styles. In America, New England has some lovely eighteenth-century houses which are open to the public, and there are early houses in many other states, too.

The next best thing is to consult one or more of the many books which are devoted to period styles in decoration and furnishing.

▲ This austere interior based on a Saxon church in England needs no furniture to add to its beauty. Light streams in through the doorway, and additional illumination is provided by cartwheel candle lights, which are electrified.

Kitchens

Period kitchens in dolls' houses can feature not only food, but replicas of gadgets which are no longer in use, such as a butter churn, a table mincer or a flat iron. We may decide upon a replica of our mother's or grandmother's kitchen as we remember it from our childhood. Going even further back in time, there are now kitchen museums where we can see how the Tudor, Georgian or Victorian kitchen was arranged.

Replicas of much of the equipment in both period and modern kitchens are made in 1/12. Victorian kitchens staffed by servants contained a huge array of gadgets, while in more modest homes cook managed with only basic cooking tools.

Even modern kitchens can be delightful reproduced in miniature, because it is always fascinating to see the equipment we use every day in a tiny size.

▲ Mrs Beeton would have approved of this neatly arranged kitchen with its well-filled store cupboard and general air of cleanliness.

▶ In contrast, this Edinburgh tenement kitchen of 1899 contains the sort of basic equipment which the average housewife would have used. The Arts and Crafts movement was well under way by this time, but the new ideas had not yet percolated through to all levels of society.

▲ Compare this French kitchen with its Scottish counterpart of much the same date. Both rooms are small, but the French version has a more airy and uncluttered feeling. It features a white continental stove rather than a black cast iron range: doubtless the French housewife has space to hang washing outdoors.

▲ Made in Japan, this unusual miniature is a Japanese rice steamer: a self-contained kitchen.

▼ An inexpensive fridge magnet which can be used in the dolls' house kitchen – complete with toast.

Bathrooms

Bathrooms are a relatively modern innovation, as frequent washing was not thought of as essential until fairly recently. The proper bathroom was a late Victorian idea, and even then they were rare. It was common for a huge house to have a single bathroom: everyone except the owners had to make do with a bowl and jugs of water. This continued until after the First World War and into the 1920s.

Dolls' houses also tend to be somewhat short on bathrooms, because when you have few rooms to arrange the bathroom is often the one to be left out. If you can find the space you will enjoy designing and decorating one to suit your house – and it is guaranteed to attract attention. A water closet with a chain which can be pulled seems to fascinate young and old alike, and one assembled from a kit might suit a period bathroom.

In the country house the bathroom has never been the most comfortable of rooms. Until the 1930s plumbing was fairly primitive, and even then hot water was provided by a dangerous-looking gas geyser over the bath.

There were occasional exceptions to the drab, unheated bathroom. In some Edwardian stately homes, lavish marble bathrooms had a freestanding bath, usually in the centre of the room, although this still had to be filled (and emptied) by relays of servants using buckets and jugs of hot water.

There would be a fire lit in the grate during cold weather, as the bathroom was usually adapted from a former bedroom with a fireplace. More workaday bathrooms were furnished with unwanted chairs and tables from other rooms in the house, in a mixture of period styles.

We all have our own idea of the perfect bathroom. A period dolls' house can manage with a washstand in a bedroom, but a modern home is incomplete without a bath or shower room, however small.

▼ A marbled bathroom which might have belonged to someone very wealthy. The bath sits on a raised marble panel and the towel is monogrammed. The interesting shower was invented during the Regency period and has been included in this bathroom for good measure: it probably belonged to an ancestor before the bath was installed.

► A marble-topped washstand with tiled back was customary in most country house bedrooms in the early part of the twentieth century. The pretty porcelain toilet set of ewer and basin has a matching soap dish with perforated top for water to drain.

'MARBLE'

■ Use thin marbled card instead of wallpaper to marble a bathroom. As a centrepiece, try adding a pictured marble panel so that the bath is raised up as the central feature. Using white tape, monogram a towel fringed at each end, and write the initials in fineline black pen or ballpoint.

▼ A stylish bath with shower handset for the modern bathroom. 'Glass' shelves on the wall or a bathroom cabinet could be added to show off toiletries and mini toothbrushes.

Tudor

Basic decoration of Tudor rooms is simple: plastered walls can be colour-washed in off-white or ochre. Other possibilities include exposed timbers or oak panelling. The floors should be either 'stone' slabs or wide oak planks.

For the walls, simulate plaster with water-based emulsion paint, thickened a little with some interior filler if you want a rough finish. As a slightly patchy effect is authentic, one coat should be enough. In a room where all the walls are left uncovered you might also choose a deep pinky-red or yellow ochre, traditional colours which give a rich effect.

▲ Timbers on a plastered wall combine with an oak screen to give this room an ancient appearance. Ceiling beams run from front to back so that they can be seen clearly.

▼ Tudor brickwork was masterly. This replica of part of the old kitchen in Gainsborough Old Hall, Lincolnshire, is a faithful copy of the original. For the hobbyist, using brick cladding in sheet form is the easiest option, but for those with patience miniature bricks can be laid in courses and grouted in. In smaller domestic rooms brickwork was usually plastered over.

Internal timbering often works best if used on one or two walls with the others as plaster. In a real Tudor house the timbers, such as the ceiling beams, formed part of the frame construction and were both heavy and strong. Adding them on afterwards is not good building practice but looks fine in miniature, and it means that thinner woodstrip can be used.

To add timbers, use woodstrip approximately ⅛in (3mm) thick and ½in (12mm) wide and distress it by denting it at irregular intervals with a small hammer. Shave the edges of the wood here and there so that it is not perfectly straight. Colour with woodstain to simulate oak before fitting.

Plan out the arrangement of the timbers using a picture of a real Tudor house as a rough guide to positioning. Cut the strips to size and glue in place.

Few of us can hope to emulate the elaborate roof structure shown above, but plain beams can be spaced across a ceiling. Use ⅝in (16mm) square dowelling (from a model shop), cut it to length, then distress and stain as before and glue in place.

▲ This magnificent roof was constructed using pegged joints in the traditional way. The windbraces form an elaborate pattern of curving oak which delights the eye.

▶ Plain oak panelling with plastered walls above. In this case the upright and crosspieces are fitted over oak veneer, but a similar effect can be achieved by using inexpensive wood and distressing and staining before gluing in place.

▶ In the seventeenth century, wall panelling became much more elaborate. Here is a splendid example of a Restoration room in the time of Charles II.

▲ An upper servant might have to sleep in the storeroom and share the bed with one or two others. Sacking on the floor or, at best, a truckle bed would be usual, but in this room a low bed is provided as the height of luxury.

Furnishing a Tudor home

Tudor furniture was sparse. Wealthy home owners might have only one good bed, a storage chest, one high chair and a number of joined stools and benches. Tables were often no more than boards which were set up on trestles at mealtimes. Servants slept on the floor and sat on benches.

Despite these limitations, the main rooms were designed to impress. The best furniture was richly carved and painted; tapestries and portraits were hung in gilded frames; and family crests, heraldic shields and weapons were displayed, often arranged to make an elaborate pattern on a wall.

Grand banquets were staged to impress influential visitors. Many courses of elaborately presented food were brought in by servants to the accompaniment of music performed on sackbuts, viols, shawms and other early instruments.

◄ A superlative example of an English 'Nonsuch' chest based on an original from circa 1580. The term 'Nonsuch' to describe these inlaid chests was invented by the Victorians. This miniature contains more than 11,000 pieces of inlay.

◄ Tudor rooms were full of colour. Use tapestries, portraits, armour, pewter, candles and food to bring the room to life. In this scene, tapestries based on millefleurs French designs add warmth above the dais in the hall. The hangings, reproduced by a photographic process, are surprisingly realistic when fitted in place.

ECONOMICAL IDEAS FOR TUDOR ROOMS

- Include some authentic early musical instruments. A lute, a recorder or a shawm would be appropriate.

- Downstairs floors can be of ceramic or resin flagstones (glue on with a rubber-based glue such as Copydex). For economy, make your own flooring from thick cardboard. Cut out some square and rectangular templates to use as patterns and cut plenty of each size. Make a card pattern to fit the floor, and glue on the 'flagstones', mixing the shapes randomly. Trim the edges neatly if they overhang the card base. Paint with grey or stone matt model enamel. Lastly, varnish with matt or semi-matt varnish and glue the floor in place in the room.

- There is nothing more attractive than the sheen of real pewter, but if the dishes and plates are to be covered with food you can economize by painting card plates with Metalcote model enamel. This dries quickly and looks good buffed up with a soft cloth. Mix two shades together to achieve the appearance of pewter: a combination of the shades representing aluminium and polished steel works well.

- ▼ Wooden buttons also make good platters. The holes can be hidden by food.

▼ Partridges nestle on an oval card plate painted to resemble pewter, and apples and pears are piled over the holes in a wooden button.

- Wooden floors should be planked. Real wood looks best in a Tudor room and, to be true to the period, it should be oak. Woodstrip for use as dolls' house planking is available in several widths: choose the widest, which is about $^3/_4$in (20 mm) wide. Cut a floor pattern in card as above, cut the planks to a variety of lengths and glue them on. Iron-on woodstrip is another option, provided it is of wood veneer and not synthetic material. Finish with a coat of matt varnish or, if the house is to be updated inside, use a satin finish.

- Shields decorated with heraldic devices will add colour. Transfers and metal blanks from a military model shop will give you a choice of coats of arms. Fix the shields high up on the walls for the best effect.

- ▼ Candleholders and tall candle stands obviously need candles. Making wax candles is time-consuming and difficult, but replicas can be made from wooden cocktail sticks. Cut to length and shave one end to a suitable shape to fit the holder. Paint with typewriter correction fluid or alternatively use a white marker pen: this is less messy than painting with a brush which then needs cleaning, and the fluid dries in minutes. In such a small size a wick is not essential, but if you do want to provide one, glue on a short strand of embroidery cotton.

◄ A floorstanding pewter candlestick with real wax candle. This design is known as a pricket candestick: the candle is stuck onto a spike in the drip tray.

Updating the Tudor interior

Many Tudor houses of the grander sort are still lived in today. Try updating a Tudor room to present its panelled and beamed interior in a new way. In time the furnishings and decorations of each historical period come back into fashion: the 1920s was a time when Tudor once again became popular.

▼ An arrangement of yellow flowers and glossy green leaves shows up well on a plain oak chest.

A modern Tudor home

Imagine one wing of a Tudor house, formerly a parlour with solar above it, originally built around 1560 for the lord and his family. The fireplaces and oak panelling remain, but now planked floors are made more comfortable by adding Turkish carpets. Candles have given way to table lamps made from Chinese blue-and-white porcelain vases topped by silk shades.

Country house furniture

Upholstered chairs in Queen Anne style (winged chairs helped to keep out draughts before central heating was introduced) now supplement the oak benches and stools, but the 'country house style' arrangements would have delighted the Tudors.

Ideas for accessories

Flower arrangements help to lighten an oak-panelled room. Use the tiny fabric flowers and leaves that are sold for trimming hats. For the English country house look, make a trailing arrangement and set the container on top of a tall wooden plant stand.

◀ In the 1920s and 1930s everyone wanted oak furniture (preferably darkened) and pewter tankards were displayed on heavily carved refectory tables and court cupboards. Additional comfort was provided by a reproduction Knole sofa.

▼ The eighteenth-century-style dummy board soldier near to the Tudor fireplace is from two centuries later than its setting but not out of place in an updated room. Chinese porcelain was also admired and collected in the 1920s and introduced wherever possible. The Imperial yellow porcelain plate on the chimney breast is a rare treasure, and even rarer in a miniaturized version.

The William and Mary influence

Period styles in Britain are dated from the name of the reigning monarch, but new ideas took many years to reach country districts far from London, so there is always some overlap.

William and Mary reigned only from 1689 to 1702, but the style of decorations and furniture they introduced continued in favour through the Queen Anne and Georgian periods right up to the Regency (see page 52–4). Chinese wallpaper panels and lacquer furniture imported by the East India Company could add a lighter touch to dark, panelled rooms. During the later Georgian period oriental lacquer was copied by English craftsmen using a technique which is known as japanning.

Another idea introduced by William and Mary was to include blue-and-white Delft pottery as a strong decorative element. Sets of five vases, known as Garniture de Cheminée, were commonly shown off on mantelshelves, with additional pots on brackets arranged on the wall, while large tulip vases might stand in a window embrasure or corner, directly on the floor. Dutch tiles served as fireplace surrounds and to decorate dairies and stillrooms.

▲ Walnut became the most used wood at the end of the seventeenth century: a William and Mary room may have a walnut floor and furniture.

► An early Georgian room in the simple and elegant style that followed the William and Mary period.

◄ A japanned double chair with cabriole legs would be suitable in a late seventeenth-century room. The original of this chair is of a slightly later date.

▶ A William and Mary table made in walnut with floral marquetry decoration in many different woods. This lovely miniature is based on an exceptionally beautiful original table which was probably made in England.

IDEAS FOR A ROOM SHOWING WILLIAM AND MARY INFLUENCE

■ Colour the woodwork with walnut woodstain, and include the skirting boards. White paint became fashionable during the later Georgian period. Use Chinese wallpaper over a dado rail or, alternatively, inset into wooden surrounds as panels. The paper shown on page 48 was a sample for a full-size pattern, but miniaturized designs are available from dolls' house suppliers.

▶ Blue-and-white miniature pottery and porcelain range from top quality individual handcrafted work to inexpensive imported pieces.

▶ This impressive tulip vase is a copy of the most spectacular piece in the Delft potters' repertoire. The miniature is handthrown and painted.

■ Choose portraits which show the correct costumes for the period and frame them with gilt picture-frame mouldings (see framing, page 81).

■ Tapestries were still used to keep out draughts. In a bedroom a tall four-poster bed can have warm-looking woollen hangings.

■ Firedogs (andirons) were used in fireplaces to support log fires: grates came into use during the Georgian period.

■ Make a small scene to frame and hang, using miniature blue-and-white ceramic tiles which can be mounted on thin wood or card. Alternatively, cut out pictured tiles from a magazine or museum postcard, provided that they are to the right scale and are printed clearly.

Georgian styles

The English Georgian and Regency periods cover a wide variety of decorative styles and the reigns of four kings. In 1714 when the first George became king, domestic interior decoration was generally unostentatious. Rooms were painted in a limited range of colours: deep red, dull green, brown and even a shade known as 'drab' were used. Fireplaces were set into the painted panelled walls without even a mantelshelf.

▲ A Tower of the Winds was a Georgian folly favoured by owners of stately homes: there are still some in existence. This 1/144th scale model of the building is hinged to open, and is painted and decorated inside as an exact replica. The room features a handpainted marble floor with a complicated design to suit the octagonal shape of the room.

▶ Georgian splendour: the magnificent saloon from Powerscourt, one of the great houses of Ireland, which was gutted by fire in the 1970s. This miniature re-creation contains eight Corinthian columns and twenty-six Ionic pilasters, all cast in resin. The elaborate gilded ceiling and railings are faithful copies of the originals.

▲ A Georgian hallway with a marble floor simulated in tiled flooring paper. The walls are painted in Adam blue.

▲ American furniture of the same period is equally elegant. These Philadelphia chairs and table in black walnut date from around 1770. The table is designed to take up little space when closed.

'Georgian style' covers more than a century. In the 1760s Robert Adam, the great architect who was also one of the first designer-decorators, instigated a huge change in decoration. Light blues and greens were picked out with white, and ceilings were often pink. Gilded details were introduced, and beautiful carpets were laid over wooden floorboards which previously had been left uncovered.

Curtains of velvet and silk were draped in elaborate folds, and ruched blinds softened large windows. Fireplaces became much grander: the surrounds were made of marble if it could be afforded, or painted in simulation if it could not.

The type of decorations you choose may depend to some extent on the size of your budget. A room can be grand without being ostentatious: use paper to simulate richer types of material. Even curtains and a pelmet can be made of textured paper which can look and feel like fabric. The paper used inside a chocolate box as packing can be suitable, as it is easy to form into pleats and drapes well. Once pressed firmly into place the folds will retain their shape.

▶ A delightfully curvaceous example of a double chair made in mahogany.

Furniture in the Georgian room must be in keeping, or the whole effect will be ruined. The simple and unequalled elegance of an eighteenth-century room with just a few fine pieces of furniture is the epitome of Georgian style.

The Regency

During the English Regency distinctive furniture and elaborate decorations were introduced by the Prince Regent, who became King George IV in 1820: after his accession the period is known as late Georgian.

The prince was fond of music, which was the most popular evening entertainment at the time. Your starting point for a Regency music room could be a dolls' house wallpaper with a musical motif. Cut out and glue panels to the walls in the manner of an eighteenth-century print room. Smaller panels can be used to emphasize a doorway, mirror or window or on either side of a fireplace.

First paper the walls and leave to dry out. Mark the position of the fireplace, plan

▲ A Regency music room is a stylish setting for fine furniture and musical instruments, which are arranged for a soirée.

▲ The original of this square piano was made by the famous John Broadwood at the end of the Regency period.

◄ The centrepiece of the Regency music room is the beautiful harp, made by an expert craftsman. The fine stringing and the use of pale, polished sycamore make it the focus of attention.

out an arrangement and fix the motifs temporarily with Blu-tack while you finalize the design. Fix them in place using solid glue stick: you need apply only a little of this to each corner. Solid glue works well, as it is possible to shift the motifs around without marking the walls while you make sure that they are straight before pressing them firmly into place.

Furnish your room with Regency-style chairs for use both by performers and audience. The chairs can be ready-made or in kit form for you to assemble yourself.

A chaise longue would have provided more comfortable seating for the most important lady in the assembled company.

Musical instruments for a Regency room can be a specialist maker's masterpiece or a readily available model, so for these you can spend as much or as little as you wish, to suit your budget.

At the top end of the range, an exact copy of a period instrument by a master craftsman will certainly be expensive, but it will give you a lifetime's pleasure. Harpsichords and square pianos are both suitable for a Regency room, although the harpsichord had been superseded by the beginning of the nineteenth century.

▼ Simple materials can be assembled to create an elegant Regency music room.

▼ Refreshments make an essential contribution to the success of a musical entertainment. A lyre-ended sofa continues the musical theme and a pedestal table is used to display dessert plates and a pyramid of fruit.

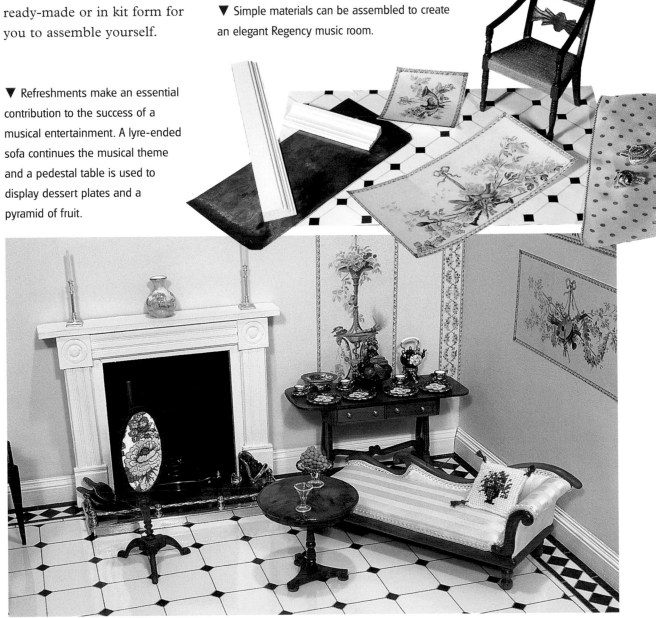

IDEAS FOR THE REGENCY MUSIC ROOM

- Refreshments are important. Provide little pedestal tables to hold wine and glasses.

- A side table can be laid for a buffet supper.

► A pole screen placed near the fire is a useful and decorative addition.

- Include a music stand: sheet music for this can be reduced on a photocopier. For clarity, choose a sheet with few notes, perhaps a piece for a beginner. Or write your own, using a fineline black pen, and reduce it in size.

► Pole screens could be moved easily to shield ladies' faces from the fire. Heavy make-up was worn, and it had a tendency to run if the heat was too intense.

▲ The Regency connoisseur admired continental workmanship. The original of this Italian cylinder desk, with a Roman scene inlaid in marquetry on the front, might have been brought back and installed in a Regency study.

▼ A Regency carver and side chair demonstrate the maker's skill in providing rope twist carving in such tiny detail. The scroll ends on the armrests are a typical Regency touch. Pale yellow striped silk is used to cover the seats.

Walls and flooring

Painted walls are an option which will allow you to hang pictures rather than use a musical motif: yellow, Adam green or blue would be suitable. Buy a sample size pot of water-based emulsion paint in an authentic 'historic' colour for a really good effect. Make sure that your framed paintings continue the prevailing Regency theme.

The flooring used to suit the formal style of the music room is a plasticized tile sheet which is easy to cut and lay in one piece. Trim to fit if necessary, and glue lightly round all the edges. Polished mahogany flooring would be another suitable choice.

Authentic scaled-down versions of Georgian skirting board give the best impression and should be mitred at the corner joins, as shown below.

An acceptable inexpensive alternative is to use plain stripwood approximately $\frac{5}{8}$in (16mm) high and butt the corners together. Paint the skirting off-white before fitting. Cornice should always be mitred at the corners. It is generally painted white but can be gilded for a decorative effect in a grand room.

Fit skirting board and cornice

Georgian-style skirting board and cornice were used throughout the Regency period, too, and make a neat finish to a room.

1 The correct angle for cutting mitred corners in wood mouldings for skirting boards: plain back of moulding upright.

2 Mitre-cut skirting boards meeting to form a corner.

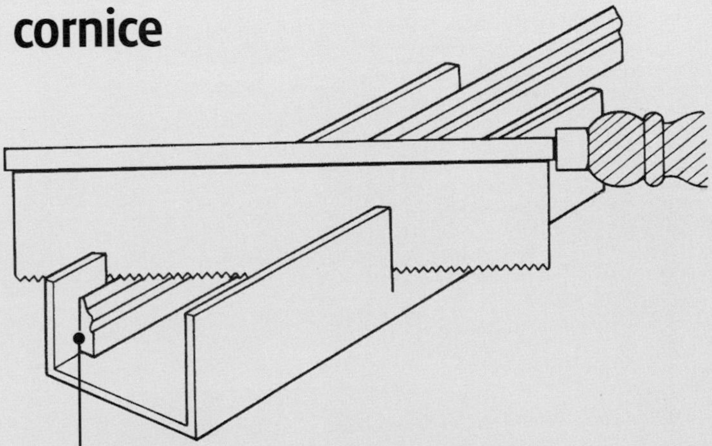

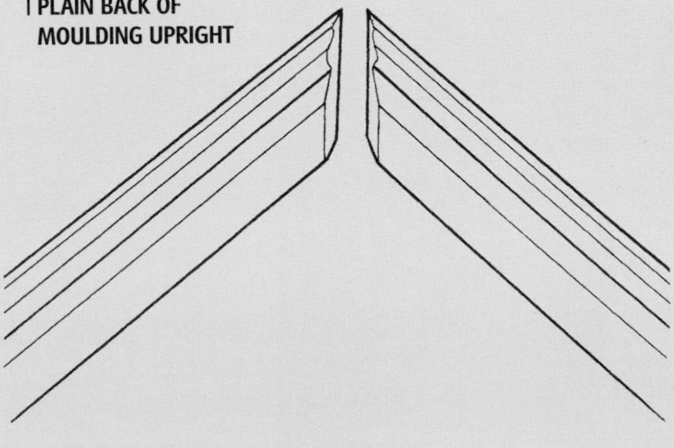

PLAIN BACK OF MOULDING UPRIGHT

The Continental influence

Even before Victoria became queen of England in 1837, decorations were becoming more fussy. Floral-patterned carpets were introduced, curtains were made of rich brocade or velvet, and wallpapers were striped or patterned and topped with a border. Stencilling or hand-painting was the latest way to add interest to floorboards.

The European equivalent of this style was known as Biedermeier, which roughly equates to bourgeois. Homes were much more comfortable for the average family, and you can be lavish with ornaments and accessories in the dolls' house room.

SILHOUETTES

■ Silhouettes depicting family and friends were popular in the nineteenth century before cameras were in general use. An effective way to frame your own silhouettes is to use jewellery backings.

▼ A cabinet filled with continental-style china and glass and a writing desk/bureau are both in the unmistakable Biedermeier style: these pieces were made from kits. The floor covering is a plasticized tile sheet which is ideal for this room style and would be suitable throughout the Victorian era which followed.

▼ Rich colours and fabrics can be used in the Biedermeier room. White satin-stripe paper is a regular wallpaper sample and the patterned ribbon edged with gold thread will give a rich effect when used as a border.

▼ This room looks more comfortable and feminine than its Georgian predecessor. A flower-patterned carpet partially covers the 'stencilled' floor, which is made of fancy card to simulate a simple design. Flowers, writing equipment and upholstered seating add to the homely effect.

How to make and drape curtains

Curtains in heavy materials were arranged in elaborate swathes during the nineteenth century. Double-sided velvet ribbon is a good choice for a rectangular or square window, as some of the fabric will be visible from outside the dolls' house. Windows with a rounded top are more difficult to curtain. The simplest method is to cut a card base to surround the window. Drape and fix the curtains to the card, which can be lightly glued to the wall complete with curtains and tie-backs.

1 Cut a card pattern $^1/_2$in (12 mm) wide to fit around the window and continue it down to floor level.

2 Cut two pieces of ribbon or fabric, each long enough to reach from the centre top of the card, across and down to the bottom, plus one-third as long again to allow for draping.

3 Start at the centre top (**A**). Fix one end of the ribbon with double-sided Scotch tape and drape to make a pleasing shape, fixing with tape at strategic points – this will allow you to make adjustments as you continue. Now repeat for the other side, checking that the two sides are symmetrical.

4 Use thin cord, gold or coloured, to make tie-backs. These can be fixed to the back of the curtains and also to the card base in order to keep them in place.

5 Make a pelmet which will cover the join at the top. Drape and fix in the same way and finish with a cord tie or bow to match the tie-backs.

6 Try the arrangement at the window using Blu-tack as a temporary fixing while you check the length. There is no need to hem, because this would add excessive bulk. Cut to length with sharp scissors and use a wooden cocktail stick to run a thin trail of all-purpose glue along the lower end to prevent fraying.

7 Finally, attach to the wall around the window with double-sided adhesive tape.

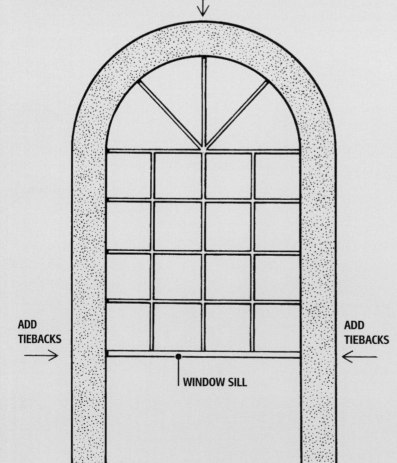

A

ADD TIEBACKS →

ADD TIEBACKS ←

WINDOW SILL

French style

French decorations and furniture have a charm all their own. A French dolls' house interior, whether it is based on the simple country look or on the grand rooms of a château, will certainly give an impression very different from an English dolls' house. French taste is conservative and thrifty: furniture is often kept for generations and fabric patterns are repeated. Nothing changes!

A country room can be sparsely furnished but still be full of atmosphere. Tiled floors in halls and downstairs parlours are almost universal, while the installation of a woodburning stove instead of a fireplace is an option. A plain wooden settle rather than upholstered armchairs, and a pretty cabinet to fill with china, can be bought from mass-produced ranges of dolls' house furniture.

A small French bedroom may have bare floorboards and pine furniture. There is usually a tall wardrobe or armoire, and an old-fashioned washstand substitutes for the lack of a bathroom. Bedsteads are commonly of brass or pine, with both head- and footboards.

▲ The bed is not made up but is instead used to lay out a fine embroidered waistcoat. There are no ornaments or clutter, and the pine furniture is plain, but this fresh-looking bedroom conveys the essence of French style.

▶ An urn on a marbled pedestal shows off an arrangement by a professional miniaturist.

◀ The Continental stove and elegant china cabinet in this room typify French provincial style.

▼ This room has been designed as the home of an artist. Art materials scattered on the table and a painting on the easel clearly set the scene.

IDEAS FOR A FRENCH ENTRANCE HALL

■ Add a bust of Napoleon: the one pictured in the room below was coloured by a professional painter of military models, but you can buy one to paint yourself.

■ Choose suitable French paintings to frame with gilt picture-frame mouldings. Landscapes such as the one used in this room (painted by Claude Lorrain in the late seventeenth century) are ideal and can be found in art gallery catalogues.

■ Paint a longcase clock. Strip and repaint an inexpensive imported model with a distressed finish to resemble an old inherited piece.

■ Arrange flowers in a trailing arrangement to stand on a pedestal: a formal arrangement will look best in this type of room.

■ Repaint a cheap metal bust or statue to simulate bronze, as shown on the corner cabinet in this room.

▼ The french hall is elegant without being ostentatious. You need only a few pieces of furniture to achieve a similar look of discreet grandeur. The armoire, table and corner cupboard are ready-made, exact copies of the real thing painted in a traditional colour. The impressive flooring is giftwrap in bronze and gold chequered squares. A bust of Napoleon in a corner is evidence of the republican sympathies of the house owner.

▲ This luxurious High Victorian room is the setting for Christmas festivities.

▼ A well-filled Victorian nursery has great appeal to the collector of miniature toys.

Victorian

The Victorian period is a favourite with dolls' house enthusiasts, whether they are concerned primarily with collecting or prefer to make their own accessories. In the early part of Queen Victoria's reign rooms were relatively restrained, but by the mid-nineteenth century clutter abounded: part of the enjoyment can be to see how many miniatures you can fit into a room.

Victorian chairs were well upholstered and made in interesting shapes, some of them reproduced from older examples. Balloon-back chairs are still popular today, while the prie-dieu (a chair designed for kneeling on rather than sitting) has gone out of fashion.

Arranging a room which shows new ideas being incorporated offers a great opportunity for the miniaturist, who can decide what to put in and what might be too forward-looking to include.

In the 1870s the growing influence of William Morris heralded new ideas in interior decoration in Britain, including white paintwork, naturalistic floral curtains instead of heavy velvet drapes, and painted furniture. This was a gradual but vast change from the dark and rich decor of mid-Victorian rooms.

Tartan carpets used by Queen Victoria and Prince Albert in their private rooms at Balmoral were soon copied, and these can be provided by using plaid woollen dress material or a wool-and-cotton mixture (see page 64). Lace curtains were still used, often combined with outer curtains made from William Morris fabrics.

VICTORIAN ACCESSORIES

■ A Victorian room is the ideal setting in which to show off your own work if you enjoy miniature embroidery or needlepoint.

■ Domed bases can be purchased for footstools, with removable padded tops to cover with your own designs.

■ Firescreens are another option: choose one where the frame can be taken apart to set in your own work.

■ Make plenty of cushions. To make them squashy and comfortable-looking do not overstuff them: the smallest wisp of synthetic wadding is sufficient. Avoid cotton wool as filling, because it will look and feel lumpy.

■ Glass domes with removable bases are inexpensive and can be used to show off an arrangement of dried flowers or tiny shells. Make a base with Blu-tack and start with a twig in the centre. Build up an arrangement, gluing on flowers or shells with impact glue, checking now and again that the 'tree' is not too wide for the glass dome to fit over it. To avoid glue on fingers, dab on the glue with a cocktail stick and use tweezers to fix on the flowers or the shells.

▶ Needlepoint and cross-stitch bell pulls and carpets will fit in well. Charts and complete kits including silk or wool thread are widely available, or you can scale down a simple full-size design by leaving out much of the fine detail and working on a small-size canvas.

▶ A needlepoint bell pull worked from a kit can be used in a drawing room or bedroom.

▲ A selection of materials used in the Victorian castle room.

▲ This comfortable parlour in a Scottish Borders castle is an example of the time when High Victorian was beginning to give way to newer styles. A fitted workbox is open ready for use, and a violin, a canterbury (to hold sheet music), a newspaper and some refreshments are all provided.

A Scottish castle room

The 'stone' walls of the Scottish Borders castle room pictured here are rendered with plaster in a pinkish tone, simulated by a plain dolls' house wallpaper, although emulsion paint would give a similar effect. In an ordinary house of the time, a William Morris miniature wallpaper might be preferable and many patterns are available. The Victorians were not afraid to mix patterns together, and even if you choose wallpaper it would still be appropriate to use patterned curtains.

The Arts and Crafts movement was in full swing by the end of the nineteenth century, and plain oak doors with handwrought iron handles were favoured. A (non-opening) double door suits this room but it can be scaled down to a single door with a handle on one side for a smaller room. This massive oak door is surrounded by copies of oil paintings by Rossetti and Waterhouse.

How to make a panelled door

To make the double door, use $^1/_2$in (12mm) wide stripwood, with a slightly wider piece for the lintel. The door frame shown is made from a shaped wood moulding with the thicker edge on the outside edge, but plain stripwood could be used. The doorstep is a block of wood $^3/_4$in (20mm) wide and $^3/_8$in (10mm) deep.

1 Decide on the height and width of the door including the frame. Cut a piece of card to this size and trim off $^1/_8$in (3mm) all round so that the card edges will not show when the wood is fitted on top.

2 Cut four pieces of stripwood to the right length and glue to the card base. Add the side frame pieces next and lastly the lintel across the top.

3 Arts and Crafts-style handles are not easy to find. For a good simulation, glue on two metal plate stands. As the part of the metal to be glued on is very tiny, use superglue which bonds metal to wood instantly. To avoid gluing your fingers, lay the door flat and use tweezers to pick up and hold the handle while you squeeze on a very little glue; then press the handle firmly in place.

4 Cut the doorstep approximately 1in (25mm) wider than the completed door and fix it to the wall. Either glue on the complete door and frame above the step, or attach it with double-sided Scotch tape.

A = $4^3/_4$in (120mm)
B = $^3/_4$in (20mm)
C = $^3/_8$in (10mm)
D = $^5/_8$in (16mm)
E = 2in (50mm)

The Arts & Crafts movement

By the turn of the century the influence of the Arts and Crafts movement was felt in the average home. The simplicity and handmade look of the new designs for furniture, the appeal of beaten copper and pewter, realistic paintings of contemporary life, and tapestries based on medieval originals gradually increased in popularity.

New influences in design

Liberty's store in London had opened in 1875, and it enthusiastically promoted the new trends. People went to exhibitions of handicrafts, and many husbands took up carpentry as a hobby and made simple tables and stools, while others tried metalwork. It was a time for learning new skills which could be used to beautify the home.

In large country houses of the kind once owned by industrial magnates, a billiard room was obligatory. In England, billiard rooms can be viewed in several houses now owned by the National Trust, and these provide a rich source of inspiration for miniaturists.

◀ A plain, sturdy chair made in oak with a drop-in leather seat. Good workmanship and strong construction followed the tradition of the country chairmaker.

▼ The billiard table and lighting are the centrepiece of this room which was made by a dolls' house group.

▶ Built-in seating on either side of a fireplace developed from the idea of a Tudor settle and became known as a 'cosy corner'.

◀ The sinuous lines of Art Nouveau were still popular: silver and pewter jugs in Liberty style looked well on new furniture. The revolving bookcase was first made in 1890, and updated designs continued until the 1950s. The one shown here is a version from the 1920s.

▼ The fireplace in the billiard room has a surround of handpainted tiles and a display of blue-and-white porcelain on the mantelshelf, which is in the taste of Victorian artistic interiors. The well-finished woodwork in this room is especially noteworthy: the plain panelling refers back to medieval interior styles.

▲ Arts and Crafts enthusiasts favoured fresh air and the simple life. Here, an open window reinforces this impression. Curtains of William Morris fabric are suitable – use Liberty dress fabric which features patterns reduced in size from those on the original furnishing fabrics.

▲ The copper picture frame and pewter candlesticks were copied from original Arts and Crafts designs by a professional miniaturist whose speciality is metalwork.

Decorating and furnishing the Arts and Crafts room

Curtains should show the pervasive William Morris influence: Liberty dress fabrics are miniature versions of the original curtain and upholstery fabrics. Net curtains were no longer in favour. In country houses, candles and oil lamps were still used, but in towns gas mantles were installed. There are some pretty miniature versions available.

Bathrooms were still not in general use. A bedroom can have a washstand complete with toilet set of ewer, basin and soap dish, like the earlier Victorian version, but by this time they might be backed with a curtain rather than tiles.

► Made in oak, this miniature version of a Cotswold-style dresser with panelled doors is similar to those made by Ernest Gimson and Sidney Barnsley, who set up workshops in the English Cotswolds.

▼ The heart-shaped cut-out was a popular motif in Arts and Crafts furniture and appeared widely on refectory tables, flanked by benches rather than chairs. This Arts and Crafts look was artistic, but like the medieval designs it reflected, not necessarily comfortable.

Modern living

The 1950s were the beginning of a great change in interior decoration. In Europe, during the years of austerity which followed the Second World War, people were starved of colour and ready to try something more adventurous.

Fabrics and wallpapers in up-to-the-minute patterns began to appear, and they were used in rooms still furnished with a mixture of traditional pieces and objects passed on by relatives. New furniture designs provided another huge style change and these were incorporated into existing room schemes. The resulting mélange may have looked a bit incongruous but it was certainly different.

▼ A reclining chair, workbox and side table with castors from the 1950s room.

▼ This cheerful room would have been very up-to-date for its time, with a brightly coloured fitted carpet and contrasting wallpapers – on the fireplace wall a miniature stripe, and on the others an art paper. It became the fashion to emphasize one wall in this way. The 1950s furniture includes a lounging chair, which can be reclined, and a 'wireless' set.

IDEAS FOR THE 1950s ROOM

- Curtains should be to the sill or just a little below. (As fabric was still in short supply, floor-length curtains were not an option.) Use a floral or brightly coloured geometric-patterned fabric.

- Make plain skirting boards from $^1/_2$ in (12 mm) stripwood, stained medium oak or painted cream or white.

- Use felt to provide a plain fitted carpet. This is authentic, as wool was not available and very thick felt was sometimes used as a carpet substitute.

- ▶ Coffee had become the fashionable drink, and almost eclipsed tea as a favourite beverage. Use a decorative fridge magnet as a coffee machine.

- Make a low coffee table. Use a small box as a base and paint it matt black. Top with shiny patterned card glued on to a piece of wood to simulate patterned Formica, which was generally favoured because it was very easy to wipe clean.

- Pictures should be bright and cheerful but not abstract.

- Leave some knitting lying around: it was a popular hobby in the 1950s. Knit a few rows on darning needles with one strand of thin tapestry wool. Transfer the knitting to long pins (preferably with coloured heads), leaving a long end of wool to wind into a ball. Fix the ball with a dab of glue to prevent it from unravelling.

◀ A decorative fridge magnet provides a 1950s coffee machine.

▶ Moulded plastic furniture was an alternative to more traditional pieces. It was light, cheerful and easy to keep clean, and it became an instant success. This set of dining table and chairs is typical of the new designs.

Contemporary styles

Today's rooms are interesting to design and complete. Many hobbyists like to arrange a room or even a complete dolls' house based on their own home, and to track down miniature versions of fabrics and floor coverings similar to their full-size counterparts. There should be no problem in finding 1/12 versions of modern furniture which, if not exactly the same, will be a good approximation to your own.

Modern styles allow free rein to the imagination: you can achieve spectacular decorative effects by using paper and card rather than expensive materials.

Colour is the key to the dramatic effect of my international-style room. The walls are painted plain cream as a neutral background for the hangings and to provide a contrast with the floor covering, a wallpaper sample in a vibrant orange-red with touches of gold. The feature fireplace is a gift box cut in half. The remaining half can be painted to give a different look in another room.

▼ Choose paper and card in vivid colours for a contemporary look.

▼ This is the sort of room you might find today in a superior apartment or expensive hotel. The woven carpet hanging over the fireplace is a 1/12 design from Turkey. The hanging on the side wall is a mosaic tile picture which has been cut from a magazine.

How to make a sofa with arms

In modern rooms sofas are more in evidence than armchairs, and may be covered in synthetic materials or leather rather than in traditional fabrics. One useful covering for the miniaturist to use is plasticized paper flowerwrap. This has a faint self-pattern and a slight sheen, which gives it a lovely appearance: it has, of course, the added attraction of being provided completely free whenever you buy a bunch of flowers. It is strong and will look like fabric when the sofa is finished.

When using paper flowerwrap as a covering you can build up as many layers as you need so that no edges of the polystyrene base show through. Two or more layers may be necessary. (See diagram and key below.)

SAFETY NOTE

Expanded polystyrene is easy to cut but liable to crumble. Use a craft knife. Start by digging the point in and then cut carefully. Remember that it will be impossible to cut yourself if you make sure that you always cut away from your other hand. Look before you cut.

1 Start with a small expanded polystyrene box approximately $3^1/_2$in (90 mm) long by $3^1/_2$in (90 mm) wide and $1^1/_2$in (40 mm) deep. These are used to pack electrical equipment and parts. As they are designed as protective packaging, the sides of the box will be around $^1/_2$in (12 mm) thick, ideal to form the sides and back of a 1/12 sofa.

2 Cut the box in half to make a matching pair.

3 Cut paper patterns for each section (see diagrams), allowing extra to fold underneath to finish off. The pieces should also be cut marginally wider than the sections to be covered and trimmed after fixing in place, using double-sided tape rather than glue.

4 To cover the base:
a) Fix on a piece of paper which has been cut to fit inside each arm.

b) Fix a strip of paper to the outside of one arm, continuing along the back to finish at the front of the second arm.

c) Cut a strip to fit over front and top of each arm, folding under at the front edge to fix underneath and finishing at the back of the arm.

d) Cut and fix on a piece of paper to cover over the back and seat, again folding under at the base of both front and back to finish underneath the sofa.

5 Using sharp scissors, trim excess flowerwrap neatly from joins.

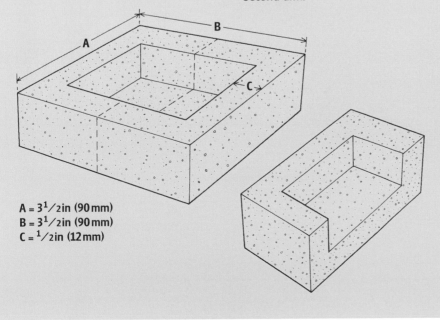

A = $3^1/_2$in (90 mm)
B = $3^1/_2$in (90 mm)
C = $^1/_2$in (12 mm)

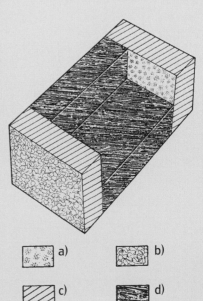

a) b) c) d)

CHAPTER 3

DISPLAY A COLLECTION

Many collectors own at least one dolls' house where miniatures are arranged in period or modern rooms. After that first house, some will decide to specialize in one type of miniature which especially appeals to them, whether it is paintings, porcelains or woodturnings.

To display a special collection, a shop, gallery or other specially designated room may sometimes provide a more suitable background than a dolls' house which is already furnished.

A collection of similar objects grouped together always looks impressive. You could start with a small arrangement on a window sill. As your collection grows it will need a larger display area.

▼ Some special collections can be housed effectively in either a formal or an informal setting. These handpainted pewter rabbits can be arranged on a nursery window sill or in a shop.

China and Porcelain

In the eighteenth century a large country house often had a china room, both to store and to show off attractive porcelain. This idea can be copied by the collector of miniatures. Walls can be used to show off sets of plates, so that even an extensive collection will fit into a small room. Larger pieces can be arranged on tables.

▲ This room is part of an antiques shop where the colour scheme and Delft-tiled fireplace were planned to complement the mainly blue-and-white china. The collection includes a bone china two-handled mug which commemorates Prince William's christening.

▼ Japanese Kakiemonware porcelain is a collectors' item whether in full size or miniature scale. The original is a rarity which was made only for a short time at the end of the seventeenth century. These lidded jars, bottles and tea bowl are handthrown and painted with delicate flowers to give an almost translucent effect.

Wooden objects

Wood is another attractive material. It is not cold to the touch like stone or marble; it feels good and often smells good; and the available range of colour and texture is immense. It isn't surprising that many collectors relish the variety of small objects which are a product of the woodturner's skill and imagination.

▲ This busy toymaker's workshop shows off wood in a number of different designs.

▼ Woodturned items on tables form part of a shop display. In the dolls' house kitchen or dining room many of these bowls and jars could be arranged as though ready for use rather than piled up for sale.

Armour

Armour fascinates hobbyists who are interested in the history of warfare or the age of chivalry. There are many distinctive types, so that it is possible to form a varied armour collection.

Some armour is made by miniaturists working in the dolls' house field, but many museum and gift shops also stock suits of armour, helmets and weapons based on historical examples and intended as souvenirs: these too, are usually in 1/12 scale.

Even at this size a suit of armour can be quite heavy, because these miniatures are usually made of pewter. It is best to provide a firm base so that the armour cannot fall over and damage small objects nearby. A really large piece of Blu-tack will solve the problem, giving added security even when a base is provided.

One suit of armour in a hallway could be the start of an interesting collection.

▲ Starting a collection: armour stands sentinel on either side of a castle door.

▼ Suits of armour are impressive standing in an oak-panelled corridor. From left to right: a suit of sixteenth-century gilded French armour; a representation of King Henry VIII's armour; and handmade pewter armour which has been finished to give an impression of age. The vizors can be raised and lowered. On the window sill, a Cromwellian lobstertail helmet and a Roman helmet complete the array.

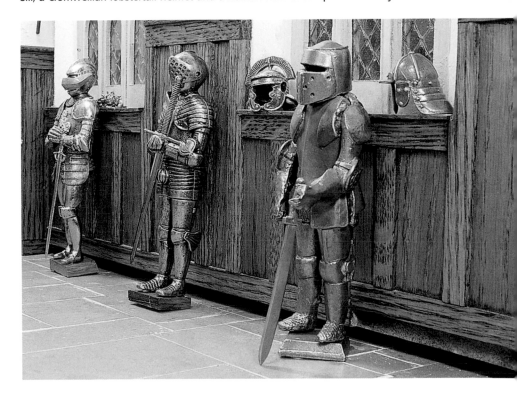

◀ A handmade cello with fine stringing. The instrument is French polished, which gives a soft sheen to the wood. Here it is shown next to a Regency chair, but a cello could be included in a modern room, too.

▼ Wind instruments displayed on a wall in a Tudor room. In the foreground, a lute is propped against an oak stool, ready for playing.

Musical instruments

Musical instruments are one speciality which can be arranged singly or in small groups in almost any room. A music room, such as the Regency example shown on pages 52–4, can be included in a dolls' house as long as the instruments are of the corresponding period.

One problem with slender wind instruments is how to fix them to prevent them rolling away. A tiny blob of Blu-tack or a thin strip of double-sided tape are two solutions. Take care when fixing them to a table or wall surface, because if pressure is applied too strongly at one point, the wood may snap.

▼ A single manual harpsichord based on an original made by Jacob Kirckman in the mid-eighteenth century. The miniature incorporates burr walnut, boxwood, walnut, amboyna and tulipwood. Fittings are of brass, and there are three sets of strings. The needlepoint cover on the music stool is worked in Florentine stitch, popularly known as flamestitch. Early period instruments will be of special interest to anyone who enjoys ancient music.

▼ A collection of period instruments is shown off on an oak table in the minstrels' gallery of a Tudor house. They include treble and bass recorders, a shawm, a lute and a psaltery.

▲ Classical art is shown in a small gallery in a Georgian house. The room decorations are also in Georgian style, with a dado rail above marbled walls, a chequered tile floor and a magnificent stone fireplace. Colours are kept pale so that the paintings show up well.

Art

One advantage of displaying paintings in a gallery is that you can rearrange the artworks from time to time without upsetting the balance of a furnished room.

Emphasize the hanging space by providing an additional 'frame' to surround the pictures. A silk cord fixed below the cornice with tasselled ends hanging on either side will add a touch of elegance in a gallery devoted to classical art. Add a few 'art objects' so that the floor is not entirely bare.

A simple, inexpensive way in which to acquire a comprehensive art collection is to use small pictures cut from exhibition catalogues or from home and decoration magazines which have art listings. It is essential that the pictures are printed with colours in register on good quality paper, and that you choose the correct type of framing for the period.

▲ What better subject for display than this 'swagger' painting by John Singer Sargent, who specialized in flattering his sitters? To emphasize its importance, the painting is framed in an impressive gilt moulding.

▲ Gilded picture-frame moulding is best for period art. A wide, heavy frame will complement an early landscape, while more delicate seascapes such as the small Turners will benefit from plainer frames, perhaps with simple beading.

Frame pictures for your gallery

Before framing, the first step is to mount the painting on thin card, using a solid gluestick in order to avoid crinkling the paper by wetting it. Scaled-down picture mouldings in plain or gilded wood can be chosen to suit the style of the picture.

You will need a mini mitre box and saw to cut the mouldings and mitre the corners. Instructions for using a mitre box and saw are given on page 82. All the pictures in the classical art gallery (left) were cut out and framed using this method.

1 Cut out your chosen picture and glue on to a piece of thin white card using solid gluestick, allowing a wide border all round.

2 Using a piece of the picture-frame moulding as a guide, lay it in place along each side of the picture in turn and draw along it with a pencil to mark out the finished dimensions of the frame on the card, then trim it to this size.

3 Cut the mouldings using a mitre box and saw. The opposite sides of the frame must be precisely the same length for a good fit. After cutting the first piece, mark

the length for the opposite side with a very sharp pencil before cutting. Repeat the process for the other two opposing sides.

4 Glue the mouldings around the picture on top of the spare card. Smear each piece of moulding with all-purpose glue and leave until slightly tacky before fixing: this will avoid the danger of getting any glue on the picture itself.

Note: The edges of the white card must be coloured or gilded to match the picture-frame moulding used. Use a gold pen or a coloured crayon.

► These frames have been chosen with care. The Rossetti oil should have a gilded surround. Japanese prints are framed traditionally in thin black moulding, while the Miró looks best in a plain wooden frame.

Use a mitre box and saw

▼ How to cut the mitred corners for a picture frame, window frame, door frame or fireplace.

▼ How to cut corners for skirting, cornice and dado.

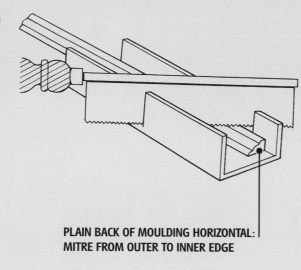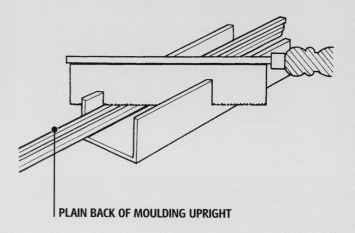

PLAIN BACK OF MOULDING HORIZONTAL: MITRE FROM OUTER TO INNER EDGE

PLAIN BACK OF MOULDING UPRIGHT

▲ Pictures in course of arrangement and the addition of some unusual modern sculpture give a lively feeling to this gallery. The sculptures, fashioned from gold wire and beads originally intended for jewellery-making, were assembled in minutes.

A modern art gallery

A gallery which is devoted to modern art might have plain white walls. It can then show a series of changing exhibitions, kept up to date with paintings taken from the latest listings and catalogues.

It may be unnecessary to frame modern abstract paintings; they often look best mounted on white card, which will also provide a natural border.

My own modern gallery (pictured below and below left) is in a room box measuring 15in (380mm) wide, 8in (200mm) deep and 11in (280mm) high. The floor and ceiling are interchangeable, so that the gallery can be used either way up. In the first version (below left) the floor is made of thick, silvery paper with a modernist design, while in the second (below) the floor is of black paper with a raised effect similar to bubblewrap. Either paper would be suitable for floor or ceiling.

▼ This exhibition has a more tranquil atmosphere: the pictures are calmer, and the tall metal 'sculptures' (from a gallery shop) were designed to hold postcards. They can also be used as a modern alternative to an easel.

Classical sculpture

The purpose of a formal gallery is to show off the collection: walls should be colour-washed to provide a background but not distract from the exhibits.

A gallery devoted to classical sculpture may be arranged in a room with Georgian-style decorations. Cornice and dado rail and a marble or tiled floor will be suitable, while the inclusion of marbled columns can add an extra dimension.

Wooden or plaster columns and capitals can be bought ready to paint as marble. If the back of the column cannot be seen, as in the sculpture gallery below, another method of simulating marble is to cover the column with thin marble-patterned card. Join at the centre back and glue it firmly in place. Paint the capitals and bases so that they match one of the colours in the marbling.

◄ Classical sculpture seen through a window of a gallery, which is set in a Georgian-style dolls' house. Ionic columns on either side of the pedimented doorway reinforce the striking classical effect.

▼ Inside the formal sculpture gallery. Walls and floor are almost covered with plaster mouldings, marble statues (simulated in cast resin) and assorted pedestals, plinths and busts. If you fix the exhibits in place with Blu-tack it will be easy to rearrange them.

Reeded columns are another idea: try using round dowelling and covering with fine corrugated card. Ensure that the join is at an indentation in the card, not a ridge, so that even if it can be seen it will not show up when painted. Paint reeded columns as stone, with light grey or stone matt-finish model enamel or with an acrylic paint mix.

Craftspeople make both classical and modern sculpture, cast most commonly in plaster or resin, but sometimes even in bronze. Look for quality in both the carving and in the material used. Busts and columns made of resin will be already coloured to resemble marble; plaster friezes and pediments can be painted using acrylic paints.

Sculpture looks best if mounted on a pedestal or plinth: it is essential to choose the size and shape to suit the proportions of the piece.

▲ A miniature of 'The Little Dancer' by Degas: it might be the focus of attention in an early twentieth-century sculpture gallery.

▶ An instantly recognizable bust of William Shakespeare, reading from one of his plays.

▶ Pedestals that include two wedding cake pillars. These are inexpensive to buy, and they can be useful where height is required.

An 18th-century sculpture room

In the eighteenth century many gentlemen returned from the Grand Tour of Europe with sculpture and paintings, and these would be arranged in a room especially designated for the purpose of showing off their splendid souvenirs.

Materials for the sculpture room

This room might have been created by an aristocratic collector who would want an original and striking setting for his works of art. Note the use of skirtings made from thin black corrugated card: black marbled card would also be suitable. Sculpture and framed paintings might both be included in a home, rather than a formal gallery collection. A frieze can be simulated in card.

▼ Plaster mouldings and other materials used in the sculpture room shown above.

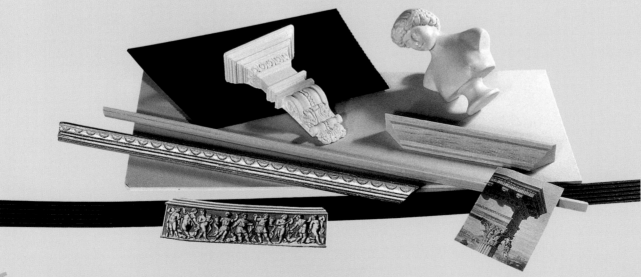

▲ This metal Chinese horse has been painted to resemble jade, using pale green model enamel followed by a coat of varnish. The ochre-coloured plinth is made in cast resin.

▲ Symmetrical arrangements were admired in the late Georgian period. Paintings and plaster casts can be arranged in pairs.

A classical colour scheme

Such a room will be more domestic in feeling than the formal gallery devoted solely to painting or sculpture. Plain walls can be painted in Adam green or blue or in a stronger colour known as 'picture gallery red'. Modern paint ranges reproduce accurate versions of these historic colours, and they can be bought in small sample pots.

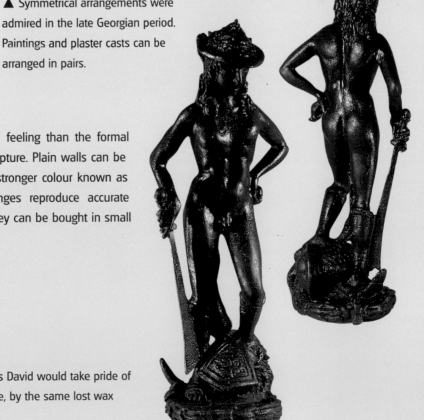

▶ This magnificent miniature of Donatello's David would take pride of place in any collection. It was cast in bronze, by the same lost wax method used to cast a full-size figure.

◄ This fireplace is designed to complement the sculpture in the eighteenth-century sculpture room rather than to house a grate. It is easy to make.

Make a classical marble fireplace

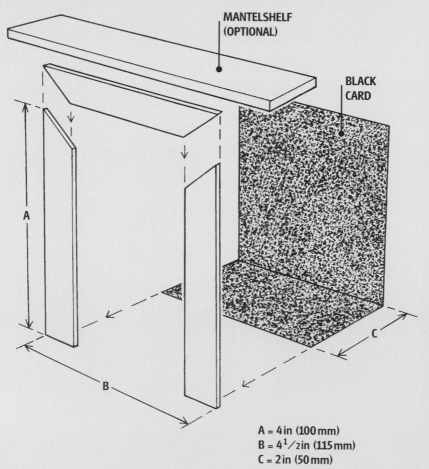

MANTELSHELF (OPTIONAL)

BLACK CARD

A
B
C

A = 4 in (100 mm)
B = 4¹/₂ in (115 mm)
C = 2 in (50 mm)

1 Cut and join mouldings as described on page 81.

2 For the marbled effect, first paint with cream or ivory model enamel.

3 To simulate veining, take a fine brush, dilute a little brown or grey model enamel with the creamy base colour, and feather on lightly, smudging a little here and there. It takes only a few minutes to produce a realistic effect. If you are uncertain about the painting, search out pictures of real marble, which naturally forms many patterns, and copy one you like.

4 Back the fireplace with black card. Cut the card long enough to be bent forward at the base to form a hearth, so that there is no possibility of a join showing.

Oriental sculpture

An original setting may incorporate something a little unusual for a dolls' house hobbyist. Your choice will be governed by the particular piece that you wish to display separately from your main collection of miniatures. It could be an American Indian artefact, a Mexican carving, a Chinese jade figure or an exquisitely beautiful shell. Foreign travel, reference books and your imagination will all provide ideas which you can use.

My own example is oriental sculpture, which appeals to many westerners who have come to appreciate the serenity and stillness associated with Buddhist images. Miniature Buddhas and other carvings may be found in tourist and museum shops which feature Asiatic art: they range from basic metal casts to gilded statues of great beauty.

Inexpensive 'stone' figures from India can be left plain, as they look natural in small size. Very cheap metal and plastic figures can be easily, and effectively, transformed by gilding (see page 91).

▲ Time for a change! This gallery devoted to oriental sculpture was used previously to show classical paintings (see page 80). Plaster mouldings in a frieze below the cornice have been added to complement the sculpture.

A Buddhist temple

Buddhist temples vary, depending on the school of Buddhism practised. They can be vast stone spaces, bare and awe-inspiring, with a gigantic Buddha figure at one end. In Tibet they are more often highly decorated, with a jewelled throne for the figure and with thangkas (traditional paintings on cloth) hung on the outside of the building. For the miniaturist an adaptation of this second option allows more scope, and can give rise to an imagined scene that will reflect a spirit of calm.

▼ Art paper and giftwrap form the basis for the decorative scheme of the temple. Gold-painted rocks add an exotic touch.

▼ The open top of this room box is covered with a bronze, self-patterned and semi-transparent flowerwrap paper which allows light to filter from above. Prayer flags made of paper are representational only, as they are normally hung on the outside of the building and would have inscriptions written on them.

Thangka paintings are colourful, lively and very exotic to western eyes. They can tell a complex story which may be difficult to fathom. Postcard-size reproductions of thangkas can be found in shops catering for Tibetan people, as well as in museum shops.

It is possible to decorate a temple using inexpensive materials. It will need no furniture; texture and colour will provide sufficient interest. Paper the walls with thick, creamy-gold woven papyrus from an art materials shop. The floor can be covered with patterned giftwrap in shades of orange and gold.

step-by-step

How to gild miniature figures

A gold or silver marker pen (of the kind that needs to be shaken before and during use) works well on metal, cast resin or plastic. It is worth practising how to use these pens before you begin.

1 Shake the pen vigorously. Then remove the cap and press the point down firmly on to some thick paper to start the metallic ink flowing. Repeat this sequence at intervals during application.

2 Press down firmly to eject a blob of ink which can be applied with the nib.

3 Leave to dry for about half an hour before touching.

Hang prayer flags on the walls

step-by-step

Prayer flags will suggest movement. Hang orange and yellow flags along each side wall. Suspend them from long green stalks cut from artificial flower sprays, to resemble bamboo poles.

1 Cut flags from ribbon or paper, roll one end around the 'pole' and secure with all-purpose glue such as Uhu. Space the flags at intervals along the pole.

2 Hang the poles, complete with attached flags, on brackets hung over the side walls. A simple bracket support can be made from a short length of the flower stalk, bent to make a U-shape. Use metal brackets if preferred, and paint them green so that they match the poles.

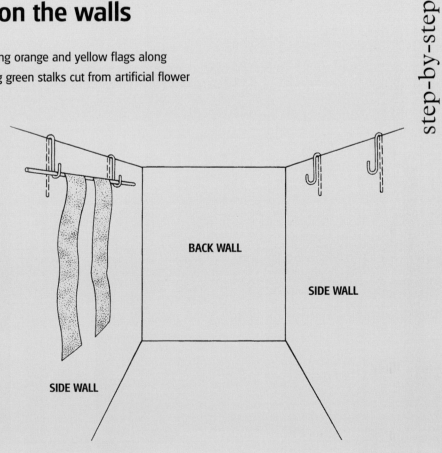

BACK WALL

SIDE WALL

SIDE WALL

Special furniture

At the very highest level of the maker's skill, unique furniture is not simply intended to be displayed in dolls' houses but may be destined for permanent exhibition in a museum. Alternatively, it may become part of a specialist collection belonging to someone who can afford and treasure such superlative work.

Few of us may own such pieces, but we can all admire them: it is inspiring to see just what can be achieved by the dedicated maker. Cabinets and bureaux are commonly chosen for reproduction, because even in full scale they are among the most complicated pieces of furniture to make. They become increasingly so as the scale is reduced, allowing the miniaturist to test his skills to the utmost; to include marquetry or parquetry using rare and unusual woods and recycled ivory; to execute minute carving; or to paint detailed scenes that are revealed only when cabinet doors are opened.

Writing desks incorporating metalwork in the form of delicate rails and working locks may include secret drawers, concealed in inner compartments that open with a touch. Table tops may be tesselated in minute fragments of marble, or inlaid with mother-of-pearl or semi-precious stones. Musical instruments will be veneered in satinwood and boxwood, crossbanded with rosewood, ebony or tulipwood, and then finished with gold leaf.

The examples shown in the following pages represent some of the finest miniature furniture ever to be made in 1/12. They are all based on historically documented pieces, and for some the approximate date of the original is given.

◀ A German bureau cabinet made by John Davenport in walnut with marquetry. The piece has a working lock on the desk flap.

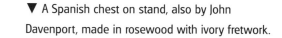

▼ A Spanish chest on stand, also by John Davenport, made in rosewood with ivory fretwork.

▲ An Antwerp cabinet on stand by Barry Hipwell, made in ebony with floral marquetry decoration. The original was circa 1700.

▲ An English cabinet on stand by Barry Hipwell: oyster veneered in laburnum, with legs in rosewood.

▲ Elizabethan 'Seadog' table by Ivan Turner. The top is inlaid with semi-precious stones to represent the marble pieces in the original.

▲ A Victorian table-desk by John Davenport, made in rosewood with floral designs in recycled ivory.

▶ An Italian folding chair of the late sixteenth or early seventeenth century. It is made by Ivan Turner in walnut and inlaid with ivory.

▶ German cabinet/bureau with marquetry architectural scenes by Geoffrey Wonnacott, circa 1775.

▼ Inside, the same cabinet has a splendid array of working drawers.

▶ English cabinet on stand circa 1775, depicting scenes of British castles and abbeys. Made by Geoffrey Wonnacott.

◄ A nineteenth-century double action pedal harp by Alan McKirdy, finished in black lacquer and gold leaf in the 'Grecian' pattern.

▼ A late eighteenth-century square piano with floral painted decoration, copied by Alan McKirdy from an original made by Longman & Broderip. The tapered legs are fitted with working castors.

◄ An Elizabethan/Jacobean court cupboard, elaborately carved in pearwood by David Hurley. In miniature scale the grain size resembles the original oak.

◀ Irish eighteenth-century breakfront bookcase with glazing in Gothic style, made by Michael Walton.

▶ This late eighteenth-century demi-lune commode, made in mahogany and inlaid with amboyna, boxwood and ebony with rosewood crossbanding, is by Michael Walton.

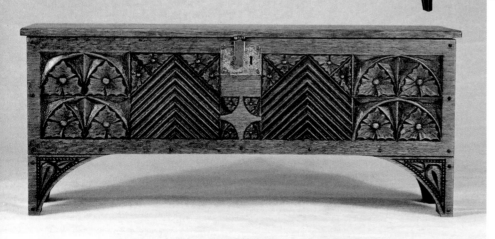

◀ An English fifteenth-century boarded chest with carved front by David Hurley.

CHAPTER 4

ROOM BOXES

A room box can be an ideal starting point for a beginner, since it provides an opportunity to practise decorating and design skills before beginning to tackle a complete dolls' house. For the more advanced hobbyist it can be a good way to try out unusual ideas.

A room box takes up little space and is sufficient for a shop or a small specialist collection. A single room setting also make an excellent project for a group, such as a dolls' house club. With each member contributing a special skill, the completed scene may contain exemplary painting, needlework and woodwork which individuals might not be able to achieve on their own.

▼ This room box has been divided in two to create a small scullery next to a larger kitchen area.

Undecorated wooden room boxes are widely available, both ready-built and in kit form. Most have a hinged or lift-off perspex or glass front. Some have a choice of period-style doors and windows and they can also be wired for lighting.

A typical room box will be the size of an average dolls' house room, approximately 15in (380mm) wide, 10in (255mm) high and 11in (280mm) deep. Double boxes with two rooms side by side can also be purchased. Smaller boxes designed to

hang on a wall will have less depth than freestanding ones. You may prefer to buy a professionally made wooden box to house a permanent arrangement, but if your woodworking skills are good enough the alternative is to design and make your own. Another variation is to construct a rear 'corridor' behind the main room so that an additional scene can be arranged. Windows and a door in an inner back wall will allow viewers a tantalizing glimpse of the background scene.

▲ A joint project by a dolls' house club, this Adam library incorporates details from two famous rooms designed by Robert Adam at Mellerstain in Scotland and Kenwood in London. The outside is painted to resemble the golden sandstone which Adam used for much of his building work. Windows and a pediment also enhance the effect.

► Inside the library great attention has been paid to reproducing authentic details.

How to make a simple room box

If you plan to experiment with a number of different arrangements before deciding on finished style and decorations, it is economical to make a room box with an open front from $^3/_{16}$ in (5 mm) foamboard (available from stockists of art materials and good stationers). Foamboard is strong and rigid and very light in weight, making it easy to carry around or take to club meetings. Most of the settings in this chapter were arranged in room boxes of varying sizes made in this material.

1 Decide on the size of the room. Measure and cut the foamboard, making sure that the edges are straight and the corners are square. Straight edges are easy to achieve if you use a self-healing cutting mat which will be marked with a grid of squares, and use a craft knife and raised-edge metal ruler.

2 Cut a floor, a back wall, two side walls and a ceiling (optional). Suggested measurements are given on the diagram but can be varied depending on your requirements.

3 Glue the pieces together, following the sequence shown in the diagram. An all-purpose adhesive such as Uhu works well on foamboard: run a thin trail of glue along one edge only and press against the piece to be joined on. Hold together for a minute or two to bond firmly together. Wipe off any excess glue immediately.

4 To finish the box, you might like to paint the outside to complement the interior decorations. Use two coats of water-based emulsion or satin-finish decorator's paint.

Cutting note: the side walls are fixed to the floor and edges of the back wall and should be cut $^3/_{16}$ in (5 mm) longer than the floor to allow for this. The ceiling will be fitted on top of the back and side walls, so needs to be cut $^3/_8$ in (10 mm) wider and $^3/_{16}$ in (5 mm) longer than the floor to allow for the thickness of the walls. The ceiling can be added after interior decorations are completed if preferred.

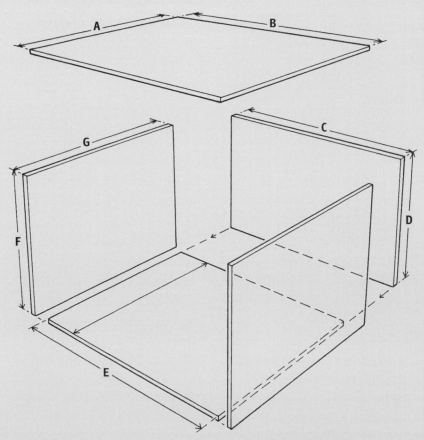

A = 11$^3/_{16}$ in (285 mm)
B = 15$^3/_8$ in (390 mm)
C = 15 in (380 mm)
D = 10 in (255 mm)
E = 15 in (380 mm)
F = 10 in (255 mm)
G = 11 in (280 mm)

▲ ◀ This large room box is 21in (530mm) wide, 12in (305mm) high and 15¼in (385mm) deep including the rear corridor. It is also available in kit form, with or without panelling, and lighting can be fitted to illuminate the background. This room is ready for decoration, with panelling fitted.

Flooring and walls

Floor covering can be fixed to a card base before it is fitted into the room box, making it easy to change at a later stage if you wish. Start with paper or thin card, perhaps upgrading to tiles or a carpet at a later stage.

For plain coloured interior walls, use artists' mounting board (Daler board, etc.) to make an inner lining to your room box shell. There is a huge range of colours, which includes silk finish and mottled effects.

Cut the board to fit inside the room box shell. Put the back wall in first, then the side walls, so that the join will be invisible. Attach with double-sided tape along the edges only, then it will be easy to change the decorations later if you wish.

A Georgian panelled room

You can arrange any scene in a room box in order to reflect your own particular interests. Here are two variations on an eighteenth-century panelled room, using the room box opposite as the starting point.

Setting the first scene in the mid-Georgian era gives an opportunity to use soft blue-and-white on the walls. Faux marble decoration adds a fashionable look. (For a marbled paint finish see page 88.) Use masking tape to cover adjacent surfaces when adding a marbled paint finish to a frieze. Test out colours on card first to try variations.

In the Georgian period, the cornice was often treated as part of the wall rather than painted the same as the ceiling. The window glazing bars and the fireplace can be painted off-white.

In the second version the decorations and furniture have been changed in order to create a fictional background for the Emperor Napoleon's abdication. The walls have been repainted a mid blue-green from a range of historic paint shades. An ornate plaster ceiling and frieze have been provided, using an embossed dolls' house paper with a scaled-down plasterwork design. The fireplace is now painted to simulate French marble. A Napoleonic torchère and a marble-topped console table provide a touch of grandeur.

▲ An art gallery print of a landscape has been added behind the windows of the panelled room on page 100. A marbled frieze fills the space below the cornice. The floorboards have been given a satin-finish varnish.

▲ In a different scene set behind the windows, the battle still rages, but Napoleon is defeated, in this variation on the same room. Outside, an officer of the 95th Rifles foils a belated rescue attempt. This is not historically accurate, but fun for a miniaturist who is interested in the Napoleonic wars.

▶ On the wall above the gilded console table, the painting shows the taking of a French 'eagle' at Waterloo. Like the painting of Wellington at the other end of the room, the picture was cut from a museum postcard and framed in gilt moulding.

A Turkish carpet emporium

Some specialized collections will look their best in a shop setting: hats and food are both particularly suitable, while furniture and ornaments can easily be incorporated into an antique shop, with the added bonus that the stock can be changed as items are moved either into a dolls' house or a designated room setting. This Turkish carpet emporium is set in an open-fronted room box.

▶ The shop is based on those in the Grand Bazaar in Istanbul, where there are rows of carpet sellers' stalls with their wares spilling out onto the ground in front. Cream woollen fringed braid provides a suitably ethnic hanging to finish off the stall.

▼ A portrait of a Turkish potentate on the shop wall makes an additional point of interest. This striking painting, cut from an exhibition listing, is framed handsomely in gilt.

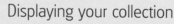

Displaying your collection

A Turkish carpet emporium is a simple but effective way to show off miniature woven carpets. These are inexpensive and are available in dolls' house shops, museum shops and tourist outlets in a seemingly inexhaustible selection of designs and sizes.

Walls and flooring

A plain background is best, as the carpets will make a colourful display. Use a white textured paper for the walls, or paint plain white if preferred.

Accessories

A low table for refreshments can be made from a circle of card glued to a round base about $1^1/_2$in (40mm) high. I used a picture of an Islamic plate to make the table top.

► Include as many carpets as you can. Carpets rolled in the corner are paper cut-outs from magazines. They might be replaced by real miniature carpets as the collection grows.

▼ One essential when haggling for a carpet in a bazaar is some refreshment, as the process is likely to take a long time. A 1/12 pewter coffee pot and two small glasses in silver filigree holders are set out on the table. The low stools are adapted from the lid and base of a small soapstone pot, topped with buttons in suitably oriental designs.

103

A Japanese gift shop

A colourful Japanese shop of the sort designed to attract tourists can be filled with holiday souvenirs for the visitor to buy. This room box is edged with a flimsy, semi-transparent Japanese white-on-white paper. The paper is creased into wings at the sides to suggest the folds of a kimono.

▼ A mini-kimono which was attached to a greetings card is the perfect size to display in the shop.

A place for everything

This busy shop layout will contrast with the sparse interior of any domestic Japanese room, where colour is generally kept to a minimum and anything not in use is stored neatly in cupboards and concealed behind sliding doors.

Wall covering

To make an authentic background for the objects on display, use a Japanese art paper. The indigo blue patterned paper used on the walls is a good example.

Traditional flooring

Tatami matting is simulated by using corrugated card. In a Japanese home this would consist of mats placed together, each of them edged in black, but in a miniature shop where so much of the floor will be covered by the stock it can be laid as a single sheet. Plain card will not give the right effect: use a water-based emulsion to paint it buff or light grey.

◀ Japanese prints appeal to art connoisseurs and tourists alike. Frame catalogue prints in thin black wood (see page 81 for framing ideas and instructions). Alternatively, they can be mounted on black card, leaving a border showing to provide a mount.

▼ Realistic cherry blossom, made in metal, is displayed on a bamboo table mat.

▼ Try to provide a variety of levels to display goods: a low box or table can be used to draw attention to special merchandise.

A Russian room

The traditional Russian 'izba' is a wooden peasant cottage. Whatever the size of the room, an essential feature is the stove. It is huge – and needs to be, in order to combat the sub-zero winter temperatures outside.

To make the Russian stove, use an earthenware pastel burner. Mount it on a round box and, for extra height, top it with a second round box. Use the card centre from a kitchen paper roll as the chimney: it can be cut to fit the height of the room. Cover it with thin card to provide a smooth finish, and glue on with the join at the back where it will not show. Glue the sections together and paint with white matt-finish paint.

▼ Wooden mouldings (purchased from a DIY store) simulate the carved wood which is always in evidence in Russian homes.

▲ A Russian stove sits in a corner of this cosy room. A bench is placed nearby for warmth.

▲ Woodcarving and music are popular Russian pastimes.

◄ Icons glow against the dark green wall. These ones are card cut-outs.

An icon in a special corner was essential, with a candle placed nearby. Some Russians like to amass a collection, and for the miniaturist this is a good decorative idea.

Because of the intense cold, every inch of the floor would be covered by overlapping patterned rugs.

The best (and possibly only) bed would be used in the daytime to show off a fine display of handworked and lace-trimmed textiles. Woven fabric or a small embroidered carpet should be hung over the bed. Scraps of lace, ribbon and embroidered fabric will simulate the beautifully laundered textiles and hand embroidery which are displayed proudly in most Russian homes.

◄ The colourful lace-edged coverlet is a machine-embroidered table mat. Plain red fabric is the background for a variety of lace patterns.

CHAPTER 5

HOLIDAY INSPIRATIONS

A holiday location can provide inspiration for an interesting miniature room or even a complete dolls' house. This will bring a remembered holiday to life more vividly than any photograph – or it may encourage you to visit that exotic location you have always planned to see for yourself.

Holidays in different places give us an insight into living arrangements in distant parts of the globe. The scenes I have chosen for this chapter include courtyards as well as rooms, and they can be arranged in single or double settings.

▼ A Mediterranean-style patio pot is ideal for a Maltese courtyard.

Colours and textiles can play a big part in such settings. Paint colours used in hot climates are often much brighter than those in cool western countries: think of brilliant, Indian sari fabrics, the delicate hand-embroidered silk hangings of China or the patterns and textures of Moroccan cushions.

A specialist dolls' house supplier is the obvious place to find furniture for period or modern rooms. Arranging a more exotic room will give a different shopping experience as you search for ribbons and braids, greeting cards and small souvenirs from tourist and gift shops and even from department stores. You will be able to make simple furniture and decorate with these materials.

◄ This Maltese courtyard is set in a very small room box and is a reminder of a happy holiday.

A seaside cottage

Most people remember their earliest seaside holiday, so my first choice is a cottage-style seaside home. Fishermen's cottages in both Britain and America are updated with the addition of modern plumbing to make desirable summer 'lets' for holiday-makers. The essence of any modernized cottage is simplicity. For a seaside home, concentrate on blue-and-white and keep bright colour accents to a minimum. Cover the walls with white rough-textured paper in order to give a plastered appearance: alternatively, paint with textured stencil paint. The floor can be covered with strong, thick paper in tones of blue. If you prefer carpet try plain blue felt or, alternatively, fit a planked floor for a natural look.

▼ A newly decorated holiday cottage, tidy and clean, ready for the holiday-makers to arrive. The traditional Orkney chair was professionally made. Scottish fishermen have made this type of chair for centuries, using driftwood from the beach, with the back and seat woven from seagrass or twine.

▼ Some of the materials used in this seaside themed room.

▲ A lobster pot and a rug with a nautical design add interest to the seaside cottage.

To make a simulated needlework picture like the one hanging in the corner of the seaside room, draw a ship on Aida linen-weave fabric, using a very fine black pen.

Frame the finished piece in plain picture-frame moulding – either left uncoloured or varnished if you prefer.

The nautical rug shown here is worked in needlepoint on fine canvas and was designed by an amateur maker. To design your own rug, draw a plan on graph paper and stitch it onto a size 18 or size 22 canvas, remembering that each square on the paper pattern represents a stitch over one thread on the canvas. The secret of success is to keep the design simple: stripes and a geometric pattern will make working it straightforward.

Complete the room with a scattering of fishing nets, lobster pots and other fishy miniatures. Add buckets, spades and model ships to suggest that the eager holiday-makers have already arrived.

◀ A corner sofa unit continues the nautical theme. A back can be added using dolls' house balustrade or, as shown, a cut-down 1/12 ladder. Leave the wood unpainted for a natural look. The wooden back can be used to display a collection of tiny shells or pebbles.

How to make a corner sofa unit

Fitted sofas upholstered in blue-and-white striped cotton are neat and give the appearance of having storage space beneath. Two sofas joined to form a corner unit make a striking feature.

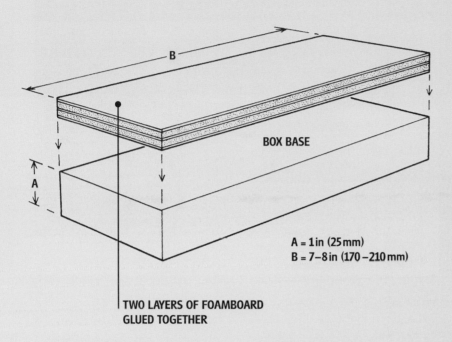

BOX BASE

A = 1 in (25 mm)
B = 7–8 in (170–210 mm)

TWO LAYERS OF FOAMBOARD
GLUED TOGETHER

COVER FOAMBOARD IN VILENE
AND STRIPED COTTON FABRIC,
AND GLUE TO TOP OF BOX

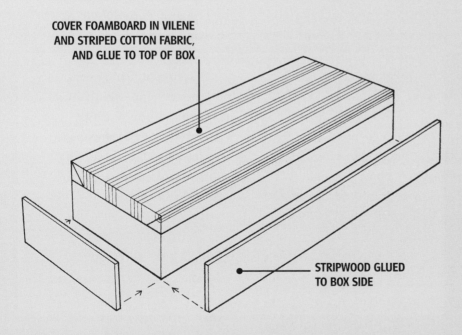

STRIPWOOD GLUED
TO BOX SIDE

1 Use a rigid box to form the sofa base, approximately 1 in (25 mm) high and perhaps 7–8 in (170–210 mm) long. Use the box for one sofa and the lid for the other, because the difference in length will be marginal.

2 Pad the tops with two thicknesses of foamboard, cut to fit the box and lid, and lightly glue together. Cover the foamboard by wrapping round with double thickness dressmakers' stiffening (Vilene) to give a soft but not squashy appearance. Turn the Vilene over the ends, neatening the corners by folding in a triangle at each corner as when packing a parcel, and glue in place underneath.

3 Cover with blue-and-white striped cotton, using the same method. Remember to match the stripes at the corner where the seats will join.

4 For the surround, use 1 in (25 mm) stripwood, cut to size and glued on to the box sides. Butt join at the corners – this is meant to look shipshape, not like expensive carpentry.

5 Finally, glue white piping cord all round the top edge of the woodstrip. Cut the cord to the exact length to fit, twist the ends firmly together and fix with a dab of all-purpose glue to prevent the strands unravelling.

▲ The Moroccan room, showing floor cushion, storage unit, and a battered-looking cupboard (see instructions on page 114–115).

A Moroccan room and courtyard

Morocco has a special attraction for holiday-makers, and the local use of colour makes a strong impact. Wonderfully bright blues and greens, bead curtains, piles of red and orange spices in the market, pink walls and green plants combine in a glorious mix whose components never seem to clash. The miniaturist can enjoy reproducing some of the excitement and colour in a small space with only minimal expense.

A Moroccan room will appear more realistic if the paint doesn't look too new. To achieve the authentic slightly shabby effect, paint the door with a coat of mid-green model enamel and, when dry, follow with a coat of French blue. Don't apply the second colour too evenly, allowing some of the green to show through. Fix a strip of braid over the top of the door.

The floor can be tiled for coolness. You can either fit individual miniature ceramic tiles or, for economy, use a card simulation.

Almost all the furniture in a Moroccan room can be homemade or adapted from inexpensive objects. A low table, some low seating (large, squashy floor cushions, perhaps), a stove or storage unit, shelves and a battered cupboard are all you need.

◄ The floor is of shiny, dark green card with a faint pattern to give a tiled effect, and is partly covered by a small carpet. A vividly striped cotton fabric is draped over one wall and finished with a coarse-textured patterned braid.

A courtyard surrounded by high walls is an oasis of cool shade in hot climates. The walls can be of rough-textured paper or card, or may be painted using textured stencil paint. The deep terracotta used on the side walls resembles reddish sandstone, while the sunset backdrop is a picture cut from a magazine, giving an extra dimension to the 'outdoor' courtyard.

There are several options for the floor: it can be tiled, painted as earth or covered with rough thick paper to look like white sand.

A pool can be any size you choose. It can be made from four pieces of stripwood, butt-joined and glued to a card or thin wood base. Paint both inside and outside as well as the top with bright turquoise acrylic paint. Fix on blue/green ceramic tiles, which are sold in craft shops, to make mosaics. You might use 'liquid water' paint for a realistic effect in the pool.

Tall palms in terracotta pots add to the oriental feeling of the courtyard and can be made very easily. A single spray of artificial greenery from a flower shop or a department store will be sufficient for several palms. Cut into suitable lengths and prune to shape. The main stem is generally wired: snip with wire cutters or pliers. The fronds can be trimmed with scissors. Alternatively, wide green plant ties can be cut and fringed to make thin palm leaves.

ACCESSORIES WITH A MOROCCAN THEME

■ Make a bead curtain to hang at the side of the door. Thread tiny multi-coloured glass beads onto nylon thread. Put the beads in a saucer, use a very fine needle, and it will be easy to pick them up one at a time with the tip of the needle. Make a large knot before threading on the first bead and, to make sure that it will not slip off, take the thread round and through twice before threading on the rest of the beads. Finish off using the same method with the last bead and, after knotting off, leave a long end of thread.

Knot all the strands together to hang several rows of beads at the side of the door. To cover the whole door you will need many more rows: sew the ends on to narrow tape and either fix over the door with double-sided tape or glue in place. Cover the tape with a strip of braid.

■ Make a hanging lamp from metal or glass beads intended for jewellery making. Thread onto a silk tasselled cord and suspend from thin chain hung across the top of the room.

■ Provide a coffee pot. It can be of copper or brass: a design with a side handle is most suitable.

■ Red lentils piled on a brass or copper dish will add a splash of additional colour. Use a button for the dish, and glue the lentils together in a pyramid shape to prevent them scattering around.

▼ Beads, buttons and scraps of braid and fabric will provide accessories for the Moroccan room.

◀ Outside in the Moroccan courtyard the double doors are painted in a similar way to the inside room door, but the colours are varied slightly and a green-painted wooden lintel replaces the braid used inside. These doors were adapted from a cheap wardrobe. The main feature of the courtyard is the pool.

How to make a Moroccan seating area

step-by-step

To make a low table, paint a small box and partially cover the sides with white braid or lace. To make a low seat, use a piece of balsa wood about 1in (25mm) high and 5in (125mm) or 6in (150mm) long as the base. Pad the top with dressmakers' wadding. Glue on a strip of braid to cover the top, and a narrower coarse braid around the sides. For the stripey floor cushions, follow the instructions below.

1 Cut a strip of striped fabric about 5in (125mm) long by 2in (50mm) wide; turn in $^1/_4$in (6mm) on each long edge and then press or tack in place.

2 Fold twice to make a square, push in a small amount of dressmakers' wadding and slipstitch the edges together. Alternatively, use striped braid and there will be no need to turn in a side hem.

3 Pummel the cushions fairly fiercely to make them look squashy before putting them into the room.

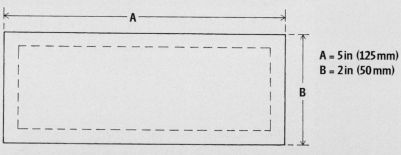

A
A = 5in (125mm)
B = 2in (50mm)
B

$^1/_4$in (6mm) TURNINGS ON ALL EDGES

FOLD   FOLD

FOLD TWICE, INSERT STUFFING, SLIPSTITCH SIDES AND END

DRESSMAKERS' WADDING

SLIPSTITCH EDGES TOGETHER

How to make a storage unit

A white, free-standing storage unit is easy to make. The old-fashioned built-in stove is often converted into a storage unit, as nowadays small portable stoves are used for cooking. A good material to use is $1/8$–$3/16$in (3–5mm) foamboard, which will not need painting. In this kind of project the exact size is not critical. It may also depend on the space you want to fill or the layout of the room. Adjust the measurements to suit your own requirements.

▲ The completed storage unit. Buttons and jewellery bits and pieces simulate brass and copper dishes and pots.

1 Measure and cut the foamboard pieces, following the diagram.

2 Cut two arched holes in the front of the lower part, and one larger arched hole in the front of the upper section. It will not matter if the holes are a little irregular in shape as this is an ethnic arrangement.

3 Glue the pieces together with all-purpose glue, being careful to centre the top section over the lower part.

A = 2in (50mm)
B = $1^1/2$in (40mm)
C = $4^1/2$in (115mm)
D = $1^3/8$in (35mm)
E = 4in (100mm)
F = $1^7/8$in (48mm)
G = 2in (50mm)
H = $4^3/4$in (120mm)
I = $1^3/4$in (45mm)
J = $4^3/4$in (120mm)

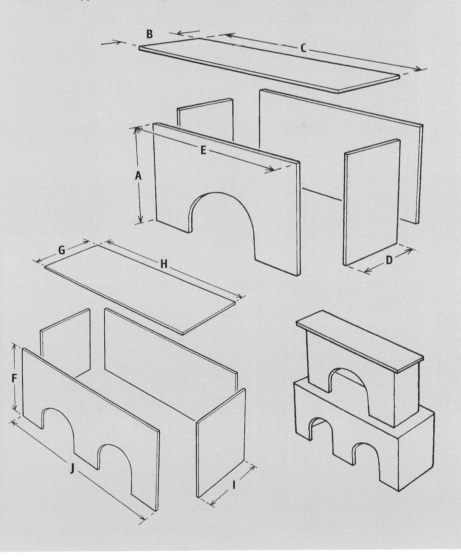

An Indian room and courtyard

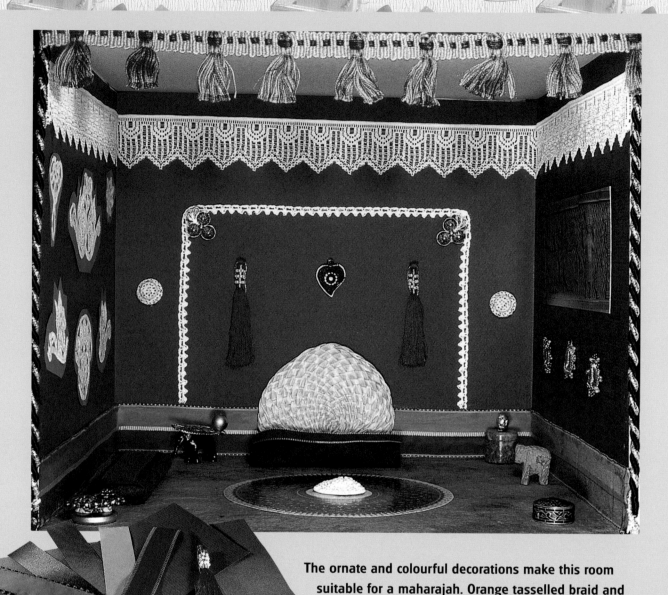

The ornate and colourful decorations make this room suitable for a maharajah. Orange tasselled braid and purple-and-gold cord finish the front of the room with a flourish. A courtyard can be arranged separately or combined in a double room box setting.

▲ A choice of vividly coloured papers and ribbons for decoration.

Walls and flooring

Although both room and courtyard are decorated in a lavish style, it is not necessary to use expensive materials to achieve this effect. The floor and walls are covered with brightly coloured textured papers, while the (minimal) low furniture and the small wall decorations can be made with a combination of buttons, beads and fancy ribbons.

In Gujarat white plaster designs make a striking effect against terracotta walls. The designs are often lace-like, sometimes geometric, and can be used to emphasize archways and doors. This rustic style is now being used again by Indian architects to decorate ultra-modern buildings.

Decorating the walls

The decoration can be achieved in two ways. One is to draw your own designs with a white marker pen. Leaves and flowers, zig-zag borders and simplistic human figures are popular and not difficult to represent.

The more complex designs resemble the crystalline structure of a snowflake, and an easy way to simulate this is to cut out part of a white paper doyley. Mount the white patterns on a roughly cut card shape in a different shade from the colour of the main wall, and glue it in place so that you fashion a random design.

The courtyard

Steps are a feature of Indian courtyards. An arrangement of shallow steps can be graduated in size to form a raised platform for the seats on top of a series of steps. Make the steps from pieces of foamboard, covered with the same paper as the main floor or painted to match. For shade, fit a card canopy covered with the same paper as the back wall over the raised platform and seats.

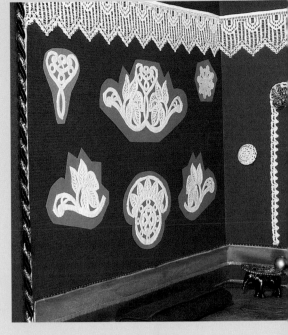

▲ Colours and patterns from India. The white cut-outs are mounted on bright orange card and contrast with the deep terracotta walls.

◄ The shuttered windows high up on the side walls of the courtyard are painted in bright blue and green. You can make it look a little shabby by rubbing off small patches of paint before it dries. The roughly carved wooden tiger came from an oriental gift shop and has been painted to simulate a sandstone sculpture.

▼ Materials used in the courtyard.

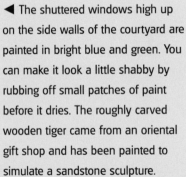

How to make Indian-style accessories

How to make bench-like seats from corrugated packing card:

1 Fold the card over several times to make a height of $^1/_2$in (12mm) and a depth of about $1^1/_2$in (40mm).

2 Trim to the desired length: the seats in the room shown are $4^1/_2$in (115mm) long.

3 Fix the card with a dab of glue underneath.

4 To cover the seat base, cover with non-fray velvet ribbon or a leather sample, with the suede side showing: leather and ribbon can both be cut neatly with sharp scissors.

5 Cut one large piece to the same length as the seat base and long enough to fold round it.

6 Join and glue underneath.

7 Finish the seat with a strip of moiré ribbon with Lurex edging.

How to make a canopy:

1 Cut the card approximately 5in (125mm) high, and to fit the width of the room plus 10in (255mm).

2 Fold back 5in (125mm) at each end to glue to the sides of the box. A card top can be fixed on top.

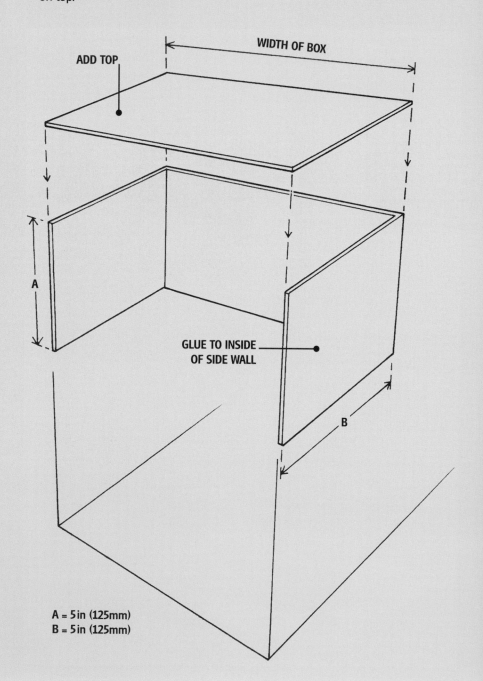

ADD TOP

WIDTH OF BOX

A

GLUE TO INSIDE OF SIDE WALL

B

A = 5in (125mm)
B = 5in (125mm)

How to make the courtyard seating:

Low seats are made in a similar way to the more formal ones in the main room but are covered with gold-trimmed Indian sari fabric.

1 Cut a piece of fabric twice the width of the seat base and long enough to wind around it several times.

2 Place the base in the centre of the fabric and fold over and over to pad and cover the base.

3 Fold the ends in neatly, making sure that some of the gold Lurex trim shows on top.

4 Glue the fabric ends underneath.

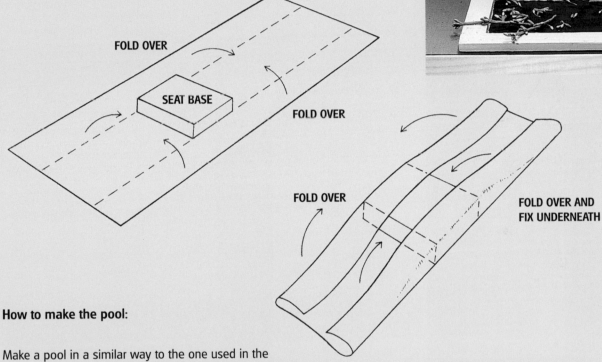

FOLD OVER

SEAT BASE

FOLD OVER

FOLD OVER

FOLD OVER AND FIX UNDERNEATH

How to make the pool:

Make a pool in a similar way to the one used in the Moroccan courtyard, but omit the tiles.

1 Cut four pieces of stripwood to make a rectangle approximately 6 in (150 mm) x 4 in (100 mm).

2 Butt-join and glue to a wooden or card base.

3 Paint with a mix of buff and pink water-based emulsion paint or an acrylic mix.

4 Rough up the surface slightly with a coarse glasspaper to make it resemble rough sandstone.

5 Cut a piece of shiny dark blue paper to fit inside the pool to simulate water.

6 Scatter with pink artificial flower petals or with small blossoms.

CHAPTER 6
OUTDOOR SCENES

A dolls' house may have a porch which can be used to link the interior with an outside space. A verandah or terrace can be treated as an extra room for garden furniture and potted plants. Even a small and drab base surrounding the house can be enlivened by the introduction of plants or garden tools.

Climbing plants can be attached to trellis on the house wall near a door or window, or fixed to a metal or wooden obelisk. Fix the support into a piece of florists' oasis to make a raised, grassy bed and dot with small flowers. This is easy to move around when you want to change the garden scene.

Freestanding garden buildings can be placed on a terrace or paved area outside a dolls' house. They extend the selection of miniatures which can be included, while taking up little extra space.

Medieval houses were sometimes fashioned from former monasteries. In a shady cloister flowering plants may be out of place, but the space can be used for livestock. Realistic miniature beasts and birds will appeal to the animal lover, and this provides a good opportunity to use them.

For a logpile, gather twigs of a suitable thickness from the garden and cut to length with a sharp knife. Glue the resulting logs together in a neat pile on a small wooden base. One coat of matt varnish will preserve the logs.

▲ The open door of a Tudor house shows a glimpse of a formal flower arrangement inside. Climbing roses in a small raised base at the side of the door link the hall and the garden.

▶ The remnant of a cloister now has a new use as a chicken run, with other farm animals among the logpiles and bales of hay.

▶ An ancient half-timbered house with an exterior covered stairway also has room for a well, a dovecote, a water butt and a small barrel containing water lilies. Well-heads can be bought ready-made or to assemble from kits.

An English garden terrace

Here is an English garden terrace assembled from a kit. It is sufficiently easy for a beginner who has never tackled a kit before, as the trellis panels are supplied ready made up.

For simplicity, paint the base and baluster section with a coat of matt stone model enamel. The wooden structure should be stained and varnished before you glue the pieces together, to avoid the possibility of any glue spots on the untreated wood: these would show up as bare patches after staining. Wood dye can be applied with a dry cloth, but use a cotton bud or fine paintbrush to work the stain into the corners of the trellis.

Alternatively, spray-paint the wooden structure after assembly using a spray-paint designed for use on models.

▲▼ A garden terrace made from a kit before and after the addition of flowers and accessories. The garden setting can be changed to suit the seasons.

The potting shed

▼ This small wooden shed stands on a firm paved base which can be used for gardening tools and plants. The horseshoe over the door is a traditional touch, fixed to 'hold' luck.

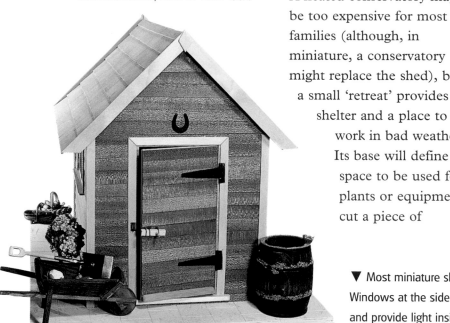

Gardening is a popular pastime, and a potting shed is essential to raise seeds and shelter growing cuttings. A heated conservatory may be too expensive for most families (although, in miniature, a conservatory might replace the shed), but a small 'retreat' provides shelter and a place to work in bad weather. Its base will define the space to be used for plants or equipment: cut a piece of plywood or medium density fibreboard (MDF) to the size you need, allowing at least 3in (75mm) all round the building.

Provide paving by marking out squares and rectangles to resemble flagstones: paint with matt stone model enamel, or glue on sheet paving with a plasticised finish.

For a lawn surround, railway modeller's grass with a peel-off backing is easy to cut and fit.

▼ Most miniature sheds have a lift-off roof to allow access. Windows at the side of the shed allow a view through to the outside and provide light inside when the roof is in place. Hats and indoor games are stored in a corner near the door, ready for use.

BOWLS

HEAVY DUTY FENCING

6ft x 3ft

For additional realism you may prefer to use ceramic or resin flagstones. To do this, measure the base wood carefully before cutting to make sure that the flagstones will fit exactly without trimming: it will look neater if entire flagstones are used.

The miniatures you put in your shed are a matter of personal choice – it has many other possible uses besides its primary role as a potting shed. Depending upon your current collection of miniatures, together with your plans for future purchases or things to make, it can be used to store garden furniture, tricycles and other children's toys, a pram or a pushchair. It might even provide a useful repository for spare furniture, especially broken items which may feature as junk 'awaiting removal' until you have sufficient spare time to repair them.

The shed can become a home office or workshop, using scaled-down office furniture and equipment, or you might like to fit it out as a toolshed, complete with workbench and miniature tools as well as the work in progress.

▲ The view into the shed through the open door shows an array of plants plus a variety of equipment for the gardener.

IDEAS FOR THE POTTING SHED

Although many of the objects in and around the shed may be purchased ready-made, there is plenty of scope for small things to make. If you are not a gardener yourself, take a look inside some of your neighbours' sheds and you will be amazed by how much they contain. Here are some ideas:

■ To provide earth or compost for plantpots, $^3/_4$-fill the pot with screwed-up paper, spread the top of the paper with glue and cover with fine tea from a teabag.

■ Some plants look more attractive if they are surrounded by small pebbles. Glue a little paper around the base of the plant, spread with more glue and cover with sesame seeds.

■ Puy lentils can be used to make gravel for box containers. Spread the base with glue and press the lentils firmly in place. The greenish-black colour is very attractive.

▼ Make wooden boxes for bedding plants from balsa wood. Cut with scissors: all you need is a rectangle for the base and eight strips of balsa glued on to form the sides.

▼ Vegetables freshly dug from the soil indicate that gardening is in progress.

A terrace in Provence

A garden terrace is another opportunity to extend display space and try out arrangements from different countries. This typical Provençal terrace is set in a two-sided room box 17in (430mm) long and 15in (380mm) deep, made from foamboard.

The house entrance

Tall walls surrounding a French Provençal terrace will be made more interesting with the addition of shuttered windows and a doorway. The doorway represents the entrance to an adjoining house. You can buy a dolls' house door but, for economy, another possibility is to use a pair from a cheap wardrobe and paint them in French blue model enamel. To make the doorway more imposing, steps to raise it can be cut from foamboard or balsa wood and then painted with matt stone model enamel. A surround of terracotta card or painted wood will enhance this impression.

▼ Basic materials for the terrace are inexpensive and easy to find.

▼ The walls are painted deep pink to represent adjacent house walls, and the base is covered with a thick, textured handmade paper in a sandy-grey colour.

▲ A seat in a shady corner near the doorway is a resting place for doves. A tub of marguerites on either side and an orange tree in a Versailles planter reinforce the idea of a lazy afternoon in France.

French windows

Windows complete with shutters which open suit the Provençal style and can be purchased ready to fit. Alternatively, provide windows with closed shutters, made from white card and blue corrugated card (from craft shops). To simulate the effect of paint which has been bleached by strong sunlight, soften the colours with a wash of acrylic paint mix.

Finishing touches

One or two sprays of artificial greenery can be used effectively as trailing plants against the walls. Choose regional plants, such as a hydrangea and an orange or lemon tree, to show off in containers.

Add chairs and a table, a bottle of wine and glasses, and perhaps a long French loaf and cheese.

▲ Paint an inexpensive rush-seated chair, and add a garden hat and a basket of flowers to suggest that the terrace is used.

Garden ornaments

For the miniaturist, siting statues and garden follies can be an enjoyable change after decorating a whole dolls' house. For the beginner, completing a setting for a gazebo or pavilion can be a rewarding entrée to the hobby before beginning on a larger project.

In the Georgian period a rotunda was often placed at the end of a long ride or on a grassy mound in the park of a stately home as a focal point. For the dolls' house owner it can become the focus of attention nearer to the house.

▲ Oriental garden buildings held a particular attraction for English landowners in the eighteenth century, and there are still quite a few dotted around landscaped grounds today. This miniature version of the genre, with its trellised fencing and thatched roof, might be equally fascinating to the hobbyist who owns a large dolls' house and has space for a folly.

▼ Garden buildings of this kind developed from Italian architectural styles. An urn on a pedestal completes the picture.

▲ Provided that it is carefully chosen, a piece of sculpture can add a touch of magic to even a small terrace or patio. This classical bronze figure is copied from the marble 'Nymph and Scorpion' by Bartolini, and on its own would furnish a small space.

▲ The coarse-grained appearance of sparkling white expanded polystyrene used as a base makes a good 1/12 simulation of rough-hewn whitewashed stone.

◀ A wedding cake pillar can represent an ancient stone column: a broken one can be used as an antique fragment.

A Greek island terrace

To create an idyllic Greek terrace overlooking the sea use expanded polystyrene packing. Any gaps in the packing can be filled in with thick card.

Set the polystyrene base into a two-sided room box. Line the walls with bright blue-green mounting board to represent the sea and sky.

You will need to make sure that the base of the polystyrene is level. Use wooden or rigid blocks as supports at strategic points to keep it steady. Arrange the supports so that the terrace simulates a sloping site, and fix with Blu-tack to keep everything securely in place.

When the base is firmly set up, cover any gaps round the sides with card or foamboard.

Add some greenery. Spiky Mediterranean plants may be cut from artificial leaves.

Chairs can be painted bright blue, while a plain white table will look more attractive if it is given a simulated mosaic top. Wine and glasses are essential. Miniature glasses can be purchased ready-filled with 'wine'. To simulate a stronger alcoholic tipple, part-fill plain glasses with cold weak tea set with gelatine.

▼ The part of the terrace overlooking the sea is reserved as a refreshment area.

127

The Modern Dolls' House

CHAPTER 7
PRACTICAL MATTERS

Creating a beautifully decorated dolls' house does not have to be an expensive or overly complicated affair. The simplest of furniture or some carefully placed accessories can bring life and interest to any miniature setting, and many can be created without special skills or materials.

In any period interior you will want to include exact reproductions of beautiful furniture in the correct style for the time. For example, look at the elegant furniture based on pieces by Charles Rennie Mackintosh (see pages 142–144) or the pretty furniture in the Edwardian rooms (see pages 146–150). Furniture made by professional miniaturists also features in the 1950s houses in shapes that would be difficult to copy, unless you have skills well above the average, as the originals were made of moulded plastic.

Economical ideas

Low-cost furniture can be made to look stunning by choosing a suitable paint finish. Many pieces of inexpensive imported furniture are supplied too thickly varnished, but the shapes are good and the finish can be transformed.

The first step is to remove the varnish with a proprietary paint stripper, using wire wool and an old toothbrush to reach into the corners. Cover your work surface with layers of newspaper, wear rubber gloves to protect your hands and keep windows open for good ventilation. Wipe the piece over with white spirit and leave it on a window sill so that the smell evaporates. Then repaint with satin-finish model enamel.

The example on the facing page is a French-style armoire – a capacious cupboard fitted with shelves that can be used to store linen or kitchen crockery in the period or modern home. To use the armoire in a bedroom, choose a pale colour, perhaps an off-white or a delicate green.

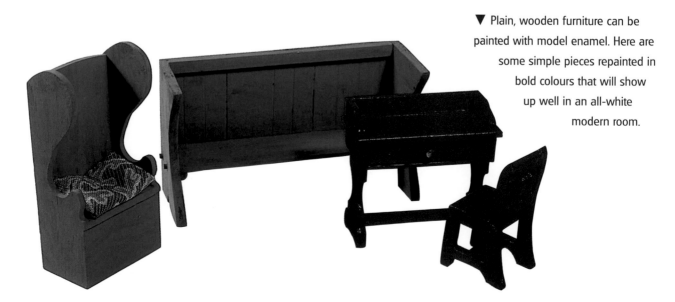

▼ Plain, wooden furniture can be painted with model enamel. Here are some simple pieces repainted in bold colours that will show up well in an all-white modern room.

◄ Before: the over-glossy finish is unsuitable in a modern dolls' house.

▶ After: painted in a mid-green, this armoire is now ideal for a kitchen. Line the shelves with wallpaper with a small pattern to set off crockery or linen.

▼ A transparent plastic box will simulate a modern glass table.

Simple furniture to make

More recently, high-quality furniture has tended to rely on clean lines and good colours for effect. For the hobbyist who enjoys making dolls' house furniture, it is not difficult to copy some of these designs at very little expense. Simple shapes can be adapted to suit many modern schemes by choosing an appropriate woodstain or paint colour or, in the case of upholstered chairs or sofas, by finding a suitable fabric to use as a covering.

On the following pages there are some basic pieces to give you a start; you are sure to think of others. These will help to complete a room setting or fill in a gap when you cannot find exactly the size of table or bed you require, and you can choose the finish to complement your scheme.

Make a plastic table with attached seat

Add a padded wooden seat to a plastic box to make a telephone or hall table.

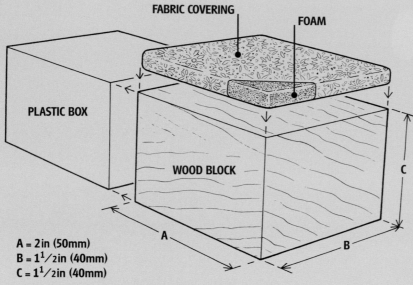

FABRIC COVERING

FOAM

PLASTIC BOX

WOOD BLOCK

C

A

B

A = 2in (50mm)
B = 1^1/$_2$in (40mm)
C = 1^1/$_2$in (40mm)

1 For the table, use a plastic box that is approximately 2in (50mm) L x 1^1/$_2$in (40mm) W x 1^1/$_2$in (40mm) H, or a square one if preferred. Small boxes used as containers for jewellery or miniatures come in a range of sizes and you may find one that is appropriate.

2 Cut a block of wood to the same size and paint or stain it. Then, pad the top of the seat with a piece of foam covered with any suitable fabric.

3 Fix the seat to the table with double-sided Scotch tape.

Make a plain modern table

This table is the correct height for a dining room. It is easy to make shorter supports to turn it into an occasional table.

1 To make the table, use ^{1}/$_4$in (6mm) thick, smooth wood – jelutong or mahogany is best.

2 Cut the pieces to the measurements shown. Glue the pieces together.

3 Stain and polish or varnish with satin-finish varnish.

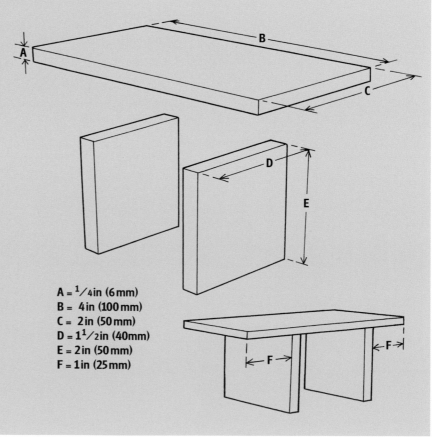

B

A

C

D

E

F

F

A = ^{1}/$_4$in (6mm)
B = 4in (100mm)
C = 2in (50mm)
D = 1^1/$_2$in (40mm)
E = 2in (50mm)
F = 1in (25mm)

Make a minimalist bed

The latest bed designs feature polished wood and a minimalist look. This style should be complemented by a duvet. Measurements given are for a large, single bed. Extend the width to $5\frac{1}{4}$in (135mm) to make a double bed.

1 Use $\frac{1}{2}$in (13mm) thick wood for the top and 1in (25mm) thick wood for the base. Cut and glue the pieces together as shown.

2 This design leaves a 'shelf' around the mattress or duvet. The bed and the base should be stained and polished or varnished in a suitable shade to suit your room.

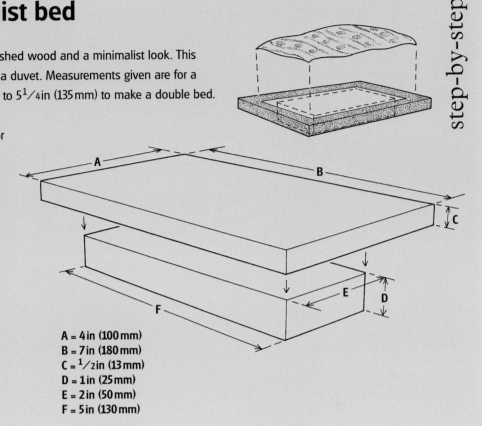

A = 4in (100mm)
B = 7in (180mm)
C = $\frac{1}{2}$in (13mm)
D = 1in (25mm)
E = 2in (50mm)
F = 5in (130mm)

Make a corner sofa unit

A sofa unit can be fitted into the corner of a kitchen or study. Painted rather than stained and polished, this design could also be used as a bed for a child. Use $\frac{3}{8}$in (10mm) thick jelutong to make this sofa unit.

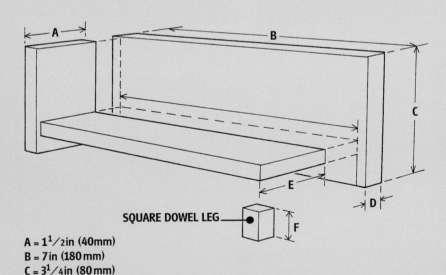

SQUARE DOWEL LEG

A = $1\frac{1}{2}$in (40mm)
B = 7in (180mm)
C = $3\frac{1}{4}$in (80mm)
D = $\frac{3}{8}$in (10mm)
E = $1\frac{1}{2}$in (40mm)
F = $\frac{3}{8}$in (10mm)

1 Cut the seat, back and side pieces to the measurements given. Glue the back to the back edge of the side piece to make an L-shape.

2 Cut the front leg from $\frac{3}{8}$in (10mm) square dowel and glue to the front corner of the seat.

3 When the glue has set, glue the sofa base plus the leg into the corner unit. Stain and polish or varnish.

4 Pad the sofa seat with fabric-covered foam. Add matching or contrasting cushions.

Make an armless chair covered with ribbon or braid

This style of chair is adaptable. The height given is suitable for a dining chair – make it lower to use in a bedroom or sitting room.

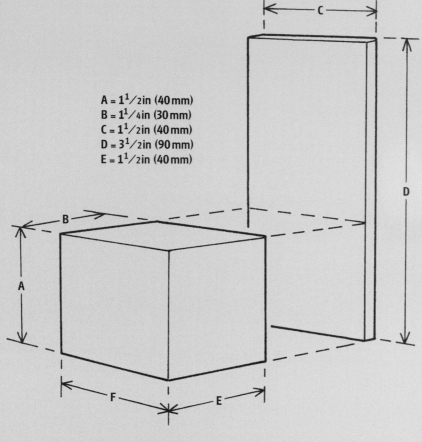

A = 1^1/$_2$in (40mm)
B = 1^1/$_4$in (30mm)
C = 1^1/$_2$in (40mm)
D = 3^1/$_2$in (90mm)
E = 1^1/$_2$in (40mm)

1 Cut the seat and back to the measurements shown. Glue the back to the seat, making sure the bases match exactly.

2 Cover with ribbon or braid as follows:

a) Spread glue thinly over the front and rear of the chair's back, and the top and front of the seat only. Starting at the base of the back, take the ribbon over the back and seat and glue underneath.

b) Spread glue on the sides of the seat. Then, starting under the base, take ribbon across and over the seat (covering the first layer of ribbon), and finishing underneath as before.

3 Slipstitch the edges of the ribbon together down the sides of the chair back.

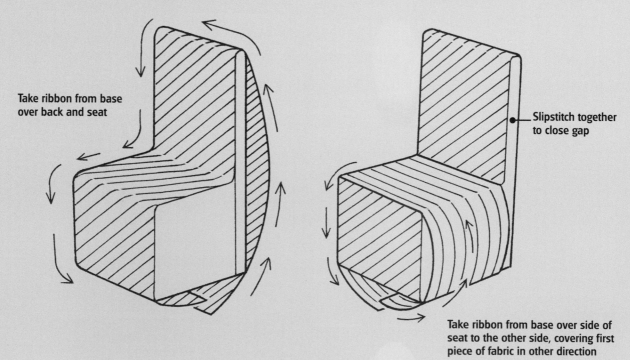

Take ribbon from base over back and seat

Slipstitch together to close gap

Take ribbon from base over side of seat to the other side, covering first piece of fabric in other direction

Accessories

Modern interior design schemes can be completed on a modest budget by the use of a wide range of materials other than those made specifically for dolls' houses. If you find something inexpensive that you will be able to adapt, do not hesitate to buy it – the opportunity may not occur again.

Be prepared to experiment and do some lateral thinking. Keep a file of pictures cut from magazines and brochures for use as backgrounds or scenes to be glimpsed through doorways or windows. Pictured carpets can look realistic, while pictures of tiles can be cut out, glued to card and then reassembled on floors or as a border on walls. Never throw away any oddments of wood: keep a box for off-cuts. Eventually, you may find a use for even the most unlikely looking shape or size.

To create original ornaments for the modern room, use beads and small pieces of fancy braid and ribbon. Picture frames, iron-on motifs, children's hair ornaments, such as slides and bobbles, giftwrap and greetings cards, bottle tops, lids from jars, small boxes, corks and fancy paper clips can all be used to make decorative accessories, and examples of such uses are shown throughout this book.

EASY IDEAS

■ An ornate classical fireplace can work surprisingly well in a minimalist room. Try an elaborate cast-resin model and see if you like the effect.

■ Make two fireplaces by cutting a plain resin or wood picture frame in half and painting.

■ Mantelshelves come into fashion periodically, such as in an Edwardian or 1980s room. They are useful in the dolls' house as a small display area for ornaments. Use plain stripwood to add a mantelshelf over a fireplace, but note that they were not fashionable in the 1930s when tiled fireplaces were favoured.

■ Use a cap from a scent bottle as a wastepaper bin.

■ Table mats have many uses: a coarse, raffia one can be used as flooring; small bamboo mats make good non-working window blinds; a textured cloth mat can be used as a carpet; a bead mat will add sparkle to an Art Deco room; and a mosaic mat can become part of a courtyard or patio.

■ Leather is generally too thick to work satisfactorily in small scale, but a cleaning cloth for spectacles, washed and smoothed out, will give a good simulation of suede for seating or bedspreads.

■ To colour decorations or miniature picture frames gold, use a marker pen of the type that has to be shaken before and during use, and avoid the tedious task of cleaning a paintbrush.

▼ Some buttons have a sturdy-looking shank on the back, but often this is of plastic, not metal, and it can be cut off with a pair of wire-cutters so that the button back is flat, making it easier to attach to a wall or use as an ornament. The buttons and trimmings pictured below are all used to simulate light-fittings in this book.

Add life to your rooms

A dolls' house without dolls may seem a contradiction. I have chosen to concentrate on design and decoration, but many hobbyists will want to enliven their interiors with some inhabitants. Professional makers of miniature dolls can provide characterful modern dolls in both 1/12 and 1/24. If you are neat-fingered, kits are also available to assemble and dress your own dolls in an individual way.

The secret of success when adding dolls to a scene is to pose them as though engaged in some occupation. Even two dolls having a conversation can bring extra life and interest to a room.

Pets

Every miniature home needs a pet dog or cat. Be careful, though, to choose a suitable breed: pug dogs or pekinese were liked in the early part of the twentieth century; for a country house a retriever or a labrador might be best; Scottish and Sealyham terriers were popular in the 1930s; and for a home of today, simply choose your favourite.

▼ This adorable pet dog is made in metal and handpainted.

◄ These attractive dolls were dressed by the maker. Alternatively, kits are available for you to costume to your own choice: they can be supplied with or without an integral wig, and also as a variety of separate parts. The flexible bodies ensure they can be posed to kneel, stand or sit.

CHAPTER 8

ART NOUVEAU

Art Nouveau evolved towards the end of the nineteenth century and flourished well into the twentieth. Essentially a European style, it was taken up in America with enthusiasm but at that time was less appreciated in Britain, where more traditional buildings and furniture were generally favoured.

Art Nouveau was a break with tradition, in sharp contrast to previous ideas. It was followed in Europe by the modernists and Bauhaus, while in Britain the Arts and Crafts movement looked backward to medieval style but also placed the emphasis on handwork and the role of the individual craftsman in producing beautiful objects.

The Art Nouveau style

Art Nouveau decorations featured distinctive, stylized designs of plants and flowers on fabrics and wallpapers, elaborate metalwork on staircases and balustrades, and curvaceous furniture embellished with symbolist details. The facades of buildings were decorated with mosaic tiles, gilding and intricate cast-iron balconies that were sometimes painted green to resemble bronze.

▲ This is a model of the elegant frontage of the Hotel Central in Prague, made in a very small scale to display on a mantelshelf or bookshelf. The area behind the balconied window provides a space that can be used to display a 1/24 figurine.

The Art Nouveau style is even more widely appreciated today. You can have a lot of fun arranging such a room and enjoy the luxury of creating its extravagant decorations. This example has all the hallmarks: vivid green wallpaper, a parquet floor (in this room, floorpaper), partly covered by a rich-looking carpet.

Decorative accessories

The Art Nouveau style was both eccentric and elegant. Green was a favoured colour for wallpapers and carpets. Pewter rivalled silver plate for ornamentation, and Liberty of London marketed the work of leading designers, which sometimes incorporated enamel insets into pewter boxes.

The feminine touch

Shopping, then as now, was a favourite pastime, especially for the lady of leisure who had both time and money to spend. Add a finishing touch to a room with some beautifully packaged purchases. Leave the lid next to a box to show off small items of clothing or a beautiful hat.

◀ The curvaceous screen with its naturalistic, plant-like tendrils gives this corner its distinctive Art Nouveau look.

▼ A characteristic fireplace incorporating beaten copper is from an inexpensive range of dolls' house furniture.

▲ The silver-plated candlesticks on the mantelshelf are based on a turn-of-the-century Liberty design, while stained glass insets in the firescreen are also typical of the period. Tiffany-style glass and the essential vase of lilies accessorize this room appropriately.

► Attractive packaging that incorporates designs by Alphonse Mucha, the symbolist artist whose posters advertised exhibitions and much besides. Hat boxes were necessities, to protect the large, fragile hats of the time.

◄ A deep frieze below the ceiling was often used as an additional decorative feature. Following the lead of Whistler's famous Peacock Room in America, completed in 1864, peacocks came to be seen as a symbol of Art Nouveau style, and were used both on friezes and in stained glass panels through to the early years of the twentieth century. Tiny, iridescent peacock stickers can be found in stationers and toy shops.

CHAPTER 9

GLASGOW SCHOOL

The work of Charles Rennie Mackintosh, the Scottish architect and designer, was key to the Glasgow School style. It was much admired in Europe and has been linked with the Art Nouveau movement. However Mackintosh's houses and furniture were entirely individual.

Mackintosh's famous straight-backed chairs and sofas, based on interlaced willow adapted to a geometric grid pattern, are the antithesis of the flowing Continental style of the Art Nouveau movement.

Sadly, Mackintosh was commissioned to build few private houses in Britain, the best-known being Hill House in Helensburgh, near Glasgow, which is now owned by the National Trust for Scotland. This was his second large Scottish house, the first being Windyhill, also near Glasgow, but many of his finest designs never left the drawing board.

Mackintosh's designs were influenced by Scottish castles, built to withstand gales and driving rain. In consequence, windows tend to be relatively small, the front door generally of solid oak, and walls are either of granite or stone or have a 'harled' finish (a typically Scottish textured render) that can be reproduced in miniature by mixing a small amount of interior filler into a matt, off-white paint. Ready-textured paints are also available in sample-size pots.

Mackintosh's work did not become generally admired in his native Scotland until long after his death, but he is now accepted as one of the leading figures of twentieth-century architecture. Dolls' houses based on his designs appeal to modern hobbyists: they are straightforward to decorate and several makers concentrate on Mackintosh-style houses and furniture in both 1/12 and 1/24.

◄ A view of Gate Lodge, a design for a house that was never built. This 1/24 dolls' house includes the massive chimney and tower that were features of Scottish fortified castles. This model was based on Mackintosh's original plans.

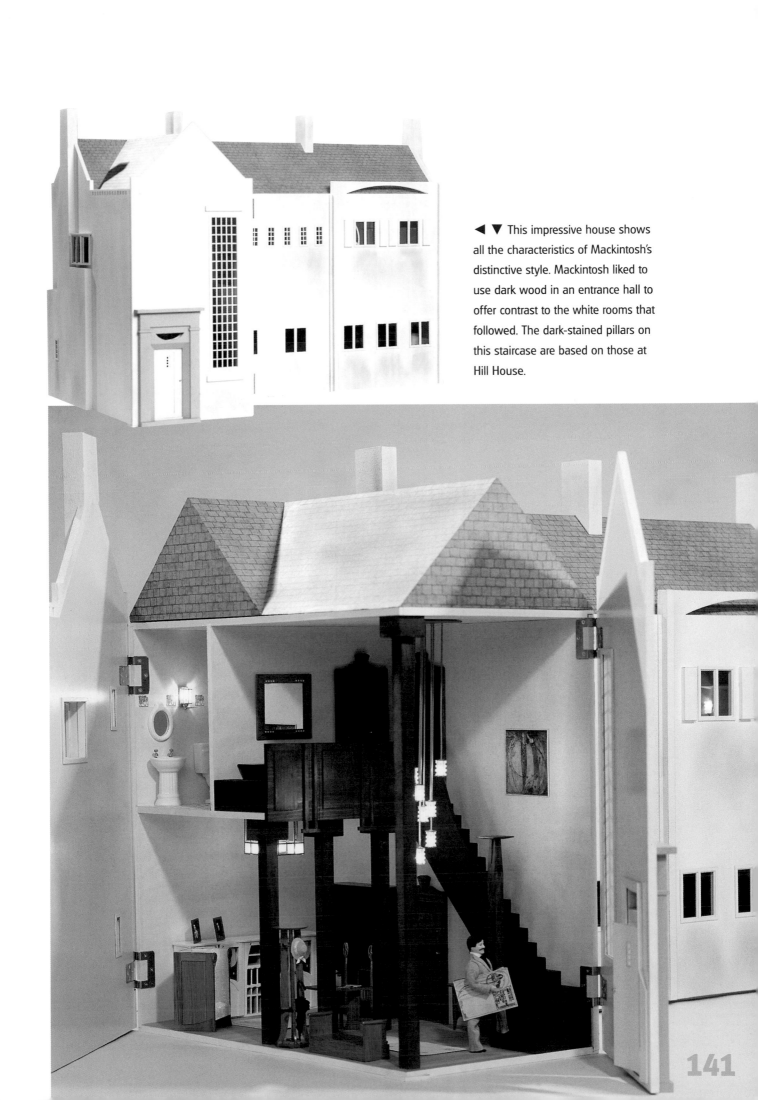

◄ ▼ This impressive house shows all the characteristics of Mackintosh's distinctive style. Mackintosh liked to use dark wood in an entrance hall to offer contrast to the white rooms that followed. The dark-stained pillars on this staircase are based on those at Hill House.

A Mackintosh room

This room is sparsely furnished to show off my much-cherished 1/12 Mackintosh-style chairs, including an oak armchair. These particular pieces are no longer available but there is no shortage of similar furniture.

▶ The pale floor of a greyish-white card makes a good background for the needlepoint carpet, which can be worked from a kit.

▶ The original Mackintosh willow chair was designed for Miss Cranston's Tea Rooms in Argyle Street, Glasgow.

Wall decoration

White walls make decorating a Mackintosh-style room a simple project. You may like to add a frieze – the one I placed near the fireplace was cut from a greetings card, but you can make your own by using a stencil or a soluble, coloured wax decorative material from a craft shop.

Japanese influence

Mackintosh was strongly influenced by Japanese ideas, and in his own home, ornaments, although strictly limited in number, included Japanese vases, which sometimes contained an exquisite arrangement of delicate foliage.

Make an impact

If you plan a Mackintosh-inspired room, aim for the effect that an astonished visitor recorded on first seeing Mackintosh's own home in Glasgow: 'On the second floor of a modest building in the great industrial smoky town of Glasgow there is a drawing room amazingly white.'

◀ The centrepiece of the room is the beautiful fireplace, which incorporates shelves for ornaments.

The interiors

A Mackintosh interior looks as modern today as when it was first decorated. In a dolls' house, mainly white rooms with pink and mauve accents and perhaps a frieze of his favourite stylized rose design (which can be assembled from cut-outs from a greetings card) will be effective and make an appropriate background for furniture based on his distinctive, decorative designs.

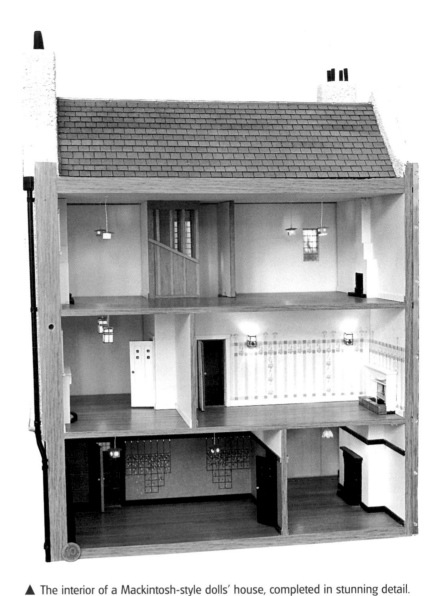

▲ The interior of a Mackintosh-style dolls' house, completed in stunning detail. The hand painted wallpaper imitates the rose-stencilled design he favoured, and the lighting fixtures are of metal with coloured insets. The room at the lower left replicates Mackintosh's design for his own dining room, in which, as a contrast to the prevailing white, he used a grey-brown wrapping paper on the walls, lightened by a stencilled rose and lattice motif.

▼ Dark, sometimes even ebonized furniture, such as these three chairs designed by Mackintosh, was often preferred in dining rooms and studies.

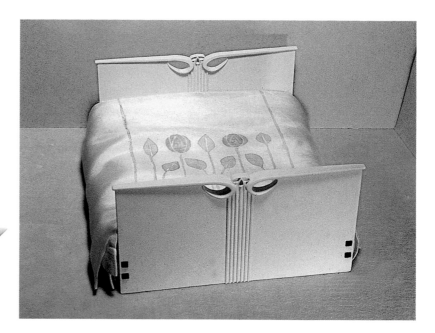

◀▲▶ Mackintosh's preference for bedroom furniture was white with insets of coloured glass. This bedroom furniture, with pink and purple glass insets, is based on designs used in Hill House.

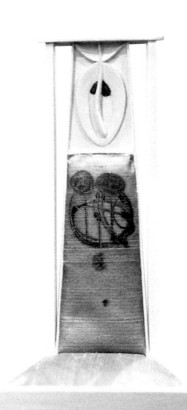

◀ This miniaturized rose boudoir chair is available in both 1/12 and 1/24. The original was designed by Mackintosh for an exhibition in Turin in 1902 and features stencilled decoration on the upholstered back and seat.

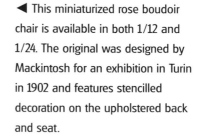

CHAPTER 10

THE EDWARDIAN ERA

King Edward VII's short reign lasted only for the first decade of the twentieth century but Edwardian style had great influence on the way in which the ordinary British home was decorated and furnished for many years to follow.

During the early years of the twentieth century a pretty, light look gradually took over from the dark and cluttered interiors prevalent at the end of Queen Victoria's reign. The average Edwardian homemaker was not adventurous enough to follow the lead given by Charles Rennie Mackintosh, who was working at this time. Many families moved to the newly built suburbs on the outskirts of the cities, where they could live close to the countryside and have their own garden. Moving to a new house was a wonderful experience after the cramped conditions in many old Victorian town houses; it was also an opportunity to change the furniture and decoration, and make a fresh start.

▲ This red-brick Edwardian house with a conservatory has many typical features: mock-Tudor timbers and pebble-dash on the facade, combined with new-style windows and stained glass in the top lights, plus a Victorian-looking porch topped by a decorative ridge. The maker has taken care with this one-off commission to get every detail exactly right.

▲ The Arts and Crafts movement, which started in the late nineteenth century, continued to develop during the Edwardian era. This Lutyens' style Arts and Crafts house has a magnificent oak-panelled door, tall Tudor chimneys with exterior chimneybreasts, and a red-tiled roof.

An Edwardian parlour

An Edwardian parlour was, above all, comfortable. Everything was of the best quality the householder could afford, and was looked after carefully. Even in the smaller home there was usually a daily maid to cope with cleaning and the all-important polishing. You could include a maid doll in her frilly cap and apron, perhaps wielding a feather duster.

▲ The delicate floral wallpaper sets the tone for this pretty room.

▼ A large, handsome oil painting is hung low over the seat, rather than from the picture rail above.

Flooring and fabrics

Fit parquet flooring, either in wood or simulated by using a plasticized paper sheet. A carpet square in a floral or Turkish pattern, or several rugs, should cover part of the floor, leaving a wooden surround. Curtains were floor-length, often in striped silk or damask, hung from wooden curtain poles. Miniature curtain sets can be bought complete with pole, finials and curtain rings. Alternatively, make poles from thin wood dowel, stain them medium oak or walnut, and use small gilt jewellery rings as curtain rings and beads as finials.

Fit an Edwardian fireplace

The fireplace in this parlour can be made from a kit with the option of a fireback to fit into a chimneybreast. Adding a chimneybreast to surround the fireplace provides convenient alcoves on either side for shelves and ornaments, a chair or a bookcase, and makes the whole room more interesting.

1 Cut the chimneybreast from balsa wood or build up layers of foamboard by glueing them together to reach the required thickness. The chimneybreast should be the full height of the room, deep enough to take the fireback and $^3/_4$–1 in (20–25 mm) wider at each side than the fireplace.

2 Cut an aperture for the grate, using a craft knife. Check that the fireplace fits well, so that it can be pushed into place after wallpapering the room and chimneybreast. Paper across the grate aperture, and use a craft knife to trim the paper neatly when the paste has dried out.

Skirting board and picture rail

Fit skirting boards and picture rails in an Edwardian room. These follow the Victorian moulding style and can be bought from dolls' house shops or by mail order. Mitre the corners, using a mitre box and saw. An off-white paint suits the period better than a modern, brilliant white, which can be toned down by adding a few drops of cream or ivory model enamel or acrylic.

The picture rails were well used. Over the fireplace an overmantel mirror was obligatory, typically oval in shape and suspended by gilt chain from the rail. Small watercolour paintings of sentimental subjects, such as children in an idealized country setting, are appropriate. Reproductions of paintings by artists such as Helen Allingham can be cut from magazines or print catalogues.

Parlour furniture

Furnish the parlour with a plethora of fragile-looking occasional tables with crochet or tatted mats to protect the surfaces. Chairs can copy Sheraton style, or you might like to include a reproduction Knole sofa. Add a footstool or two and a piano for evening entertainment.

▲ A tall plant-stand with elegantly curved legs shows off a green plant.

The bedroom

Bedrooms were decorated with pretty floral wallpapers, silk curtains and lacy accessories. Furniture could be fussy: the most elaborate pieces included fretwork, and the Edwardian dressing table might have a large mirror topped with a Chippendale-style pediment and swing mirrors on either side. Whether plain or fancy, it was usually made of mahogany.

Even mass-produced furniture was well made and durable. In 1903, you could buy a bedroom suite of dressing chest, wardrobe and washstand for £8/10s and it would last a lifetime. The bed cost extra!

Central heating had not yet arrived for the average home, and bedrooms were very cold. This was considered

▲ The brilliant colour of this hand-quilted silk eiderdown would make it a splendid centrepiece in an Edwardian bedroom.

healthy, and a window was always left open at night to let in extra fresh air. A thick eiderdown was essential for comfort, usually made in silk or satin with a quilted pattern. One placed over the 'counterpane' (the term used before 'bedspread' was adopted) will make a

decorative addition to the Edwardian bed.

For children's and maids' bedrooms, plainer white-painted furniture was favoured. It looked clean and fresh and, unlike polished mahogany, could be wiped over easily with a damp cloth to remove fingermarks.

▼ ▶ The classic bedstead with wire base is fitted with brass castors. A capacious wardrobe with delicate decoration has two deep drawers at the base as well as hanging space. The details on these miniatures were reproduced from top-quality furniture of the period.

◀ ▶ A single wardrobe with a drawer, and a dressing chest topped with a swing mirror in a simple style. Although plain, the mirror frame and the detailing on the wardrobe indicate that these pieces are of fine quality.

A bathroom

When you allocate room functions in an Edwardian dolls' house, unlike those from earlier periods, you can at last include a bathroom. Many households still had a washstand with ewer (a large jug with a wide mouth) and basin in the corner of the bedroom, and if your house is small then this is the option to choose. Even huge country houses might have only one or at most two bathrooms for the family, while for weekend guests the washing facilities remained severely limited.

Add plenty of accessories to the bathroom: a wooden towel 'horse', glass shelves on gilt or wooden brackets to hold toiletries, and a soap dish to hang over the edge of the bath are decorative.

A bath mat with the word 'bath' can be worked from a needlepoint kit in stranded cotton. If you are short of time, a good substitute is to make a bath mat from a piece of facecloth and print 'BATH' using a black ballpoint pen.

▼ This charming bathroom has a high-flush water closet. Brass taps are fitted on the free standing bath and deep washbasin, and a potted palm emphasizes the period style.

◄ Conservatory furniture in painted metal. The Edwardians liked reproductions of earlier styles: the elegant chair is derived from early nineteenth-century chinoiserie and the double seat has Gothic details. These handmade pieces are available in both 1/12 and 1/24.

Edwardian accessories

An Edwardian dolls' house or room setting can look really delightful; it should be pretty, neat and homely. Finish the room with your own personal choice of ornaments and embroideries, but not too many, as much Victorian clutter had been swept away with the beginning of the new century.

► An elegant lady looks for new garden furniture. She has a ravishing hat, which, at that time, would also have been worn indoors when company was present.

◄ These two elegant ladies are dressed to pay an afternoon call. They could be posed entering or leaving a house, apparently deep in conversation.

CHAPTER 11

ART DECO

A radical new style always feels exciting, and at the cutting-edge of design, and none was more so than Art Deco, originally known as the Moderne style. It flourished during the 1920s and 1930s, and was introduced to a global public at the 1925 Paris Exhibition of Decorative Art, from which it gained its eventual name.

Despite being viewed initially with reserve by the more traditionally inclined homeowner, the art deco style influenced house design for many years to follow. In Britain especially, houses built during the 1930s often included details such as curved bays, porthole windows and sunray designs on garden gates.

The style was particularly successful when used for apartment blocks and hotels, where the structure was large enough to show off the exterior decoration.

In 2003, a mammoth Art Deco Exhibition at the Victoria and Albert Museum in London led to increased public interest. The style is appreciated by many dolls' house hobbyists, and, as always, makers have responded to demand by producing furniture and accessories to complete both 1/12 and 1/24 dolls' houses.

▲ This apartment block is typical of those built in garden suburbs and some of the more prosperous parts of London in the early 1930s. For the hobbyist it would be a dream to complete internally, as each apartment could be decorated in an individual style and accessorized accordingly. The model consists of three flats plus a roof terrace.

◄ This enchanting statuette is a copy of 'Con Brio', sculpted by Ferdinand Priess in 1935. It epitomizes the sense of movement that was so admired at the time. Priess was famed for his technical virtuosity and the miniaturist, in turn, has produced an exceptional figure, painted to resemble the original bronze and ivory.

Art Deco architecture

Art Deco was taken up rapidly in America, especially in California where flat-roofed houses with curving walls, roof terraces and light, spacious interiors were built along the West Coast. There the climate was ideal for sun roofs that could actually be used;

in Britain, the true Art Deco house is a comparative rarity, as they sat less easily in a grey landscape with frequent rain. Flat roofs tend to leak and were viewed with suspicion – rightly so, from a practical point of view.

In Britain, surviving Art Deco houses are most

commonly finished in white. With curving walls, balcony railings and the occasional porthole window, they lie in the landscape like ocean-going liners. On Miami Beach, Art Deco hotels have been restored and painted afresh in vibrant combinations of turquoise, pink and mauve, and, once again, make an extraordinary impression.

▶ (facing page) Distinctive, applied decoration was a feature of Art Deco buildings. On this British house, it is confined to a restrained motif over the bay window. The front entrance makes its own strong statement. The stunning interior has an elegant curving staircase with the typical balustrade of the period. This example is in 1/12 scale, but 1/24 house designs by the same maker are also available.

▲ ▶ A striking Art Deco beach house modelled on those at Malibu, California. An Art Deco house still looks extraordinarily modern today; the latest furniture suits the interior just as well as reproductions of 1920s and 1930s classics. The large windows offer good views of the ocean and there is a generous sunroof.

Decorate in the Art Deco style

◄ This room leads off a hallway where a stained glass window in the distinctive style of the period (cut from a magazine picture) looks spectacular. Wall lights are simulated by fancy buttons. The floor is of slightly shiny cream card; fine wool would be equally suitable as a floor covering.

My reception room might have featured in an exclusive apartment in the early 1930s. It is designed to receive and impress visitors and there is a distinctly snobbish statement made by the cream flooring and sofa. It would be obvious to a visitor that such luxury could be kept pristine only with the attentions of a maid.

The latest fashion

In the late 1920s, new decoration schemes were initiated in the homes of fashionable society ladies who could afford to employ an interior decorator, and were taken up by others anxious to be in the forefront of home design. Syrie Maugham (the wife of Somerset Maugham) pioneered the idea of the all-white room when she had the music room of her Chelsea house decorated entirely in white; furnishings in the room included white satin curtains and white velvet lampshades.

This was perhaps a little extreme but the idea filtered down to the less wealthy, and a scheme that is mostly in cream or beige with colour accents in green or vivid orange contrasted with glossy black will provide the essence of the Art Deco room. One much-copied fad of the time was 'Regency stripe' wallpaper, although this bore no relation to genuine Regency designs. I used giftwrap in white with a thin gold stripe to give the right effect.

◄ The electrified standard lamp is positioned behind the sofa to cast a gentle glow on the occupants. The painting (from a prints catalogue) is by Albert Gleizes, who had begun as an Impressionist painter but became a noted exponent of Cubism during the Art Deco period.

◄ Simple and inexpensive materials can give a room the Art Deco look.

▶ Buttons and trimmings can be used as cushions or other decorative accessories. A fancy silk-covered button represents a jewelled purse laid on the table.

Textures

Textures are doubly important in a room with a pale colour scheme. Try to add some sparkle: in my room I used a black mosaic glass mat to represent a small rug, and this produced the brittle effect I wanted to achieve. Shiny satin cushions show up well against the plain fabric-covered sofa.

A Noel Coward touch

If space permits, a desirable addition to an Art Deco room could be a white baby grand piano, to give a Noel Coward effect. Inexpensive miniature pianos are widely available and a black one can be repainted with white, satin-finish model enamel.

Make an Art Deco table

For a low table, use a small, transparent plastic box; make the top of thick white card and cover it with leather-effect shiny plastic. In general, it is best to colour the edges of card to match a table top, but in this example the edge was left white deliberately to emphasize the contrast between shiny black, white and translucent 'glass'.

step-by-step

Bathrooms

The Art Deco bathroom displayed as much originality as the rest of the house: the suite could be coloured, shapes were more streamlined and low baths were fitted with matching side panels.

▲ Black and white might be used in a bathroom, but as an alternative, a shade of green known as eau-de-Nil could be chosen. The shapes and detailing of this 1930s suite are characteristic of the period.

Art Deco essentials

A piece of sculpture, generally in the form of a stylized figure, was a much-admired ornament. Less expensive at the time but now extremely collectable, the bold and distinctive pottery of Clarice Cliff added colour and gaiety to even the most ordinary homes.

▲ ▼ Clarice Cliff became the best-known designer of Art Deco pottery, and her patterns look equally well in miniature. Here is a selection of her instantly recognizable tableware, reproduced in porcelain in 1/12 scale.

CHAPTER 12

THE TRADITIONAL LOOK

In the late 1920s and early 1930s, another type of house emerged – one that was to become known as 'Stockbroker Tudor'. Comfortable modern homes for the moderately wealthy took elements from the designs of Charles F.A. Voysey, the respected British architect who had incorporated vernacular features into his designs at the beginning of the twentieth century.

The new houses were built in leafy suburbs where the occupants could enjoy the advantages of country air. They were set well back from existing roads and given privacy and an air of exclusivity by tall boundary hedges and, typically, a 'spinney', a small wooded area beyond the formal gardens. Such a house was approached by a driveway so that, in the manner of a stately home, the building was revealed only after entering the formal garden.

These houses were finished to a high standard internally, with solid oak-panelled doors and staircases, a legacy of the Arts and Crafts movement.

▲ A beautiful porch and front door that derive directly from Voysey's style.

◄ A stone birdbath was a much-liked garden ornament during the 1930s.

▲ 'Fairbanks' is a fine example of the Stockbroker Tudor genre, with six rooms and both front and side openings. This large dolls' house measures $33^3/4$in (860 mm) wide, $27^1/2$in (700 mm) deep and $28^3/4$in (730 mm) high, and also has a garden area.

The inside is as detailed as the facade. Stained glass in the top lights of the windows and the front door, with its impressive surround, all add colour, while the deep window sills allow for further miniatures to be arranged to complement the adjacent rooms.

► A house assembled from a kit can be customized to suit your own inclinations, provided you have the necessary skills. This adaptation from the 'Fairbanks' kit shown opposite was built by a hobbyist who enjoys the hands-on approach.

Suburban housing

Charles Voysey would have been amazed to see the miles of ribbon development of 'mock-Tudor' houses that adapted his country house ideas to the smaller home during the 1930s. Such houses were in great demand: they looked back to the past but had neat, well-designed interiors and were not too expensive for the average family. In 1936 the price of a basic semi-detached house was less than £1000. The semi-detached house always had three bedrooms, although the third was very small, often referred to in the estate agent's particulars as a box room but more often used as a child's bedroom. Kitchens and bathrooms were half-tiled, and French windows from the dining room led to the back garden, with a paved area next to the house. There was a small front garden for show, but the back provided a private space to sit out, garden or play games.

▲ A popular garden ornament was a brightly painted gnome. They are great fun in a miniature garden. These two cheery little fellows are of pewter, which you can paint for yourself.

▼ This model is a superior house with a generous quarry-tiled porch, topped by brick facing, again following Voysey's lead. The windows on either side of the front door let plenty of light into the hall, which would have had a parquet floor, or, at the least, oak planks. The front gate is in the Art Deco sunray pattern. This dolls' house can be obtained in 1/12 or 1/24 and kits or plans are available for the 1/12 version.

▲ Tintin and Snowy, whose adventures began in 1929, are spending a lazy afternoon before setting off on a new expedition. Transport awaits on the brick parking space.

Make a terrace

It is easy to add a terrace extension to the wall of a suburban-style house; some homes will already have a wall that extends to form the side wall of a terrace, but, if not, one can be fixed in place. The terrace can be of any size to suit your dolls' house.

1 This terrace measures 12 in (305 mm) long by 7$^{1}/_{2}$ in (190 mm) wide and is fitted against one wall of a brick-finished house. The added side wall is of wood, 12 in (305 mm) long by 9 in (230 mm) high, covered with textured white card.

2 Owners of suburban houses in the 1920s and 1930s favoured straight, neat borders. Edge the borders with stripwood or narrow brass trim. Make a slightly raised border of simulated earth or gravel, so that flowers or shrubs can be fixed in easily.

▲ White flowers snipped from a larger spray of plastic flowers are placed in a neatly edged border; they show up well against the brick wall.

Interior decoration

Decoration and furnishing of the average home followed traditional styles rather than Art Deco, although Clarice Cliff pottery, or ceramic flying ducks on the walls, can be included. Walls should be painted in plain colours: cream was most commonly chosen downstairs, while pink was favoured for bedrooms. Paintwork was generally cream, although there was a short-lived fashion for wood-graining.

The dining room

Reproduction Tudor or Jacobean furniture was favoured for dining rooms, so Tudor-style dolls' house furniture is appropriate. The average dining room had a dark oak dresser or an 'Elizabethan' court cupboard, a gateleg table that could be opened out when needed, ladderback chairs with leather or rush seats, and pewter ornaments.

Tudor-style wall lights were simulated by antique-finish metal wall brackets and shades made of parchment placed over candle-shaped bulbs. To harmonize with this period look, a model of an Elizabethan galleon completed the scheme.

▼ A dining table with extending leaves and a set of Yorkshire-style ladderback chairs, which includes two carvers, would add distinction to a dolls' house dining room.

▲ The 1930s lounge (the new buzzword which replaced sitting room in the suburban home) was designed for comfort. The three-piece suite or sofa and two matching armchairs appear inviting as afternoon tea is about to be served.

▲ A mahogany tea trolley fitted with brass castors, complete with beehive-shaped honey pot and a teapot with the obligatory tea cosy.

The sitting room

Furnishings were standardized in the 1930s home. As well as the matching three-piece suite, you can include a period 'wireless', a standard or table lamp and a small bookcase. Plain fitted carpet (use woollen dress fabric) or a patterned carpet square centred on a stained wood surround are both suitable for a 1930s dolls' house.

Afternoon tea was still a fixture. Brought in from the kitchen on a tea trolley and served in the lounge, this typically consisted of tea and buttered scones with jam or honey and small fancy cakes. The teapot was covered with

▲ The red-brick fireplace (ready-made) is cosier than a tiled one, and gives an impression of the much-admired Tudor look. The china 'crinoline lady' figure on the mantelshelf featured in many homes. The up-to-date electric fire saved a lot of work in laying and lighting a traditional coal fire, as well as clearing up the resultant ash and dust.

a tea cosy to keep the brew warm. It is interesting that nowadays we seem to have hot tea without this accessory. However, if you plan a teatime scene in a 1930s dolls' house you can make a tea cosy easily from a short length of bobble braid. Sew it into a circular shape with tiny stitches and gather the top ends together to fit around and over the teapot.

The bedroom

In the 1930s bedroom there should be a freestanding wardrobe and a dressing table. The dressing table would be fitted with a mirror with two additional side sections. A low stool with an upholstered top was always provided so that make-up and hair styling could be attended to in comfort.

▲ Bedrooms were still cold, so a warm eiderdown or quilt was essential. This hand-embroidered silk quilt features the well-known crinoline lady design, which also appeared on crockery, trays and tablecloths throughout the 1930s.

Teatime

In the words of a popular song of the time, 'Everything Stops For Tea'. A miniature tearoom is an enjoyable project to make and can be set in a room box.

Tea and gossip

Teatime vanished from the home scene with the onset in 1939 of the Second World War, but the 1930s high street tearoom, where ladies met for a gossip and refreshment, continued in use and remains virtually unchanged in many British towns and villages today.

Walls and flooring

Use a pretty wallpaper and a patterned carpet, and add bought or home made furniture. Such places usually have lots of pictures on the walls and a scattering of ornaments to interest the customers.

▼ A 1930s-style tearoom in 1/24, serving tea and home made cakes in an unsophisticated setting. It is based on surviving examples of tearooms, which both locals and visiting tourists love.

Make round tables with cloths

To provide a number of tables in your tearoom, one economical method is to make round tables from empty cotton reels topped with thick card.

1 Draw round a suitably sized jar lid as a pattern for the card tops. Cover with circular, floor-length tablecloths made from fine cotton.

2 To make a pattern to cut the floor-length tablecloth that will hide the cotton reel base, draw round a saucer or tea plate to mark the size and try it out in tissue paper first to make sure that the measurement is just right. It is surprising how large such a cloth needs to be to cover well. Damp the cloth, fit on the table, and use masking tape to hold it in place until the folds have dried without sticking out too far.

3 Add teatime food, pretty china and a vase or two of flowers to complete the scene.

◀ A 1/12 porcelain tea set in Blue Roses, a typical pattern and shape from the 1930s.

▶ Small pewter objects are popular as gifts. This fancy box, complete with a tea service on the lid, is exactly right for a 1/24 room. Painted with model enamel, using a fine brush, even the tablecloth looks realistic.

The kitchen

A 1930s kitchen is now a real period piece. The latest labour-saving device for dealing with the weekly wash was an electric washing machine with integral hand wringer. The machine was filled from a hose attached to the kitchen tap, with a tap at the bottom to empty it. It needed constant attention during the wash period.

▼ An electric washing machine was a great improvement on the old-fashioned outdoor tub, rubbing-board and heavy mangle.

▲ In most middle-class homes, a 'daily' woman and a gardener-cum-handyman came in once or twice a week to help with the chores. The cleaning woman in this kitchen is working at an old-fashioned Belfast sink, and it is interesting that these are again considered desirable in twenty-first-century kitchens.

Gas cookers were already in general use in the 1930s; electric cookers had just arrived on the scene but were considered expensive to run and somewhat alarming. A refrigerator was a new luxury that gradually replaced the old-fashioned larder.

Kitchen storage cabinets were surprisingly capacious – dry goods such as sugar and tea were kept in the lower cupboards and everyday china at the top. Pale green was the standard colour: this looked attractive against cream walls and a red quarry-tiled floor.

◀ A 1930s kitchen cabinet with a central fold-down shelf that could be closed up when not in use.

CHAPTER 13

THE 1950s

In the 1950s new decorative schemes were limited initially by the scarcity of fabrics, furniture and all the accessories that we take for granted today. People longed for bright colours and patterns after all the years of 'make do and mend'.

A surge of optimism and new ideas was inspired by the Festival of Britain in 1951, promoting innovative interior styles for the second half of the twentieth century.

Decoration and fabrics

Fabrics in vivid colours enlivened the 1950s room. Magazines such as *Ideal Home* showed their readers how to create the new look.

Walls were decorated in contrasting styles, with just one wall papered and the others plainly painted. Another new idea for wall covering was to use hessian – a rich tan colour was a popular shade – which also had the advantage of deadening sound. This, too, was generally just used on a single wall or perhaps on a cupboard front.

▼ This room is arranged for a pleasant evening listening to the long-playing vinyl records that preceded compact discs, and its decorations are very up to date for the time. The pictured curtain fabric, used here as wallpaper, is 'Calyx', designed by Lucienne Day in 1951. The chairs, made from mobile phone holders with a retro 'look', are based on a design that would have been at the height of modernity during the 1950s.

Make a record player

To make a record player suitable for the 1950s room you need a small flat box, large enough to take a turntable on which to fit miniature records: these are available in packs complete with copies of old record sleeves.

1 A box about 1^1/8in (30mm) square and ^{1}/2in (13mm) deep will be suitable, either black or in a dark colour.

2 Fit a square of ^{1}/4in (6mm) thick black card into the box as a base and add a washer, also painted black, to simulate the turntable.

3 To make the arm to take the gramophone needle, bend a small piece of metal into a curve and glue it into the corner of the box so it is poised above the record. Almost any small piece of metal can be used – part of a paper clip, a short nail that can be bent into shape with pliers or, my choice, part of the metal clip from the back of an old brooch.

A = 1^1/8in (30mm)
B = 1^1/8in (30mm)
C = ^{1}/2in (13mm)

▼ Swedish glass and stylish ceramic ornaments accessorized the plain teak furniture. These handkerchief vases are made in porcelain.

On a dolls' house wall, use linen or linen-look fabric to suggest the texture. Make a card template and glue the fabric onto that before fixing it to the wall with double-sided Scotch tape.

Patterned carpets featured geometric shapes rather than the unimaginative florals used in the typical pre-war home. It is worth checking out the table linen

department of your local store to find place mats that can be used to simulate floor coverings. You should find a good selection of designs, including linen, plastic, printed, embroidered or woven, with many colours and patterns to choose from. Most are sold singly, so the cost of carpeting an entire dolls' house will be minimal.

▲ The overriding impression left by furniture designed in the 1950s is of straight, spiky legs. Here are two typical tables, one with a glass top that allows an interesting view of the cross-braces below. The other has a marble top, but Formica, a new wipe-clean material that could be patterned to resemble marble, was preferred to the real thing at the time, and was much cheaper.

Furniture

Teak was the most widely used wood for the new furniture, supplanting oak and mahogany. Scandinavian design had a strong influence: shallow cupboards were fitted with sliding doors and plain sofas were perched on thin, straight legs.

A coffee table became the focus of many sitting rooms. This was a relatively new piece of furniture, to cater for an increase in coffee drinking and the prevalence of low seating. For young people, the coffee bar rather than the pub (public house) was at the heart of the new social scene outside the home.

Make a coffee table

A replica 1950s-style Formica-topped coffee table is simple to provide. The measurements can be adapted to suit the size of your room.

1 For the base, use a small box approximately $^3/_4$in (20 mm) tall, 2 in (50 mm) long and $1^1/_2$in (40 mm) wide and paint it black.

2 Cut stiff $^1/_4$in (6 mm) thick card to make the table top, $2^1/_2$in (65 mm) long by $1^1/_2$in (40 mm) wide. Cover with a suitably patterned, shiny card to simulate Formica. Colour the edges of the table top to match or tone with the 'Formica' pattern.

3 Glue the completed table top to the base.

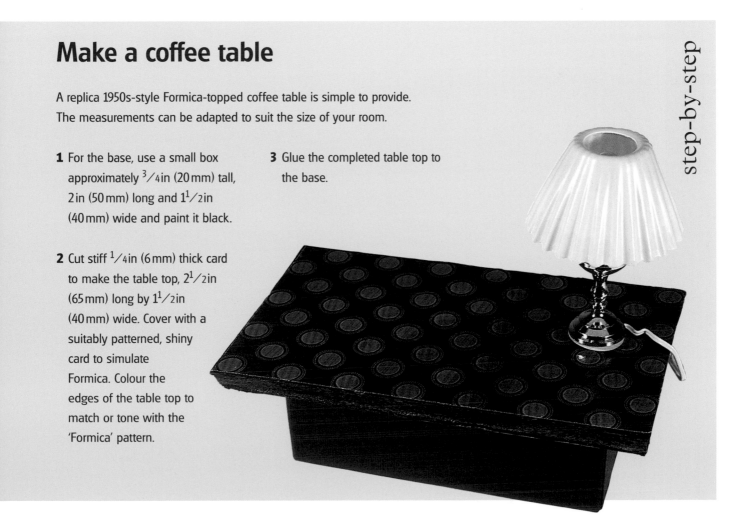

step-by-step

The bedroom and nursery

Built-in bedroom furniture began to replace free-standing pieces. One novelty of the time was an extended headboard that linked cupboards on either side of the bed without taking up floor space.

Traditional nurseries were still popular, and the furniture was decorated with rabbits, ducks or teddy bears.

▲ The bedhead and bedside cupboards could be painted to suit the colour scheme. The wardrobe shown resembles the popular G-Plan furniture that superseded wartime basic utility furniture. Although still plainly styled, the quality was generally excellent.

▶ A nursery will look its best with the addition of some child dolls. This adorable little toddler is by a French doll maker.

A new look for the nursery

▲ The yellow-and-white colour scheme is fresh and appealing, and the candy-stripe wallpaper is exactly right for this period.

▼ The artist-maker who decorated the nursery furniture also produced this delightful oil painting to add a colourful note to the room.

With the introduction of so many new ideas on home decoration in the 1950s, the nursery was not entirely left out.

New colour schemes

Yellow-and-white as an alternative colour scheme to the prevailing pink for a girl or blue for a boy was introduced in the late 1950s and at first was considered quite daring. This had advantage that the nursery could be decorated and ready before the gender of the baby was known: by the 1950s many parents did their own decorating and were not as quick as professional decorators.

Furniture and accessories

The furniture in this room is handpainted in a Noah's Ark design and the frieze at child's eyelevel continues this theme. The play furniture (by a different maker) is also handpainted and is designed in a size to suit the 1/12 child doll.

◄ Accessorize the nursery just as you would for a real baby or toddler. Bear in mind that wooden toys suit the period better than today's plastic.

CHAPTER 14

THE MODERNIST HOUSE

The first modernist houses in the 1920s and 1930s were greeted with astonishment. They were built for wealthy clients by architects such as Le Corbusier and Mies van der Rohe. In Britain, the majority of people preferred traditional homes to gleaming white walls and expanses of glass.

In Britain, the preferred home for the wealthy in the early twentieth century was a centuries-old manor house: the new modernist homes seemed to provide little privacy for the occupants, even though many such houses were raised up on columns or pillars. Modern designs were accepted more readily in Spain and in California, where the climate is better and where these minimalist structures seemed to suit the landscape.

By the 1950s, the priority in Britain was to provide inexpensive housing to replace that which had been destroyed in the Second World War; architects were designing concrete blocks of flats rather than innovative one-off designs. In America it was a different story. Some beautiful homes were built in the 1950s; ground space was not at a premium and many were spacious one- or two-storey houses incorporating glass, brick, concrete and steel to provide light-filled rooms.

Make a modernist house

A modernist house is the perfect display unit for the dolls' house hobbyist who enjoys modern furniture. Collecting and minimalism may seem contradictory but it is rewarding to make your own modernist house and create a perfect setting for a few well-chosen pieces.

I have chosen two iconic designs to miniaturize: both built in America in the mid-twentieth century. They were considered so special that they have recently been renovated, and are still admired by architects throughout the world today. Houses derived from these designs can now be seen in Britain, although it has taken until the twenty-first century for minimalism finally to become accepted.

These houses are easy to make – particularly if foamboard is used rather than the more difficult-to-cut plywood as the main component. I hope you will enjoy choosing and making one of these designs.

◄ This sculptural-looking Egg chair is perfect for the modernist home. It was designed by Arne Jacobsen during 1957–1958, with a moulded fibreglass seat shell that, in the original, swivels on a cast aluminium base. They were not especially comfortable but still look modern today.

Make a 1/24 scale modernist house

Here is a small-scale model adapted from the Farnsworth House by Mies van der Rohe. The completed house measures $23^1/_2$in (595mm) long by 7in (180mm) deep by $7^1/_2$in (190mm) high. This dolls' house is an almost transparent, elongated pavilion with an open front.

No electric lighting is necessary, as the effect of the model displayed in a well-lit room is magical. It is made of foamboard, acetate sheet, semi-transparent envelope stiffener and wood dowel.

Materials

- Two A0 size sheets of 3.5mm (approx. $^1/_8$in) foamboard.
- Two A4 sheets of acetate.
- One A4 sheet of reeded envelope stiffener.
- $^1/_2$in (13mm) square wooden dowel, usually supplied in 36in or 1m lengths. You will need approximately 45in (1150mm) to make pillar supports.

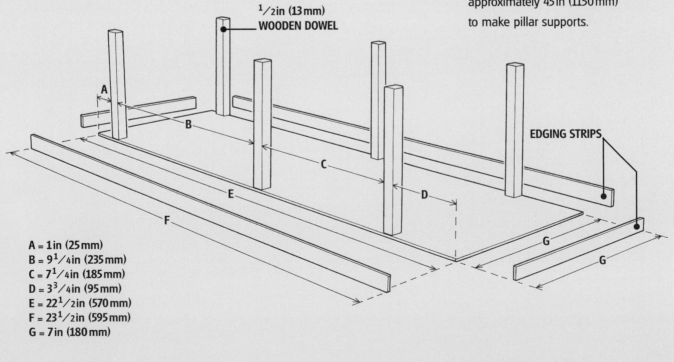

$^1/_2$in (13mm) **WOODEN DOWEL**

EDGING STRIPS

A = 1in (25mm)
B = $9^1/_4$in (235mm)
C = $7^1/_4$in (185mm)
D = $3^3/_4$in (95mm)
E = $22^1/_2$in (570mm)
F = $23^1/_2$in (595mm)
G = 7in (180mm)

1 Cut one piece of foamboard 22½in (570mm) L x 7in (180mm) W for the floor. To edge the floor, cut two strips of foamboard 23in (585mm) L x ³⁄₄in (20mm) W, and two strips 7in (180mm) L x ³⁄₄in (20mm) W.

2 Glue the edging strips to the floor in the sequence shown, with the lower edges level with the base of the floor.

3 Cut six pieces of dowel, each 7in (180mm) L, and paint white. If preferred, the wood can be painted before cutting, as the cut ends will not need painting.

a) Measure and mark the positions for the wooden pillars as shown. This will give one large room and one smaller room, plus a terrace extending a further 3³⁄₄in (95mm) beyond the pillars at one end.

b) Glue the pillars to the base and inside of the edging strips, making sure that the pillars at the back are exactly opposite to those at the front.

4 Cut and fit the glazing to represent glass walls. A mixture of plain and reeded will enhance the effect.

a) Cut two pieces reeded, both 7in (180mm) H x 1in (25mm) W to fit left-hand end spaces, and two pieces plain, both 7in (180mm) H x 7in (180mm) W for each end of the house. Glue the 1in (25mm) wide strips of glazing to the pillars at the left-hand end, then glue the 1in x 7in (25mm x 180mm) W piece to the glazing strips and to the floor and inside of the edging strips.

b) Glue the second piece of 7in (180mm) W glazing at the right-hand end of the house inside the pillars. This will leave an open terrace beyond.

c) To glaze the back of the house, cut one piece of plain glazing 13½in (345mm) L x 6½in (165mm) H and one piece of reeded glazing 7in (180mm) H x 4½in (115mm) W. Glue the plain glazing on top of the base edging at the back of the house and to the pillars. Then glue the 4½in (115mm) W piece of

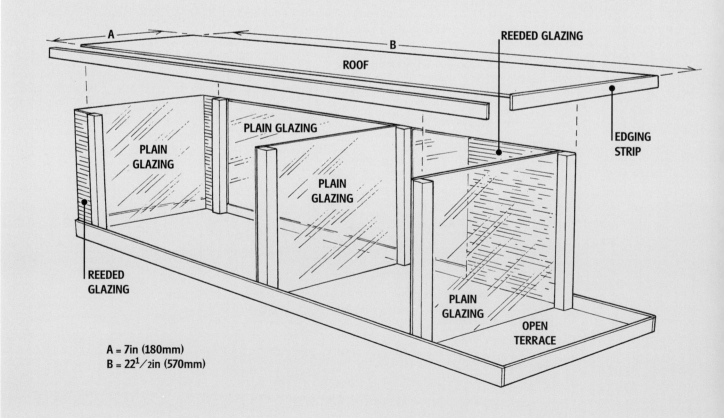

A = 7in (180mm)
B = 22½in (570mm)

reeded glazing to overlap on the inside to give the impression of a sliding door.

d) Cut one piece of plain glazing 7 in (180 mm) H x 7 in (180 mm) W. Glue to left-hand side of the off-centre pillars to form the room divider.

5 Cut one piece of foamboard measuring 22$^1/_2$in (570mm) L x 7 in (180 mm) W for the roof.

6 To edge the roof, cut two strips of foamboard 23in (585mm) L x $^1/_2$in (13mm) W. Glue the edging strips to the roof as shown, then glue the completed roof in place to the tops of the pillars and glazing.

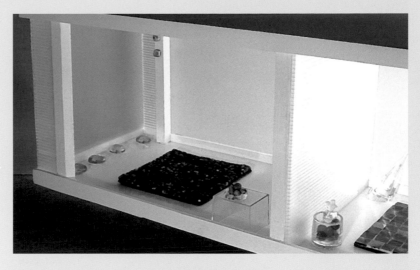

▲ This shows how the glazing is fitted to the walls.

Add a plinth

The house should appear to float above the ground rather than rest on it. I substituted a plinth for the pillars that raised the real house above the ground, as I felt they would be vulnerable to accidental damage in such a small scale. The plinth base gives a similar feeling.

For the plinth, use a block of wood approximately 8 in (205 mm) L x 5$^1/_2$in (140 mm) W x 2 in (50 mm) H, centred under the house. This will not show around the edges and gives the desired effect of a light, almost floating structure. If you do not have a suitable piece of wood, use a box of similar dimensions (with a weight inside) to stabilize the house.

▼ Floating in air! The almost transparent house appears weightless.

▲ The terrace extension with just one pot plant and glass exterior 'lights'. The string of lights by the sliding door entrance is a thin wire bracelet, strung with blue glass beads. The miniature birds are of hand blown glass. Blue glass mosaic coasters used as tiled areas and plastic furniture and glass accessories are delicate and add sparkle.

Furnishing the 1/24 scale modernist house

Furniture for the modernist house needs to be carefully chosen to give the best effect. The architect obviously didn't consider that his clients might want to hang pictures when he designed this house, although it would be possible to display a painting on an easel. Ceramic objects or small sculptures are shown to advantage.

In my model I decided to emphasize the sparkling crystal effect with clear plastic furniture, glass accessories, and only a hint of colour. Ready-made 1/24 furniture would also look well, either special craftsman-made pieces or inexpensive furniture that you can paint in the colour of your choice.

THE FARNSWORTH HOUSE

■ Le Corbusier began the trend for the all-white house, but Mies van der Rohe went one stage further with the amount of glass he used in his 'see-through' houses, of which the Farnsworth House is, perhaps, the most famous example. It was designed and built in Illinois during 1945–1951, restored twenty-three years later, and again renovated during 1997–1998.

Make a 1/12 scale modernist house

My second choice is based on a home in Connecticut, designed and built during 1955–1956 by architect Philip Johnson and restored in 1998. It is open-fronted, making it easily accessible, and with no door frames or hinges to fit, it is straightforward to make. The completed house, including the small base extension, measures 31 in (790 mm) L x 14 in (355 mm) D x 12 in (305 mm) H.

1 Cut one piece of foamboard 31 in (790 mm) L x 14 in (355 mm) W for the base, then cut two pieces of foamboard, each measuring 29 in (735 mm) L x 12 in (305 mm) W to make a double-thickness floor. Glue together.

2 Centre the floor on the base and glue, leaving a 1 in (25 mm) extension all round. Cover the base extension with brick paper, folding and glueing the edges underneath the base; allow a 2 in (50 mm) overlap underneath.

3 Cut the supporting pillars from foamboard, which should be used double-thickness for strength.

a) Cut four pieces 11 in (280 mm) H x $2^1/2$ in (65 mm) W for the centre pillars. Glue two pieces together to make each pillar.

b) Cut eight pieces 11 in (280 mm) H x $2^1/2$ in (65 mm) W and eight pieces 11 in (280 mm) H x 2 in (50 mm) W for the corner pillars. Glue two pieces together to make double-thickness foamboard of each width.

Materials

- Two A0 size sheets of 5 mm (approx. $1/5$ in) foamboard.
- Seven 36 in (915 mm) lengths of $1/2$ in (13 mm) wide stripwood (to paint black for roof trim and window frames).
- Two large sheets of dolls' house brick paper. (Note: when buying brick paper, select a good-quality one with a matt finish; cheaper versions are too shiny, do not look realistic and will easily tear.)
- One sheet of cream artists' mounting board to fit as a floor (or an alternative colour if preferred).
- Two pieces of acetate sheet for glazing, each 9 in (230 mm) W x 11 in (280 mm) H.

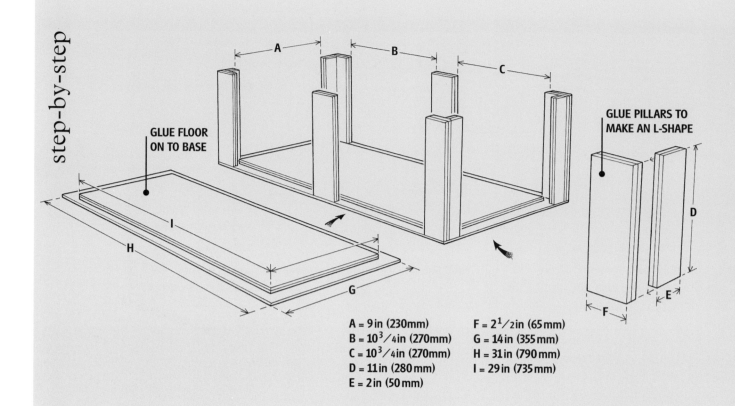

GLUE FLOOR ON TO BASE

GLUE PILLARS TO MAKE AN L-SHAPE

A = 9 in (230 mm)
B = 10^3/$_4$ in (270 mm)
C = 10^3/$_4$ in (270 mm)
D = 11 in (280 mm)
E = 2 in (50 mm)

F = 2^1/$_2$ in (65 mm)
G = 14 in (355 mm)
H = 31 in (790 mm)
I = 29 in (735 mm)

c) To assemble each corner pillar, glue 1 x 2^1/$_2$ in (65 mm) width to 1 x 2 in (50 mm) width to make an L-shape for each corner.

4 Cover each of the pillars with brick paper, glueing in place with a neat join at the inner corner of the L-shape, and along one inner edge of the two flat centre pillars.

a) Glue corner pillars to each corner of the floor and to the base extension.

b) Glue flat pillars, to create a central division for two room spaces, to the edge of the floor and to the base extension. Equally spaced, each room will be 10^3/$_4$ in (270mm) L.

5 Cut two pieces of art mounting board, each 10^3/$_4$ in (270mm) L x 11 in (280 mm) H to make back walls. Paint or paper the walls.

a) Mark a vertical line down the centre of each side of the back pillars and glue the walls in place, leaving an equal amount of brick showing on both the outside and inside of the house.

b) Cut two strips of foamboard each 1 in (25 mm) W x 10^3/$_4$ in (270 mm) L. Glue along top of back walls between pillars inside the house.

6 The side walls are glazed with rigid acetate sheet.

a) Cut two pieces, both approx. 9 in (230 mm) W x 11 in (280 mm) H. Check the space between the pillars for any slight variation in the structure before you cut the glazing, so that it fits exactly.

b Glue the glazing in place down the centre of each pillar, taking care not to smear glue onto the glazing.

7 Fit the inner floor using mount board, or any surface of your choice.

8 Cut eight pieces of ^{1}/$_2$ in (13 mm) stripwood (painted black), each 9 in (230 mm) L, and eight pieces 10^1/$_2$ in (265 mm) L to make the inner and outer window frames. Attach with double-sided Scotch tape. Fit the base strips first, then side and top strips. Before fitting, check each measurement and trim length if necessary.

a) After fitting the exterior window frames, cut two pieces of foamboard 9 in (230 mm) L x 1^1/$_2$ in (40 mm) W and cover with brick paper, joining at one edge.

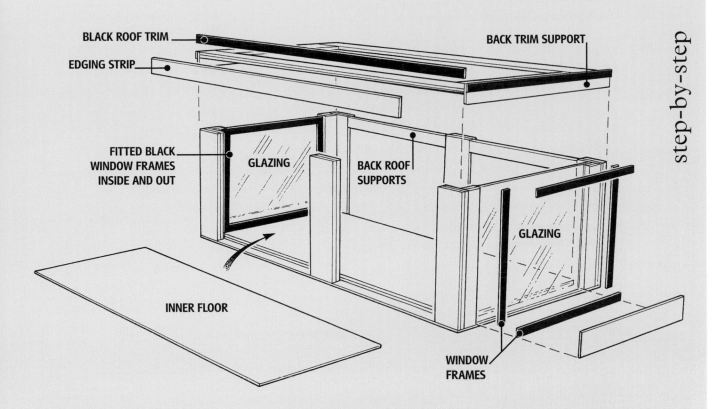

BLACK ROOF TRIM

EDGING STRIP

BACK TRIM SUPPORT

FITTED BLACK WINDOW FRAMES INSIDE AND OUT

GLAZING

BACK ROOF SUPPORTS

GLAZING

INNER FLOOR

WINDOW FRAMES

Fit at the base of each window, outside between pillars.

9 Cut one piece of foamboard 30 in (760 mm) L x 13 in (330 mm) W for the roof. Check the measurements before cutting the roof to allow for any slight variation. It should cover the tops of the pillars exactly. Glue on top of pillars, back walls and side glazing.

a) Cut two pieces of foamboard each $30^1/_2$ in (775 mm) L x $1^1/_2$ in (40 mm) W and two pieces 13 in (330 mm) L x $1^1/_2$ in (40 mm) W for front and side roof edging. Glue side edging to pillars and edge of roof. Glue front and back edging, to cover the ends of the side edging.

10 Cut two strips of foamboard each measuring $29^1/_2$ in (750 mm) L x 1 in (25 mm) wide and two strips 9 in (230 mm) L x 1 in (25 mm) wide. These will act as supports for the roof trim.

a) For the roof trim, cut two pieces of black-painted $^1/_2$ in (13 mm) woodstrip, each 30 in (760 mm) L, and two pieces each $13^1/_2$ in (345 mm) L. Glue the black trim

to the top of the white roof edging. Glue the side pieces first, then front and back to cover the side edges of the roof trim.

b) Glue the 1 in (25 mm) wide foamboard strips flat to the top of the roof and to the black trim. These will act as a support. Check measurements and trim to fit exactly if necessary before glueing.

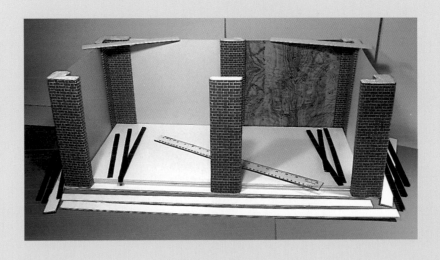

PHILIP JOHNSON

■ The 1/12 scale house is based on a design by the architect Philip Johnson. It is modern in style but not aggressively so and follows the lead of American Frank Lloyd Wright and, in England, Edwin Lutyens. Both designed homes that included traditional elements and liked to use materials such as brick, stone and wood.

This house was designed for a wealthy client, and set in a green space rather than hemmed in by other homes. It has space, light and the warmth of brick, and will appeal to the hobbyist who wants to include furniture of any period from the 1950s to the present. The idea is to bring the outside indoors; wood cladding is used on some walls, while pale floors provide an airy, spacious feeling.

▼ The rear living-room wall is coloured plain cream to take a card reproduction of a large painting of trees. The effect is, as the architect intended, to bring the outside indoors and visually link the interior with the surrounding woodland.

Inside the 1/12 scale house

This house has an open-plan interior with two 3in (75mm) wide wooden walls fitted against the central pillars to make partial room dividers without spoiling the open-plan effect. The 3in (75mm) wide rear divider screens off the stove from the bedroom, and can be covered with brick paper before fitting. You can buy a ready-made stove, but for economy and a splash of colour I used a red tape dispenser standing on its end, and added logs to provide a realistic touch.

The house is intended primarily as a display unit for miniature furniture and does

not have a separate kitchen. If you want to include a kitchen area, the space can be subdivided by adding an extra room divider where you wish. Similarly, an en suite shower could be fitted into a corner of the bedroom.

Colour coordination is important in an open-plan house. Cream and taupe contrast well with brick and wood-grain walls, and rugs in each room are rust-coloured. Keep to a few basic soft shades and then add furniture in a brighter colour so that it shows up well, such as the sofas featuring a deep, bright blue.

Furniture

This is a house that was designed for twentieth-century modern living, but it remains equally suitable for the twenty-first century. Whether it is furnished with retro-1950s furniture or in the latest minimalist style, it will look attractive and comfortable. In either case, keep the furniture and accessories to a minimum to make the most of the spacious interior.

To supplement bought furniture, make some modern pieces of your own; the colour or finish can be adapted to suit your scheme. The black Wassily chair in the living room was designed by Marcel Breuer in 1925 and is still manufactured today. The seating furniture is from an inexpensive range from a mail order supplier.

▲ The square table in the living room has a leather-effect top – a suitably textured art card – glued to a square box base. It is simple to make and effective.

▼ The Tulip table and chair were designed by Eero Saarinen during 1955–1956. His avowed purpose in designing single pedestal supports was to clear up the mess of legs in domestic interiors – and he succeeded brilliantly. These miniature versions are in 1/12.

▼ The log-burning stove gives a comfortable feeling to the living room.
The room divider at the front of the house is covered with wood-effect paper
to match the back wall of the bedroom.

▲ The bedroom is spacious enough to take a sofa as well as the bed. The duvet is a lavender bag, which also adds fragrance to the room, and is covered in taupe linen, while the bedside tables are small boxes with an interesting texture. The back wall is covered with wood-effect paper, which continues the theme of the woodland pictured on the living-room wall.

Make a modern bed

step-by-step

You will need a plain box approximately 7in (180mm) L x 4in (100mm) W to form the bed base.

▲ A padded headboard is easy to make. The wall lights on either side of the bed are gilt buttons.

1 Make the headboard from $^1/_4$in (6mm) thick card, wood or foamboard. Pad the front of this with a piece of thin foam.

2 Cover with fabric, fold the edges over the headboard and foam and glue in place at the back.

3 Make a valance to match and fit around the bed base.

CHAPTER 15

THE 1960s

House building returned to pre-war levels during the 1960s, and those who could afford them employed architects to design spacious modern homes. Renovation of older houses was a popular alternative and this was seen especially in London, where so much of the existing housing stock was (and still is) Victorian.

To create more spacious rooms, it was common practice to 'knock through', which involved demolishing a non-structural dividing wall to make two small rooms into one large one. This was also a good way to reinvent a 1930s home, which invariably had a lounge and a separate dining room, and it spelled the beginning of the end for formal dining rooms.

▲ Skips (dumpsters) became an everyday sight in the streets throughout the 1960s. This well-used-looking model would add that extra touch of realism outside a 1960s dolls' house.

▼ This 1/12 scale version of a large detached house built in the 1960s is made in three sections. The specially moulded 'stone cladding' reproduces the York stone used to build the real house.

The dual-purpose room

There were two ways to create and use the new large room. One was to make the sitting and dining room into one, by placing a table and chairs at one end, and the other was to combine the sitting room and kitchen, sometimes with a low room divider between the two sections: eating in the kitchen soon became acceptable for dinner parties as well as for breakfast. When a home was renovated, curved walls were sometimes introduced as part of the reorganization. This can be arranged in a dolls' house room to avoid a box-like effect. It looks attractive and a little unusual.

▲ ▶ This typical 1960s room is decorated in cheerful colours; the dining table is placed at one end. The room is accessorized with a new-style floor light with a glass shade and a tall metal stand, from an inexpensive range of dolls' house electric lighting.

Make a curved wall

step-by-step

Art card is stiff enough to make a curved wall, and it has a suitably smooth surface. Select the right colour from the wide range available and there will be no need for further decoration. What you lose in reduced floor space, you will regain with an original and pleasing effect. Accessorize the 1960s room with pop art by well-known artists such as Andy Warhol and Roy Lichtenstein. Suitably sized reproductions can be cut from a prints catalogue or a magazine gallery guide.

1 Cut the card to the height of the room and long enough to cover the back wall and one side wall.

2 Glue it along most of the back wall, then curve the card around the corner and glue it again, firmly, to the front edge of the side wall.

3 Trim when the glue has set.

Retro style

Another facet of 1960s decorations was retro style, which updated 1930s ideas. Instead of the all-white room, shades of lavender and grey with purple accents looked fresh and appealing, especially to those who enjoyed a more restrained and elegant decor.

Decoration

This room is a blend of styles, all reproduced in the 1960s. The fireplace reinvents Art Deco style while the rug is a 1950s design and the striped sofa was thoroughly up to date for the time. The print over the fireplace is a copy of a painting by Yves Klein, who specialized in painting blocks of solid colour, particularly in a distinctive deep blue. A reproduction is easy to achieve in miniature size.

Fireplaces

With the increasing use of central heating during the 1960s, fireplaces were no longer considered essential: beautiful period designs were ripped out in their thousands, and the walls were replastered. Much too late, it was realized that a fireplace could be an important focal point even in a modern room, and during the 1980s and 1990s period fireplaces became sought after and reinstated. This was the start of architectural salvage as big business.

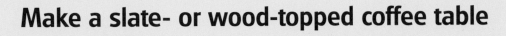

Make a slate- or wood-topped coffee table

A slice of tree trunk or slab of slate was a clever idea for a coffee table. This miniature version is made from a wooden coaster, mounted on a small circular base – a cardboard tube from the centre of a roll of kitchen towels, painted dark grey.

Use a small slice of jagged natural slate – mine fell from the roof of my home – or an offcut of wood. A slate coaster could be used to make a round or square table top. Note that for a large table you may need to provide two supports.

▶ It had become acceptable to use mugs rather than cups and saucers, even when guests were present.

A porthole window

A porthole window is another period idea resurrected from the 1930s, but by the 1960s an oval shape looked newer and more interesting. Cutting out a perfect, small-size oval accurately is not easy. Solve this problem by using a card picture mount on one wall, with the shape already cut out. Fix a pictured view behind the 'window' before glueing the wall in place.

◀ A room with a view: gentle colours harmonize in this room, while the slate coffee table provides a contrast in texture against the smooth surfaces of walls and floor.

How to make a 1960s fireplace

Modern fireplaces are straightforward to make, as they rely on plain shapes rather than elaborate mouldings. You can buy a ready-made fireplace in a choice of styles, but it is economical and also fun to make your own. This fireplace measures 5³⁄₈in (135mm) L x 4in (100mm) H. The size can be adjusted to suit your room.

1 Cut a piece of ¹⁄₂in (13mm) thick balsa wood, 5³⁄₈in (135mm) L x 4in (100mm) H. (Alternatively, you can use foamboard: you will need two layers glued together.)

2 Choose an art card in a colour to suit the room: I used a mottled grey. Cut the following pieces:
- one piece 5¹⁄₂in (140mm) L x 4in (100mm) H for the front of the fireplace
- two pieces 4in (100mm) L x 1/2in (13mm) W for the sides
- one piece 5¹⁄₂in (140mm) L x ¹⁄₂in (13mm) W for the top
- one piece 5³⁄₄in (145mm) L x 2¹⁄₄in (55mm) W for the hearth.

(Note: the card for the front and top are both fractionally longer than the balsa wood so that the side edges will be covered.)

3 Use part of a picture-mount oval as a pattern to cut the grate aperture. Centre it carefully and mark out the shape on the reverse of the card front, extending the lower edges slightly (see picture). Cut out the space.

4 Place the card over the balsa wood base and draw around the aperture. Cut out a space in the balsa slightly larger all round

than the marked opening. Glue a piece of black card to the back of the fireplace to act as a fireback. Glue the coloured card to the fireplace as shown in the sequence below.

5 Colour the edges of the hearth with a matching or toning felt-tip pen. Position the hearth and fix it to the floor with double-sided Scotch tape. Centre the fireplace on top and attach it to the wall and hearth with double-sided Scotch tape: this is preferable to glueing it permanently in position, in case you decide to change the room at a later date.

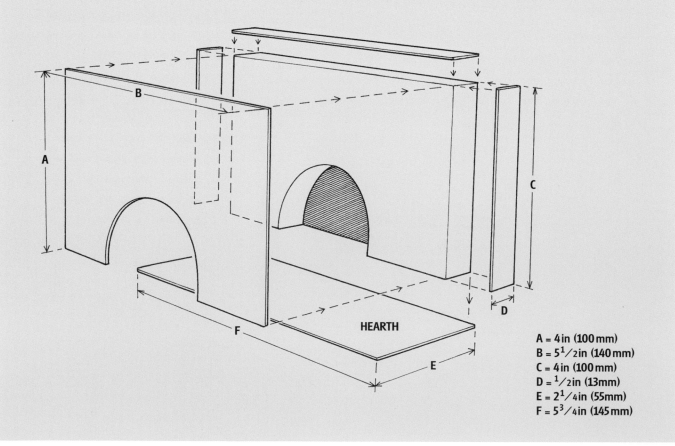

HEARTH

A = 4in (100mm)
B = 5¹⁄₂in (140mm)
C = 4in (100mm)
D = ¹⁄₂in (13mm)
E = 2¹⁄₄in (55mm)
F = 5³⁄₄in (145mm)

CHAPTER 16

THE 1970s

A 1970s newbuild home made of concrete may not be very appealing when reproduced as a dolls' house. A common alternative was to update the interior of an older property, and you may prefer to arrange a home for the 1970s in a period dolls' house. Victorian houses, for example, are remarkably adaptable, and were frequently converted for twentieth-century family living.

Colours used in the 1970s were often bright, even brash; purple and orange were both liked. Although the rooms might be startling, they suited the mood of a time when adventurous schemes were carried out and enjoyed. Geometrically patterned carpets or shagpile were both in fashion and added further interest.

▲ A replica of a real home, a snug 1970s bungalow in 1/24, set on its own plot of land. Although small, this one-storey dwelling makes the most of the available interior space, as there is no staircase to work round. You could also enjoy planning the garden.

▼ An attractive conversion of a cottage and adjoining agricultural buildings to make a spacious family home, reproduced in 1/12. This type of conversion was very popular in the 1970s (as it is today) and rooms decorated in the latest style would be appropriate.

A traditional look

A calmer, more restful look also flourished to cater for conservative taste, and for this the favoured paint colour was the soft cream called 'magnolia'. This shade showed off furniture and accessories to advantage, and was above all safe for the less adventurous decorator – though eventually, so many interiors were painted magnolia that it became something of a joke.

Use cream to achieve this effect in a dolls' house, as true magnolia is a little dark in a small room. It would be suitable in a conventional bungalow like the one shown at the top of page 189.

▲ The flooring used in this room is giftwrap. Op Art rather than Pop Art was in vogue; striking prints based on spirals enliven the scene. The wall-hung bookcase is a card box, attached to the wall with double-sided Scotch tape. The miniature books are light in weight but if you want to display a heavier ornament, you will need to glue the box to the wall for additional security.

Furniture

New furniture designs changed the appearance of the 1970s room, and the growing popularity of flat-pack furniture meant that homeowners could buy pieces more cheaply than in the past. One innovative concept was to have small cupboards and shelves screwed to the wall rather than standing on legs. They appeared to float weightlessly and made the room space seem larger, a helpful effect in a miniature room, too.

Kitchens

The fitted kitchen had arrived, with plenty of cupboards and appliances that slid in under countertops. British kitchens were typically still rather small, and this arrangement made the most of the limited space. American kitchens, on the other hand, are nearly always more generously sized, but fitted kitchens were adopted there, too.

▼ A 1970s fitted kitchen with ample work surface above the storage cupboards. The wall cupboards have glass and mesh fronts so that the contents can be seen at a glance.

Bathrooms

Bathroom design took a leap forward in the 1970s. The now old-fashioned plain bath was fitted with side panels made of marble-patterned Formica. Bathrooms and sometimes even the bath side panels were often carpeted which was not a great success. The carpet could get very wet and soon became stained.

▲ The status symbol for the 1970s bathroom was a corner bath with gold-plated taps. Avocado green was the most popular colour, but black was more striking. Fitted shagpile carpet often featured in the bathroom, too – you can make your own from a face flannel.

Bedrooms

Bedrooms could be pretty and feminine or modern and colourful, according to taste. Both versions were considered fashionable.

▲ A cottage-style window in this charming bedroom is emphasized by curtains with a pelmet. The dressing-table shelf with a triple mirror and a curtain to conceal a storage area underneath was considered suitable for a young girl.

▼ A more modern style for a sports-loving teenager contains furniture with contrasting coloured panels. The look is much bolder and gives a completely different effect. A check duvet with matching pillowcase is bright and cheerful.

A teenager's room

Most teenagers had a room of their own by the 1970s and were allowed to choose the decorations. You might like to include such a room in a 1970s dolls' house or apartment, and if there are internal doors, a notice saying PRIVATE or KEEP OUT on the door would reflect the rebellious attitude of the time.

Home entertainment

A record player or a radio was essential in a teen room. As yet, the only television set was in the main family living room but music was allowed, often played at top volume to the irritation of anyone else at home. 'Hi-fi' was in its infancy compared to today's sophisticated equipment, and the CD player was yet to come. A rather old-fashioned-looking record player is appropriate, as it most likely would have been a hand-down from parents rather than newly bought. (See 1950s, page 168, for how to make a record player.)

Wall decorations

The posters of pop idols on the walls were cut from advertisements. An alternative way to display them is to provide a cork pin-up board: cut a slice from a thin cork table mat to make one.

▼► A lively room, with the type of decorations chosen by the 1970s teenager is arranged ready for a party. Shiny, black, plasticized paper makes a suitable floor, while patterned giftwrap with a silver background and a brightly coloured design gives a disco effect to the back wall.

▲ A decorative wall plaque made from eight novelty buttons in the shape of bottle caps, with 'cola' printed on each. Mounted on a shiny red base, they might be recycled tops from the teenager's favourite drink.

A recording studio

A visit to a recording studio was a teenager's idea of heaven in the 1970s. If you enjoy pop music, you might like to make a small studio in a room box. Mine was inspired by finding the striking black patterned giftwrap to use on the walls and the iridescent plasticized sheet, which was easy to cut with scissors, to fit as a floor. There are always lots of cables trailing around when music is being recorded, and these can be simulated with black cord. Add inexpensive musical instruments as you wish: a keyboard is particularly useful for this setting. To simulate loudspeakers for either a teen room or a recording studio, use two small blocks of wood of a suitable size and paint them a matt black.

▼ A recording studio with plenty of atmosphere.

CHAPTER 17

THE 1980s

In the 1980s, the traditional country-house 'look' was once again fashionable, whether in a country or a town house. This was largely due to the lead given by Laura Ashley, who had introduced a whole generation to an updated version of the country style.

One possible way to show off traditional style in its 1980s reincarnation is to arrange rooms as though the house has been in the same family for generations: this gives an opportunity to include a mixture of furniture, with some that might always have been present and newer pieces introduced from time to time over the years, in a variety of period styles.

An updated Elizabethan sitting room

I chose to set this 1980s-style sitting room in an Elizabethan room box made from a kit plus a panelling kit, and found it a very enjoyable exercise. To convert the room into a country-house library, one wall is covered with bookcases. This is a trompe l'oeil effect (the art of painting views and objects to make them appear three-dimensional) using a picture, but wooden shelves with real miniature books would fit equally well against the panelling.

▲ An Elizabethan room furnished with a mixture of Tudor and modern pieces looks stunning.

▶ The portrait of Queen Elizabeth I which hung over the fireplace before the room was updated.

The planked oak floor would have been there originally, but a Turkish carpet creates additional comfort. Large sofas – one a Victorian reproduction of a Knole sofa and one modern – and a low table to hold drinks and cigars make this a gentleman's retreat.

The tapestry remains, but the portrait of Elizabeth I has been banished to a corridor. In its place is a portrait of the present owner's wife, painted by Matisse soon after their marriage, a commission that I imagine he occasionally regrets.

The newly decorated room

A room decorated and furnished in the 1980s to simulate the country-house ideal was somewhat different but equally comfortable and attractive. Expensive patterned wallpapers were complemented by lavishly draped curtains with tasselled tie-backs, a little over-length and allowed to trail on the floor. Pale carpets and traditional furniture styles featured strongly.

For those who had them, inherited antiques, landscape paintings and portraits of ancestors decorated the walls. Huge squashy sofas were considered essential and a grand fireplace looked both welcoming and impressive.

The essence of this look was casual comfort.

The country-house style works best in a reasonably large room; mine measures 11in (280mm) H x 15in (380mm) L x 9½in (240mm) D. The room has a full-length French window fitted to the back wall, giving a view on to a pretty courtyard beyond: both window and courtyard are a trompe l'oeil effect.

Reproduce pale-coloured fitted carpet with woollen dress fabric; a sample of a full-size wallpaper with a scroll pattern will be more suitable than a miniaturized version. Fit Georgian-style skirting board and cornice, painted white.

▼ This room has all the key elements of 1980s style. There is a lovely blend of pastel colours and just the right mixture of over-scale ornaments.

Create a view

A good view through a fake window can be arranged to enhance any dolls' house room – a variety of suggestions appear throughout this book. Choose a townscape or countryside view from a magazine picture to suit your room.

1 Glue your chosen picture onto card, using an all-purpose glue (not paper glue, which causes crinkles). Then fix the pictured scene, on its card backing, to the wall. Cover with acetate sheet to simulate window glazing.

2 French windows do not need a complete window frame, as the sides can be hidden by curtains and held in place by a wooden or fabric pelmet at the top.

3 Make a small step at the base of the window to give a neat finish at floor level.

4 Use a sample of upholstery fabric to make curtains to give the appearance of heavy drapes. A slightly over-scale pattern will add to the lavish effect. Turn in the side edges and a hem at the lower edge, and glue in place rather than stitching, which on thick fabric might make a ridge.

▼ The blue-and-white china is French; these pieces came from the souvenir shop at Monet's Garden at Giverny. As arranged on the mantelshelf and hearth, they emphasize the summery look of the room.

▲ The exotic elephant ornament simulates an expensive souvenir that might have been brought back from a trip to India.

Fit a fireplace in the newly decorated room

step-by-step

A ready-made fireplace in cast resin could be used; for example one with an Adam-style 'marble' surround. Another good choice could be a plainer Georgian style. I decided to be economical and provide my own, using pieces of wood moulding left over from other projects.

This fireplace was designed for show rather than to appear functional; it is fitted directly onto the wall without a chimneybreast or aperture for a grate. This is a convenient and effective arrangement if you want to add a fireplace to an existing room without having to change the wallpaper. For greater realism, fit a chimneybreast to allow depth for a grate before papering the walls, following the method given in the Edwardian section (see page 147).

1 Cut a backing of grey card approximately $5^1/_2$in (140 mm) L x $4^3/_4$in (120 mm) H.

2 Cut three pieces of wood moulding to fit on top of the card edges and mitre the corners before glueing in place.

3 Mark out a rectangular central space to represent the grate aperture; cut and fit marbled card to make the surround.

4 Cut a mantelshelf 6 in (150 mm) L from wood moulding that is approximately $3/_4$in (20 mm) W and glue to the top of the fireplace.

5 To make the hearth, cut $1/_4$in (6 mm) thick balsa or foamboard $5^3/_4$in (145 mm) L x $1^1/_2$in (40 mm) W. Cover with marbled card. Colour the front and side edges with a felt-tip pen to match or tone with the marble-effect card.

6 Fix the hearth to the floor with double-sided Scotch tape. Centre the fireplace on top and fix to the wall and to the hearth with double-sided Scotch tape.

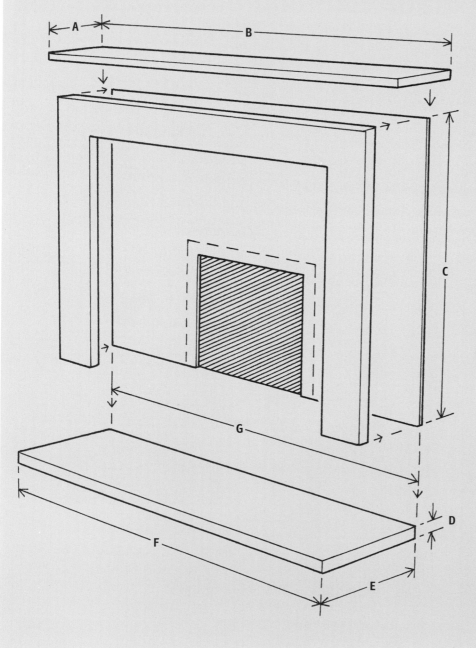

A = $3/_4$in (20 mm)
B = 6 in (150 mm)
C = $4^3/_4$in (120 mm)
D = $1/_4$in (6 mm)
E = $1^1/_2$in (40 mm)
F = $5^3/_4$in (145 mm)
G = $5^1/_2$in (140 mm)

Lighting

A chandelier, whether working or non-lighting, is almost obligatory for the 1980s room. It became fashionable to twine the chain with ribbon in imitation of eighteenth-century practice. The non-working chandelier in my room is a ready-made trimming of glass beads attached to ribbon, from a haberdashery department.

Large table lamps with drum shades were also used in the 1980s, and it is quite easy to make a non-working version of such a lamp at minimal expense.

▲ Some examples of non-working table lamps with bead bases and shades made from ribbon.

Make a 1980s table lamp

step-by-step

1 Choose a suitably shaped bead for the base and 1in (25mm) wide velvet or thick silk ribbon to make the shade.

2 For the shade, cut a piece of cork ³/₄in (20mm) H – this will be covered with ribbon to create the cylindrical shape of the drum shade.

3 Cut a piece of 1in (25mm) W ribbon, long enough to go around the cork. Glue it on, taking care not to mark the ribbon – it is best to spread the glue on to the cork, leave it to become slightly tacky, then fit the ribbon. Butt the ribbon ends together and keep the join at the back when placing the lamp in a room.

4 Cut a piece of thin metal rod the length of the bead and shade, plus a little extra. Check the height of the bead base and smear a small amount of glue on to the metal rod to slightly less than this measurement.

5 Now push the rod through the central hole of the bead and tape over the lower end to hold the rod in place while the glue sets. Finally, push the top of the metal rod into the centre of the cork, using a thimble for safety.

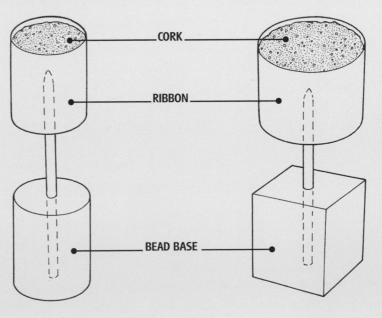

CORK

RIBBON

BEAD BASE

The country kitchen

▶ A country-style kitchen was desirable, whether the home was actually in the country or in town. This furniture is hand-painted with farmyard animals and birds.

The Laura Ashley influence extended to the kitchen, which came to be recognized as the focus of home life, used for family meals and dinner parties as well as for cooking. More people really did cook in the 1980s; convenience food in the form of ready-meals had not yet become accepted and people enjoyed giving dinner parties and preparing elaborate dishes.

▲ A kitchen table looks its best if it is laid out with some fresh food in preparation.

Walls and flooring

For realism, use ceramic tiles for the kitchen floor; floorpaper printed with a tile design is an acceptable alternative. Plain walls decorated with a floral or leafy border will continue the 1980s countryside theme, and the border can also surround a window so that curtains will be unnecessary.

Traditional appliances

In the American kitchen you would find the latest modern cooker, but a British country-style kitchen was incomplete without an Aga (a modern range) if it could be afforded. It was a status symbol, but it did also keep the kitchen warm. The Aga in the kitchen shown is a double-oven version from an inexpensive range of dolls' house furniture.

It was in the 1980s that the Belfast sink made its comeback. Twenty years earlier, people had been anxious to dispose of them as Victorian relics and install a new stainless steel model.

◄ A well-filled dresser is the centrepiece of the 1980s country kitchen. Crockery and accessories by several makers are displayed on the shelves.

▼ The latest four-oven Aga with lids that can be opened would add distinction to any kitchen large enough to accommodate it. It is available in similar colours to those used on the real cookers, and can be supplied fully finished or as a kit.

► The open window provides a view on to a pretty courtyard. The matching set of washing-up bowl, bin and plate rack adds an authentic touch, as dishwashers were not always present in the British kitchen in the 1980s. The shelves below the sink provide convenient storage for baskets or pots.

Bedrooms and bathrooms

A bedroom lavishly draped with floral-patterned fabric is appropriate, and a quilt on the bed will be the centrepiece. There was a revival of interest in patchwork at this time, and it became a popular hobby for those keen on sewing.

▲ ▶ English eighteenth-century japanned furniture, made to mimic Chinese lacquer, suits the country house and can be used in a sitting room, hall or bedroom.

▶ This fine example of 1/12 hexagonal patchwork was professionally made. If you're skilled with a needle, you can sew your own from a kit which includes tiny templates.

◀ The country-house ambience can be extended into the bathroom. A ready-made fitment with a deep washbasin set into a marble-topped cupboard will provide a suitable feeling of opulence.

CHAPTER 18
THE 1990s

During the 1990s the trend to renovate older properties continued, and some new homes were built in the style of former periods. Like the conversions, they were fitted out with the latest in modern technology. Homes that follow original Shaker style were built along the eastern seaboard of America. Few people are lucky enough to own one, but you can achieve your wildest dreams in miniature.

You may like to model the interior of a modern dolls' house on your own home as it looked through the 1990s. What you include will be limited by the number of rooms. Decide on your priorities before you begin.

▶ Inside the Shaker house spacious, light-filled rooms are as seductive as an empty loft space to even the most committed modernist. It would look equally good furnished with Shaker-style miniatures or the latest twenty-first-century designs.

▼ This 1/12 scale Shaker house has external clapboarding and working sash windows.

Updating the period house

Here is an ancient-looking dolls' house that has been converted for modern living. It is modelled on a sixteenth-century yeoman's dwelling, that has even earlier origins.

Mix and match

If you already have a period-style dolls' house and plan some alterations to the interior, it is worth bearing in mind that you can change the decorations and include contemporary furniture in a miniature home of any date from Tudor to nineteenth century, while leaving the facade untouched. This can revitalize a tired-looking scheme or transform a house that needs interior decoration and renovation.

Family life

The house has been arranged to suit a modern family, with a country-style kitchen complete with Aga, a cottage-style living room and a bedroom, which include some antiques. The nursery has plenty of children's toys and the pushchair in the hall adds to the lived-in effect. The old Victorian range in the inglenook has been kept as an attractive feature.

▼ This appealing, timber-framed dolls' house is in 1/24 scale but can also be made in 1/12. The brickwork and plaster finish, hand painted in realistic colours, is delightful.

▼ The interior of the 'Yeoman's house' is now arranged as a family home in a country style that has a mixture of old and new furniture.

Open a gallery

Another use for an updated period dolls' house is as a combined work and living space. A good way to display a small collection of similar miniatures, furniture or accessories left over after a change of style, is to begin a gallery. Accommodation can be arranged in a room above or below the display space, provided there is a well-placed staircase for access.

Such a gallery might specialize in antiques, art, ceramics, 1930s furniture, crafts ... choose your own theme. During the 1990s a record number of art and craft galleries opened and most seem to be still thriving, so this is a topical project.

▼ This comfortable living room is part of a conversion of a medieval mill house as a weekend home which would provide rest and relaxation for city dwellers.

▶ Later, I transformed the room to make a gallery to display handmade pottery. This is mostly in 1/24, although the floorstanding pieces are in 1/12. The room has a quiet, timeless quality and is just right to show the work of a country potter.

The home office

The modern trend of working from home and for computers to become part of our lives means that the home office is now commonplace. It can be in a hallway or on a landing, in a corner of a larger room or extended to fill the whole of a small room if you can spare one.

Home computers, photocopiers, filing cabinets and filing systems are all available in 1/12 scale so that miniaturists can reproduce their home office in their dolls' house.

◀ All the essentials for the home office can be fitted into a small space.

Kitchens and bathrooms

Most new homes were built with state-of-the-art kitchens and bathrooms. Each family used the available space differently to suit their needs, but a home office and a television room became more common than a separate dining room or a designated guest room, and children's playrooms replaced traditional nurseries.

▶ Deep blue storage units and the latest range-style cooker complete with aluminium hood suit the upmarket modern kitchen.

▲ In a family home, a childproof bathroom is essential. This simple arrangement would suit a country house, with its plain tiled floor (squared paper) and tongue-and-groove panelling. The splashback behind the basin is a piece of textured card.

▶ The dark blue porcelain bowl looks striking against the black-and-white background. The floor covering is squared paper.

Children's rooms

A modern children's playroom can be fun to decorate. Choose bright colours for the walls and floor, and add stickers and cartoon-character images from television shows, films and books. These are available from most stationers and toy shops.

▼ Transform a plain cupboard into a magical one in minutes by adding stickers showing wizards and conjuring tricks. The wizard on the cupboard front is an appliqué motif from a haberdasher's. For economy, this cupboard is of white card.

◄ Inexpensive dolls' bunk beds are supplied complete with bedding. In the dolls' house they can be used to display toys or to accommodate child dolls.

▼ There is plenty to keep children occupied in this playroom. Animal stickers on the walls are placed at a low level for a child's eye view, and the bunk beds allow two children to share the space.

Miniature shops

And now we come to the great pastime of the 1990s – shopping. This era saw the transformation of shops, especially department stores and malls, so that what had been simple retail outlets additionally became places of entertainment. Families took to shopping together for a day out, not only to make essential purchases but to admire the displays and in-store demonstrations and to stop for refreshments.

▲ The fascia board and bright paint colour on the facade of this fancy dress shop will attract attention.

Creating a miniature shop

A shop is a useful display space for the miniaturist, and shops are often chosen as a project for a dolls' house club, so that the members can enjoy themselves making their own speciality, whether it is tiny hats, woodturnings or food made from Fimo. A shop can be arranged in a very small space, and one idea that has become popular recently is to make a shop in a stationery box-file. The main part of the box can be used for shelving and some of the stock, while a larger floor area can be provided by the box lid. It is necessary to remove the spring clip to allow the floor to lie flat.

▲ A sweet shop can be filled with beautifully packaged confectionery and chocolates.

Resurrect an old idea

Toy sweet shops, generally made of cardboard, used to be popular with children and were given as Christmas presents in the 1930s, stocked with a variety of real sweets in tiny glass jars that could be refilled. I have not seen one of these for many years, but a sweet shop is an unusual idea for a miniature project.

▶ A pet shop is an idea that will appeal to an animal lover. A non-opening door at the back suggests a storeroom beyond.

CHAPTER 19

THE NEW CENTURY

At the beginning of the twenty-first century, houses designed to look to the future rather than the past are at last widely accepted – both full-scale and in miniature. Miniaturists who had previously concentrated on earlier styles now also make ultra-modern dolls' houses and furniture as well as period designs, and this has been welcomed by hobbyists eager to try something new.

◄ A rooftop swimming pool set in the calm atmosphere of a Zen garden is both attractive and unusual.

▼ One appropriate way for a miniaturist to celebrate the start of the third millennium was to make a scale model of a church. This beautiful interior is based on an ancient English church in Oxfordshire.

The start of a new millennium seemed to make us all more adventurous. The modern dolls' house has many features that simplify decoration. For example, a flat roof is easier to deal with than a sloping roof. The complication of slates or tiles is largely avoided; a parapet of plain stripwood makes a neat finish, and the flat roof space can be turned into a garden or even be used to add a swimming pool.

▶ ▼ Commissioned by a London dolls' house shop to encourage hobbyists to look to the future, the most striking feature of this 'high-tech' house is the central, full-height glazed area which allows a tantalizing glimpse of some of the contents. It has six rooms and incorporates the most up-to-date lighting and designer touches that any modernist could desire. It can be made to order, to furnish to your own choice.

▼ The bedroom has a calm atmosphere, adaptable lighting and a hint of Japanese style in the wall covering, which resembles a shoji screen.

▶ The kitchen has stylish aluminium wall panels and ceiling-mounted spotlights. Naturally, there is also a dishwasher and a capacious wine rack waiting to be filled.

Make a town house

Affordable houses in towns are designed to suit limited spaces. Many three-storey homes are built as infill, just like the Victorian terraced houses that may flank them, but designed in a minimalist style that is easy to maintain.

As a contrast to the spacious modern dolls' house shown at the start of this section, here is a project to make a small town house in 1/24 scale that is easy to assemble, decorate and furnish. No tools are needed.

By definition, a dolls' house with two or more rooms is made up of a series of boxes. There are many possible variations, but the most straightforward is the two- or three-storey house with a single room on each floor. The house can be open-fronted so that the interior will be on show to make a decorative addition to your home. The house demonstrates what can be achieved by using three similar-sized boxes. Each measures 9¼in (235mm) wide by 6in (150mm) deep; two are 6¼in (160mm) high and the third 7in (180mm) high, allowing a useful variation in room height. These boxes once held sets of books, but you can use any strong, rigid boxes of a suitable size. They all need to be the same width and depth so that they make a neat house when stacked.

Boxes all of the same colour will give a uniform appearance to the house exterior; the alternative is to colour-coordinate each room to the outside of its box, which will emphasize the modern style.

I imagined a small executive-type house designed to suit a young professional couple, who in real life would probably move on to something larger when they start a family. The conventional upmarket decorations mean that it would be easily resaleable, so again this house is true to

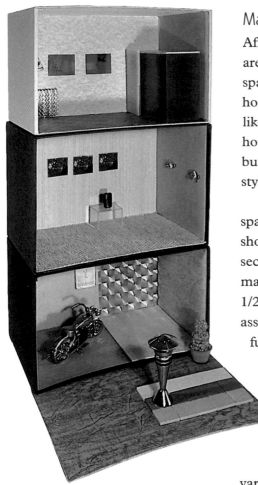

▲ Decorated and fitted with wall lights (non-working), this house is ready to furnish. It is intended as a setting for miniatures rather than a working home, so a staircase that is out of sight must be assumed.

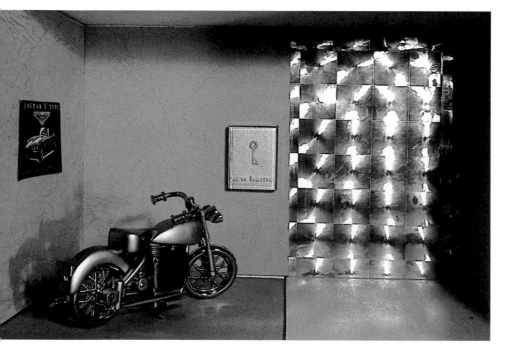

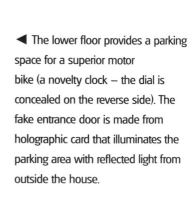

◀ The lower floor provides a parking space for a superior motor bike (a novelty clock – the dial is concealed on the reverse side). The fake entrance door is made from holographic card that illuminates the parking area with reflected light from outside the house.

▲ In the sitting room, thick textured paper makes a floor that simulates sisal carpet. The wall lights are children's hair ornaments.

modern life. I see it as a show home, so have included only token furnishings to convey a lifestyle image.

The lower storey is treated as a parking space plus utility room and entrance. The middle floor is the main sitting room, and the top floor is the bedroom with en suite shower.

Decorating the town house

All the rooms are finished using art papers, wallpaper samples and textured card, rather than more conventional materials or paint. The ceilings are papered with plain white paper to reflect light. I chose a variety of subtle shades and textures, bearing in mind that the house is open-fronted – sudden colour clashes might spoil the overall effect. Colour accents are provided by small pictures on the walls.

In such small rooms, neat, modern radiators are preferable to fireplaces as they take up little space: this is standard practice in many new town houses. In the sitting room, the radiator attached to the wall is a

picture of a new design, taken from an advertisement. The bedroom radiator is made from a set of coloured hairgrips, fixed on to a pastel-coloured card backing. Near to the gleaming fake entrance door on the lower floor, there is a glass key

plate engraved with the words 'New Home'. You may find something similar in a craft gallery or gift shop. It prompted the thought that this house project might make an unusual present for friends or family who are moving house in real life.

▲ The shower is a semi-translucent, resin candleholder, with a door added at one side to extend the fitment to make an en suite shower room. The door is made of white reeded card, which is also used to make a top for the fitment.

Interior design in the twenty-first century

By 2001, interior decoration had settled into a new style: uncarpeted hardwood floors, neutral colours and oriental influences became key features of a different look for the home. The work of leading interior designers was well publicized in home decoration magazines, read by a growing number of people, and the ideas shown in turn influenced displays in furniture stores.

Off-whites, taupe, brown and beige, spiced up with dark brown and orange or red, made a calm, restful background. Clutter was swept away, and just a few carefully chosen ornaments, preferably oriental vases, bowls or perhaps Buddha figures, could be seen to advantage in rooms with a minimal amount of furniture. The oriental influence was immediately apparent: restful and calming, so that the home could become a retreat from the ever-busier and perhaps more threatening world outside.

Natural materials had returned to favour: in the most expensive kitchens, stone floors replaced vinyl, and granite or solid wood worktops were preferred to the synthetic worktops that had lasted for years (losing some of the advantage of wipe-clean surfaces which did not stain).

These decorative ideas all look wonderful in miniature rooms, without the sometimes prohibitive expense of the originals. Neutral does not mean dull: the blend of pale colours can be given variety by the use of textured fabrics. The most expensive sofas are covered in suede and strewn with velvet or shaggy cushions, sometimes adorned with tassels; fabrics that glisten with gold thread are another subtle way to complement a predominantly beige room. These ideas are all easy to scale down.

DECORATING THE MODERN DOLLS' HOUSE

The modern dolls' house has many features which simplify decoration:

- External door casings and window frames can be made of plain stripwood rather than elaborate mouldings, so it is not essential to mitre corners.

- A painted finish to represent plaster or concrete instead of brick or stone cladding makes completion of the facade straightforward.

- Internal doorways may have simple cut-out spaces, so there is no need to provide a door frame.

- Skirting boards are an anachronism: instead, the walls of a full-scale twenty-first-century house may be indented at the base to avoid scuff marks. In 1/12 or 1/24, this detail is unnecessary, as it will be too small to need emphasis.

- Fireplaces are optional: if you prefer, you can install a central heating radiator based on one of the latest models.

► The low table and minimalist flower arrangement create a peaceful effect against the beautiful woodwork. This restful corner is part of a prize-winning room for the twenty-first century, created by a Scottish Miniaturist Group.

▼ The latest bathrooms are provided with freestanding bowls of glass, porcelain or even stone. In this design, the tap would no longer need to be turned on and off: the water would flow when a hand is placed beneath it. This is an arrangement that is sure to be here to stay.

A zen-style apartment

Colloquially, the new decorative ideas became known as Zen style. It reached inner cities first, where old industrial buildings continued to be converted into expensive and well-designed apartments. The modern minimalist apartment gives another opportunity for the hobbyist to make and decorate scenes in room boxes as an alternative to a complete dolls' house.

The rooms in my 'apartment' convey the essence of oriental-influenced style. Each room is $10^1/_2$ in (270 mm) high by 10 in (265 mm) deep; the sitting room is $12^1/_2$ in (315 mm) wide and the bedroom slightly smaller at 11 in (280 mm) wide.

The sitting room

The pale woodstrip flooring is paper, and the textured cream wallpaper on the back wall is a sample of regular-size wallpaper that has a slightly raised pattern resembling foliage. To achieve a similar look, add variety with a mix of textures and keep furniture to a minimum, so that what is there can make an impact.

Add a bowl fire

The ultra-modern feature is the flame-effect fire with tiny pebbles, rather than the more usual simulated coal, arranged in a shallow bowl. Arrange your own 'flames' with red or orange paper: I used a cut-out from a picture advertising this type of fire, but red and orange cellophane is a good alternative. The fire stands directly on the hearth where it shows up well, rather than being set back.

▼ The flame-effect fire bowl filled with a layer of pebbles is simple to arrange.

The bedroom

Like the sitting room, the bedroom has a contrasting paper on the end wall, in this case a pale orange art paper with a textured finish. The doorway towards the back of the room is fitted with an acetate screen that allows plenty of light to filter through from the sitting room. In modern loft apartments, doorways are sometimes left completely open and no door is provided, but in a dolls'-house-size apartment the transparent infill can make it look properly finished, although this is an optional feature.

Furniture and accessories

In the sitting room, the low, armless sofa has a wooden base topped with bronze gauzy ribbon over silver upholstery (a metallic pan cleaner) which shines through the gauze. The soft, shaggy cushions are made from children's hairbands. A bed and a table are all that is needed to furnish the bedroom. A wooden soap tray makes a base for the bed. Add a bamboo headboard – mine was part of the handle from a soft brush (made in China) – or you can cut one from a thick bamboo table mat. I used a bought lavender bag, made of brown velvet, as a duvet: this has the advantage of scenting the room.

▲ The low table is the top of an ornamental soapstone box, used to display the delicate orchid in a translucent porcelain vase. The leaves attached to the wall are from an Indian peepul tree; they can occasionally be found in shops that stock art papers, or in gift shops.

▼ Florists' buckets, each containing a single large lily, are a typical designer touch.

◀ The completed fireplace with the latest style of fire bowl. The miniature pots on either side are based on modern Japanese porcelain. The fireplace wall is papered in cream with a faint stripe to emphasize this arrangement.

Make a fireplace for the zen-style apartment

As is so often the case, the focal point of the sitting room is the fireplace. Make one to suit the zen-style apartment from thick black card (or wood, painted matt black). The hearth is of black and gold marble-effect card, while the fireback is pale grey to provide contrast and lighten the effect.

1 Cut balsa wood or foamboard approximately $1/2$in (13mm) thick, $3^1/4$in (80mm) H x $3^3/4$in (95mm) W. Cut out a central rectangle $1^3/4$in (45mm) H x $2^1/8$in (53mm) W for the grate aperture.

2 Colour all the edges with a black felt-tip pen, including the edges of the aperture.

3 Cover the fireplace with black card. (Note: when cutting the pieces for front, sides and top, they should be fractionally larger than the base so that the card joins do not show.)

4 Cut a piece of pale grey card $1/2$in (13mm) larger all round than the size of the grate aperture and glue to the back of the fireplace to make a fireback.

5 Cut a hearth from $1/4$in (6mm) thick card or wood, $1^1/2$in (40mm) W x 4in (100mm) L, and cover with marbled card. Colour the edges with a gold pen. Fit to the floor with double-sided Scotch tape. Fit the fireplace centrally over the hearth.

CHAPTER 20
ETHNIC INFLUENCES

An interest in miniature scale can extend to a variety of subjects. In the main, hobbyists tend to concentrate on projects that they can study in their own locality, but it can be rewarding to try schemes based on more exotic styles. This gives an opportunity to plan a decorative scheme that may be very different from those nearer to home, and to gain a small insight into other cultures.

A Chinese temple

A temple interior is a place for calm concentration, richly decorated with symbols of Buddhism and containing gilded artefacts. One room from such a temple makes an interesting project that can begin with a choice of background paper (giftwrap) showing Chinese characters and symbols, and allow for the inclusion of a few small objects obtained from gift or museum shops.

▲ A miniature lacquer screen from China, with panels that depict the four seasons. The screen is in 1/10 scale, but not too large to use in a dolls' house.

▼ The gilded Buddha figure was sculpted by a professional miniaturist, and the Chinese-style carpet is one from a dolls' house range. The soapstone lions guarding the entrance came from an oriental gift shop.

219

▲ Irises in a shallow bowl are displayed on a red silk-covered box in this traditional-style gold-and-black room. The print on the wall was cut from a magazine.

▲ Made in Japan: two handmade lidded jars bought at a miniatures fair.

▼ An updated Japanese bathroom: this bathtub is a deep soapstone box. The porcelain basin sits on a wooden shelf and there is a view of the garden.

Japanese style

Japan is a contradiction; alongside the traditional home with its sparsely furnished, low-ceilinged rooms and small courtyard there are modern apartments that are equipped with the latest technology.

The Japanese love miniature replicas of dolls, furniture, houses and gardens, and just as in the west, the dolls' house hobby is popular. It differs in that because homes in general are small, 1/24 is the preferred scale and, using traditional origami techniques, even young children are adept at making tiny replicas of dolls and furniture in exquisite detail.

A traditional Japanese room

To get the best effect with minimal decoration, choose textures and colours of papers carefully. Real Japanese papers can be found in shops specializing in art papers.

The bathroom is a very important part of any Japanese home. If you decide to extend your Japanese room box by adding on further rooms, this should take priority. A deep tub is essential and typically would be rectangular and made of wood. But even though many Japanese keep to a traditional style in part of their home, a more modern bathroom may now be chosen.

A playroom for a Japanese child

With home space so cramped in many parts of Japan, it would be a lucky child who had a designated playroom. Japanese toys are so appealing that it seemed a pity not to make such a room which I felt a Japanese child would enjoy – but the room is necessarily minimal compared with a western playroom.

Japanese children are fascinated by cartoon characters and video games from an early age. Therefore, in a room designed to suit a slightly older child it would be appropriate to include a television set or computer.

▼ Bright colours enliven the room for a Japanese child. The tiny Emperor and Empress dolls are traditionally displayed for the annual Girls' Festival.

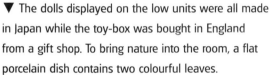

▼ The dolls displayed on the low units were all made in Japan while the toy-box was bought in England from a gift shop. To bring nature into the room, a flat porcelain dish contains two colourful leaves.

▲ Extra rooms can be added to this project easily. The bathroom might be next in importance: here is an idea to suit a modern city apartment.

◄ This room includes both a modern painting and a Japanese print depicting a Kabuki Theatre actor. The tiny figure of a Samurai warrior is a startling contrast to the miniature robot clock.

◄ Miniature lacquerwork is still made in Japan, copied from full-size traditional pieces. This set of stacking boxes on a tray is a typical design.

A modern Tokyo apartment

An apartment in Tokyo is often a tiny space and will probably belong to a young professional person.

Decorations should feature grey, black or brown, with red, orange or yellow colour accents. The floors may be of wood or of matting. Japanese woodwork is beautifully finished, so if you choose wood, a piece of veneer from a craft shop would be preferable to a paper simulation. Alternatively, use part of a woven straw table mat to provide a textured appearance similar to tatami matting (thick, rectangular, woven straw mats, used as floor covering in traditional Japanese rooms).

For the walls of my room I decided on a glossy bronze paper with a hint of mauve to suit the sophisticated city apartment. Pale grey would also make a good background.

Of necessity, such a tiny living space has to be kept tidy: this is often difficult in reality, and the modern Japanese apartment can be cluttered. However, this is not a problem in miniature, where boxes or low cupboards can be assumed to hold anything that does not have to be kept out for immediate use.

Use a small box to make a cupboard. I used a black card box with a grey pull-out inside. Punch a hole in the centre of the pull-out drawer, as handles are not attached in Japan. A low shelf can be arranged as a display space.

To make the shelf, use a piece of wood or a long, shallow box, painted grey.

Japanese rooms frequently consist of a curious mixture of treasured objects and quirky, modern items. Given the general admiration for pop music and footballers, there may be anything from a poster with a picture of David Beckham to a collection of mechanical toys. Whatever you choose, remember that the obligatory television set is always placed on the floor or a low shelf, where it will be at eye level for someone sitting on a cushion or mat.

◄ A bamboo blind allows light to filter into the room from the courtyard.

1 Cut a baseboard $9^1/2$in (240mm) L x 7in (180mm) D. This will allow a space $2^1/2$in (65mm) W x 7in (180mm) D for the courtyard.

2 To make the courtyard walls and ceiling, first cut the glazing: one piece $2^1/2$in (65mm) W x 7in (180mm) H for the back wall, two pieces 7in (180mm) L x 7in (180mm) H for the side walls, one piece $7^1/4$in (185mm) L x $2^3/4$in (70mm) W for the ceiling. (Note: the ceiling is larger as it will cover the back and side walls.)

3 Glue the glazing to the side of the room, as shown below.

4 Next, make the gravelled floor.

a) Cut a piece of card $2^3/8$in (60mm) W x $6^7/8$in (175mm) L.

b) Spread evenly with white PVA wood glue and cover with florists' decorative sand in a grey-green colour, pressing down firmly and evenly to make a flat surface.

c) When the glue is dry, turn the floor upside down and shake it gently to remove any surplus. Repeat the process if necessary to fill in any bald patches.

d) Slide the gravelled floor into the courtyard space.

5 Glue the completed room plus courtyard on to the base board.

A courtyard for the Tokyo apartment

However tight the space, even a single-room apartment might have at least a token courtyard to provide the essential link with nature. It could be just a narrow, gravelled strip against one wall, with three strategically placed rocks or a single pot plant.

To make a room with an attached courtyard you will need to omit one solid side wall from the main room. This will be replaced by a wall of reeded envelope stiffener or acetate sheet to divide the room from the courtyard. The room size is 7in x 7in x 7in (180mm x 180mm x 180mm).

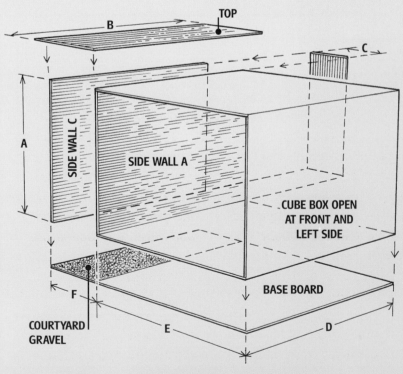

TOP

B

C

A

SIDE WALL C

SIDE WALL A

CUBE BOX OPEN AT FRONT AND LEFT SIDE

BASE BOARD

F

COURTYARD GRAVEL

E

D

A = 7in (180mm)   D = 7in (180mm)
B = $7^1/4$in (185mm)   E = 7in (180mm)
C = $2^3/4$in (70mm)   F = $2^1/2$in (65mm)

An Indian extravaganza

India is another country that always seems exotic to westerners. The heat, the colours, the noise and, more recently, the influence of 'Bollywood', a film industry that now attracts worldwide attention, are all a great contrast to western-style living.

A Bollywood-style room

Replicating a Bollywood-style room allows the freedom to include far more blatant luxury than in most miniature scenes. This room setting is based on the apartment of a famous Indian film star. It is lavishly decorated in vivid colours, filled with silver furniture and accessorized with silk cushions, mirrors and jewels. Part of the enjoyment in recreating this room is in the ingenious use of non-dolls'-house bits and pieces to complete the effect.

▼ Art papers and giftwrap are used for the floors and walls. Purple, orange and hot pink combine well, and tassels and braid add authentic finishing touches.

Jewel-encrusted furnishings

The silver furniture is inexpensive white wire furniture transformed with silver model enamel. The centrepiece of the room is an elaborate bed with its jewelled headboard. To recreate this, use a gift box as the bed base, preferably in deep pink or purple, or cover a plain box with shiny paper. The bedcover is a metallic pan cleaner, while jewelled finials are plastic hair ornaments. A jewelled Indian mirror frame is used as a headboard.

▼ The leopard is a toy shop animal, painted silver to look like a statue, while the jewelled boxes were from a gift shop.

► The completed courtyard looks suitably exotic. The remarkably inexpensive elephants came from an ethnic gift shop.

The Indian courtyard

In India, an apartment of this degree of luxury would have its own private courtyard, probably floored in marble and with a canopied area to provide shade. For the flooring I used a textured paper with a raised pattern of flowers and leaves which look as though they are scattered on the surface. An alternative could be mosaic tiles, which can be simulated with paint, paper or card. The rough-textured background paper combines colours in a manner that is almost three-dimensional to achieve a scenic effect.

▼ Transformation scene! The courtyard looks extraordinarily beautiful by moonlight, an effect achieved by a change of backdrop – a dark blue paper sprinkled with silver – and low lighting. The silver gazebo and seat are an irresistible invitation to a moonlit tryst.

Santa Fe room and courtyard

Santa Fe in New Mexico is a magical place combining Central American Indian culture with North American influences and has a charm all its own. The adobe (sun-baked clay) houses in earthy colours are a major part of the attraction of Santa Fe and interesting to reproduce in miniature.

Most houses today have been updated for modern living and have sophisticated interiors. I chose to reproduce a rustic, fairly primitive home, which conveys the feeling of an original, unmodernized dwelling.

Decorating the interior

Line the walls of the box with soft card or 3.5mm (approx. $^1/_8$ in) foamboard and cover with thick, coloured paper. Vary the colours: terracotta, orange, buff or ochre would all work well. Wrap the paper round each piece of lining and fix it at the back with glue or sticky tape. This covering over a semi-soft base suggests the thickness of the adobe walls, as do the curved edges produced by using this method. Next fix the walls in place with double-sided Scotch tape along all the edges.

▲ The one-room home is set in a large, ready-made box measuring 11in (280mm) H x 10in (255mm) D x 15$^3/_4$in (400mm) W. This is a standard size of box; alternatively, make one to suit your own requirements from foamboard.

▼ The low bed is a wood and raffia soap stand and the typical Mexican musical instruments came from an ethnic gift shop. The flooring looks very realistic, although it is actually a pictured surface.

Build a Santa Fe corner fireplace

Corner fireplaces are a noticeable feature of Santa Fe homes. They, too, are of adobe and look chunky with rounded corners and a thick hearth.

1 First, you need to make a corner chimneybreast.

a) Cut a piece of 3.5mm (approx. $^1/_8$in) foamboard or soft card 5in (130mm) wide and $^3/_4$in (20mm) less than the height of the room. Cut the side edges at an angle of 45° so that they will fit flush against the walls when fitted across the corner.

b) Cover with thick coloured paper to blend with the other walls.

2 Next, make the hearth and fireplace. Set the chimneybreast aside while you make the hearth; the chimneybreast will fit on top of the hearth.

a) Cut a triangular hearth to fit into the corner: $6^1/_2$in (165mm) W x 5in (130mm) x 5in (130mm) each side. You will need to glue together several layers of foamboard to make a hearth about $^3/_4$in (20mm) deep. Round off the front corners.

b) Cut the fireplace 5in (130mm) W x 3in (75mm) H from foamboard; glue layers together to make a thickness of approximately $^3/_4$in (20mm). Cut out a space to take the fire.

c) Paint both hearth and fireplace with stone model enamel; apply two coats for a smooth effect on the fireplace, but aim for a rough finish on the hearth.

d) Next, cut out a space in the chimneybreast that is slightly larger than the aperture in the fireplace.

3 Glue the hearth in place, and then glue the chimneybreast on top. Finally, glue the fireplace in position against the chimneybreast and hearth and stack the logs upright, not horizontal, following local style.

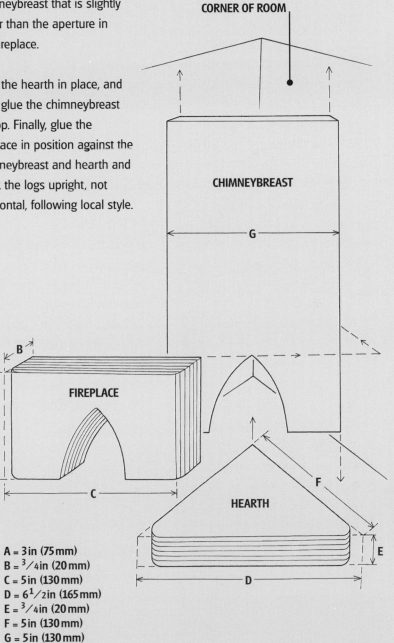

CORNER OF ROOM

CHIMNEYBREAST

G

FIREPLACE

A

B

C

HEARTH

D

E

F

A = 3in (75mm)
B = $^3/_4$in (20mm)
C = 5in (130mm)
D = $6^1/_2$in (165mm)
E = $^3/_4$in (20mm)
F = 5in (130mm)
G = 5in (130mm)

◄ The materials used to make both room and terrace are colourful and varied. It is worth looking in gift shops and haberdashery departments to search out suitable beads and braids.

The ceiling

The ceiling can be treated in the same way as the walls. In some houses ceilings are of wood, and a quick way to reproduce this alternative effect is to use a slatted table mat. It will look realistic and is easy to cut and fit in one piece. Turn the box upside down and use PVA wood glue to fix it in place. Leave until the glue is thoroughly dry before putting the box the right way up.

Fit the flooring

A picture of a stone floor in earthy tones taken from a brochure may be ideal for the floor. If you prefer, simulate an earth floor by painting card with a reddish-coloured paint (brown and red make a good blend) thickened with a little interior filler to give it a grainy texture.

Peruvian and Mexican souvenirs as ornaments

Miniature animals and figures to complete the room are widely available in ethnic gift shops. Braids and woven purses with typical designs are inexpensive and can be cut up and used for blankets and floor rugs.

Remember to include a plain wooden religious cross on the wall and some earthenware pots or jugs. A metal candlestick with a candle, and perhaps an exotic flower or a cactus in a pot, complete the room.

◄ A wide selection of miniature figures can be found in ethnic gift shops and will add real character to your room setting.

A Santa Fe terrace

You might like to add a terrace to your one-room house. I used the lid of a cardboard box measuring approximately 15 in (380 mm) long by 12 in (305 mm) deep, with an edging 1¹/₂ in (40 mm) high. Alternatively, make a base from wood or thick card and add a wall of stripwood to provide a typical fence.

▲ The terrace seems full of warmth and colour. Stepladders were used by the Pueblo Indians to reach other parts of the buildings rather than internal staircases – entry from outside was through a window aperture. They are still features of Santa Fe life today, although homes now have doors.

step-by-step

Add steps to the terrace

One authentic touch is to add steps to join the terrace to the house. Make steps from blocks of roughly cut balsa wood; the painted finish can be rough for this purpose.

1 Mask out the position for the steps on the terrace floor but glue them in place after the floor is complete.

2 Paint the floor and steps with an ochre-coloured matt paint. Add a tiled area near to the house: I used part of a wallpaper sample with a mosaic tile effect. Mark this area while you complete the rest of the floor.

3 To add texture to the painted surface, use ornamental sand (sold for flower arrangers and use in fish tanks) and apply as for the Japanese courtyard (see page 223).

4 Finally, fit the steps in place on the terrace and add some large stones and fake cacti.

CHAPTER 21

PUBLIC SPACES

I have chosen a variety of projects as examples of some of the public spaces that can be enjoyable to reproduce in miniature. Each allows the development of a theme in a very different way from that required for a purely domestic interior.

Open a museum

In real life, the seriously wealthy often build up a vast collection, and some decide to endow a museum or help out with a loan exhibition. In the same way, the hobbyist with a specific interest will collect miniatures that particularly appeal to them, whether it is paintings, sculpture or a group of related objects. Such a small collection can be shown off to advantage in a specially designed setting.

You could choose any special interest for your museum, from miniature dolls' houses and reproductions of period toys to aeroplanes or boats, and enjoy gradually building up an individual collection. For a more intimate feeling, perhaps for a costume museum, a period-style dolls' house may provide the perfect display space. I decided on a transport museum with the emphasis on vintage motorcycles.

▼ The 1/12 modern house (see page 177) is an adaptable building and can be used for a wide range of purposes. In this second version, it has become a museum of vintage transport with a self-service café attached. Simple alterations to the finish and interior decorations create an entirely different impression from the first, domestic version.

The Café

Vintage Transport Museum

MUSEUM OPEN

A transport museum and café

My museum was made from the instructions given to make the modern open-plan house (see pages 177–179) but the pillars and stepped surround to the entrance are faced with textured white card instead of plasticized brick to give it more the appearance of a public building. In place of the plain glass window walls at either end in the original version, I fitted coloured acetate sheet, and blue and purple card rather than a pale colour for the floors. The rear walls are white to show off transport posters, cut from advertisements.

The museum setting

Do a little landscaping around your museum and café. A green space or a paved area, a path of small tiles or gravel and a few tubs of flowers make an attractive surround. This also provides a place to set up signs. Choose coloured paper that will stand out against white, and use a computer to design your own museum and café fascia boards. Select these from the wide range of fonts available on most computers: try printing in several type sizes on different-coloured background papers to decide on the best effect.

Once you are satisfied, cut out the sign and glue it to card before fixing it to the front of the building or onto a freestanding signboard.

▲ The motorcycle display area is sure to interest any enthusiast. The Italian scooters are miniatures of vintage models dating from the 1960s. A modern television provides an interactive display, while the pictures on the wall were taken from a newspaper.

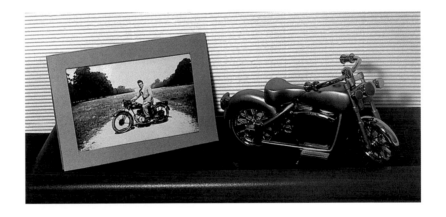

▲ The sepia photograph of a rider in the early 1930s is an original family photograph – snapshots taken by box cameras at the time were often very tiny and can be useful in a miniature setting.

◄ The Michelin Man advertising figure next to my Museum Open sign at the entrance is sure to attract the visitors' attention.

▲ The table and chairs and also the crockery are all inexpensive and the food looks delicious. A water jug, glasses and cutlery are laid out on the checkout desk with a mini-computer to add up the bill.

The café

Most museums provide refreshments for their visitors; a self-service café is a good idea, as it allows more time to look at the exhibits. Start with a long table or fitment on which to lay out the food. Plastic box lids make good trays so that the sandwiches and cakes can be arranged in sequence for the customers to help themselves, while bottles of soda water and cola look best in their own special 'cool' unit.

◄ Here is the beginning of my next specialist museum.

A hotel foyer

We all stay in hotels from time to time, on holiday or on business. You may prefer the small, intimate, private hotel or the grand, deluxe version. Either way, a hotel project is immensely enjoyable, even if you get no further than the reception area. Base it on one where you spent a fantastic holiday, or maybe one you have visited to attend a memorable function.

A luxury hotel will have a reception area that is intended to impress or amaze guests as they arrive. There need not be a lot of furniture, although, if you wish, you can provide comfortable (or stylish) armchairs and small tables.

The soft glow of working lights will create atmosphere, although in this case I dispensed with electric lighting and relied on the dazzling effect of tiny stranded metallic beads suspended across the room (an inexpensive necklace). The reeded blind is a table mat made of plasticized hollow rods.

▶ This palatial hotel foyer is based on one in a New York hotel in Manhattan where luxury and glamour combine. It is set in a two-sided, open-fronted room box 12 in (305 mm) wide x 15 in (380 mm) deep x 12 in (305 mm) high, with the third wall covered by a blind to let in light or sunshine.

▲ ▶ The flooring is giftwrap in an unusual striped pattern. The reception desk is covered with the reverse side of the same paper, a pale bronze, ensuring perfect colour coordination.

Set up a reception desk

To make the large reception desk, use $^1/_4$in (6mm) thick wood.

1 Cut one piece 2in (50mm) H x 10in (255mm) L x 2in (50mm) W for the desk front. Cut two pieces each 2in (50mm) H x 2in (50mm) D for the ends. Cut two back supports each 2in (50mm) H x 2in (50mm) W to fit at the back corners.

2 Glue the pieces together in the sequence shown.

3 When the glue has set, cover with a thin card that has a metallic finish.

4 The desk top is a piece of 2in (50mm) wide brass strip (from a model shop) which looks both functional and impressive.

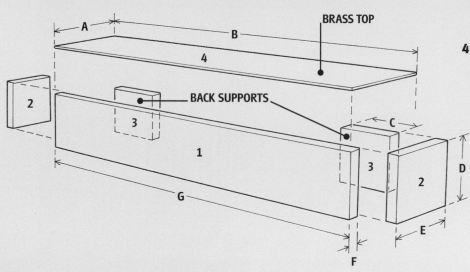

BRASS TOP
BACK SUPPORTS

A = 2in (50mm)
B = 10in (255mm)
C = 2in (50mm)
D = 2in (50mm)
E = 2in (50mm)
F = $^1/_4$in (6mm)
G = 10in (255mm)

◀ Light shining through the blind makes a dazzling effect in the richly decorated reception.

The blind

The type of place mat used for the blind is available in a choice of colours. It is quite heavy and needs to be anchored securely above the ceiling. Use a heavy-duty cloth tape that is very strong. After fixing the blind in place, cover the fixing tape by adding an additional layer of foamboard to form the top of the room box.

Accessories

One or two large, striking pictures are all you need to decorate the walls. Choose 'paintings' to complement the colour scheme. Add some imposing flower arrangements and antique ornaments to complete the extravagant and luxurious effect.

▼ Some luggage will indicate the presence of hotel guests. This trunk and suitcases are of fine-quality leather.

Make a low table

As mine was to be a modern hotel, I decided on the minimalist look. The low table is an open box. The inside is painted matt silver and the outside covered with bronze-coloured paper. Use a ready-made box or make one.

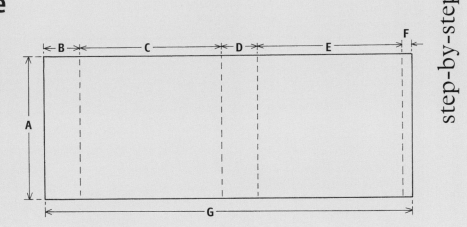

1 Cut a strip of strong card that measures $10^{1}/_{4}$in (260mm) long x 4in (100mm) wide. Paint one side of the strip. This will form the inside of the table space.

2 Score, then fold and glue together, as shown in the diagram.

A = 4in (100mm)
B = 1in (25mm)
C = 4in (100mm)
D = 1in (25mm)
E = 4in (100mm)
F = $^{1}/_{4}$in (6mm)
G = $10^{1}/_{4}$in (260mm)
H = 4in (100mm)
I = 4in (100mm)
J = 1in (25mm)

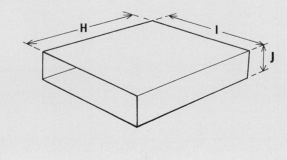

A spa salon reception area
Luxury hotels may have additional health facilities, such as swimming pools or keep-fit centres. This tiny reception is designed for a spa salon and is made in a shallow box 7in (180mm) long by 5in (130mm) deep by 8in (200mm) high.

Both flooring and back wall are wallpaper samples, while the end wall is silver-grey card from a brochure. The door to the spa is a green plastic paper knife, which was presented in a white card pack with a small 'window' to show the green. It works well when fitted at an angle into the corner of the room.

▲ A calm, cool space is appropriate for a spa reception area.

◄ A combination of different papers was the inspiration for the spa reception area.

▲ The simple but effective colour scheme is based on black, silver and an orange-red to give a suitable Chinese 'look' to the restaurant. The gleaming back wall has a repeated pattern of slightly recessed circles.

A Chinese restaurant

A large hotel will have several top-class restaurants: a breakfast room, a tearoom, a function room, a grill room and often an oriental restaurant, so there is plenty of choice for miniaturization. To continue the theme of the grand hotel foyer, I decided on a superior Chinese restaurant, again set in a large room box.

In many new-style restaurants, the chefs can be seen preparing and cooking the food behind a glass screen, and this can be an entertainment in itself. Use a curved photograph frame as a screen: these are fitted with transparent plastic, rather than glass.

Make a 2 in (50 mm) high partition wall as a base for the frame; the top should be about 2 in (50 mm) wide to form a shelf. Arrange cooking pans and utensils behind the frame to suggest the kitchen area beyond.

◄ This restaurant is intended as a smart city venue; the large circular window shows a view of tall buildings with plenty of glass. This is a trompe l'oeil effect that can work well if the picture is chosen with care.

The table and accessories

The dining table is made from two silver-grey boxes mounted on a wooden plinth painted orange-red.

This restaurant does not feature miniature food – there is enough drama in the spectacular interior decorations. In the kitchen behind the screen there is one token piece of salmon, but copper pans show up well and indicate that cooking will commence when the customers arrive.

Used matchsticks make good chopsticks. Cut the matchstick into suitable lengths and then split each lengthwise into half and then in half again. One matchstick will make two pairs of chopsticks.

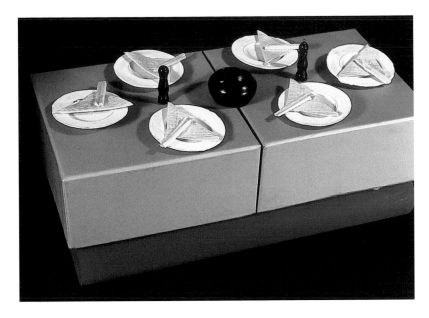

▲ A perfect table-setting, ready for the meal to begin, with a folded paper napkin and chopsticks laid neatly on each plate.

Make accessories for the Chinese restaurant

To make banquette seating

I have not included chairs as I wanted to show the whole scene without obscuring the table, but you might like to make banquette seating to suit the size of the table.

1 Cut a piece of wood 1¼in (30mm) high and the same length as the table and then paint it black.

2 Cut a piece of foam padding the same size as the top and cover it with black imitation leather, joining it underneath.

3 Glue the padded seat to the banquette base.

To make the napkins

Use thick coloured paper from a roll of kitchen towels. Cut a strip that is ³/₄in (20mm) wide and then cut it into ³/₄in (20mm) lengths. Fold each napkin diagonally to make a triangle and secure with a tiny piece of double-sided Scotch tape inside, which will not make a bump.

A = ³/₄in (20mm)
B = ³/₄in (20mm)

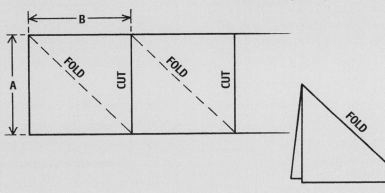

I was attracted to the idea of a minimalist working space of the kind favoured by eminent architects. It is set in an open-fronted room box with a transparent coloured plastic stationery file as part of the arrangement to provide an end wall that suggests an elevator beyond.

▲ One large modern armchair is ready for the client, while the desk chair is a Wassily chair, designed by Marcel Breuer and much admired by contemporary furniture designers.

A room with a view

This office is designed as though in a penthouse suite. A series of cloud pictures against a matt blue background link it with the view outside. The room size is 12in (305mm) high, 10in (255mm) deep and 12in (305mm) long plus a 4in (100mm) long floor extension to take the stationery file at one side. The file is lined on the side facing into the room with blue holographic paper to add depth of colour and give the impression of a lit space beyond.

Furnishing the office

The office follows the minimalist ideal of an uncluttered desk, a great view from the window, and luxurious seating for the client. Smooth, reflective surfaces predominate to give a modern appearance.

The outlook from the office is an important part of the scene. Cut a large rectangle for the window space and fit a picture behind it. The one I used is a panoramic view of London and the Thames, and emphasizes the suggestion that this office is set in the prestigious Docklands area of new development. For the partly lowered blind I used card with a striped pattern in graduations of colour. The floor is grey marbled card.

Make a sleek office desk

To make the desk, you will need a wooden or strong card box approximately 5$^1/_2$in (140 mm) long by 2$^1/_2$in (65 mm) deep by 2$^1/_4$in (55mm) high.

1 Cover the box with satin-finish grey card, curving the corners for a sleek effect.

2 Make the desk top from $^1/_4$in (6mm) thick card or wood and cover it with matt grey card. I was lucky enough to find a piece with a neat blue grid pattern to add interest. However, any geometric design would be suitable to glue onto plain grey card.

▲ The large desk is suitably impressive.

◄ The desk top is left bare, except for a mini-computer and a paperweight, ready to use when the architect spreads out his plans.

1/24 Scale

CHAPTER 22

THE SCALE

My reaction when I first saw a 1/24 dolls' house was one of delight – but then a moment of doubt. How could anyone with average-size hands manage to decorate and arrange furniture in spaces so tiny? Naturally I wanted to see if I could achieve this and was soon hard at work.

To anyone who shares my initial feelings about 1/24, I can offer reassurance. After only a few hours thinking out revised approaches to interior design, and then actually tackling these smaller decorative schemes, the reduced scale seemed perfectly normal. When I then went back to look at one of my 1/12 dolls' houses, it seemed huge. It is only a matter of adjustment, which you will find is quickly made.

Scale comparisons

The 1/24 scale is not always fully understood; in fact, at one time it was termed 'half-scale', which added to the confusion. What was unclear from this was that the measurements of a piece of miniature furniture need to be halved in all directions to give only $\frac{1}{8}$ of the volume – or overall size – of a similar piece in 1/12.

It may be useful to look at some pictures of similar miniatures in each scale to help you to adjust to 1/24. While looking at the close-up pictures, you will be able to see the miniatures in a way that would be impossible without using a magnifying glass. Some remarkable work is made by leading miniaturists who enjoy the challenge of making a piece as meticulously in 1/24 as in 1/12, but carving, for example, can be so small that the fine detail is almost invisible to the naked eye.

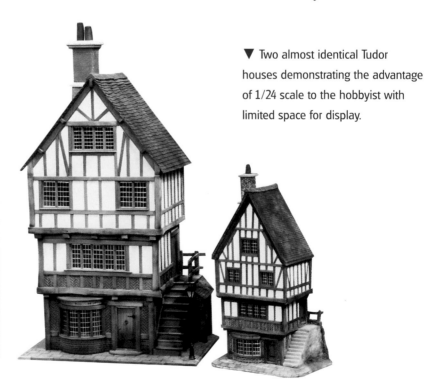

▼ Two almost identical Tudor houses demonstrating the advantage of 1/24 scale to the hobbyist with limited space for display.

WORKING IN METRIC

■ If you use metric measurements you may prefer to work in 1/25 scale. In this case, $1\frac{5}{8}$in (40mm) represents $39\frac{1}{2}$in (1m). For all practical purposes, 1/24 and 1/25 are the same, as the difference cannot be distinguished by eye.

EXAMPLES OF 1/24 MEASUREMENTS

Measurements are approximate, because individual items will vary.
If in doubt, measure up objects in your own home and scale them down.

ROOMS (typical size)	Depth	$6^1/_2$–7in (165–180mm)
	Ceiling height	5–6in (125–155mm)
	Width	$6^1/_2$–7in (165–180mm)

FURNITURE		
Four-poster bed	Length	$3^1/_2$in (90mm)
	Height	$3^3/_8$in (85mm)
	Width	$2^1/_2$–3in (65–75mm)

| Single bed | Length | $3^1/_4$in (81mm) |
| | Width (3ft bed) | $1^1/_2$in (38mm) |

| Dining chair | Height to seat | $^3/_4$in (20mm) |
| | Height of back | Varies |

| Armchair/Sofa | Height to seat | $^5/_8$in (16mm) |
| | Height of back and length | Varies |

Dining table	Height	$1^1/_4$in (31mm)
	Length and width	Varies
	Diameter of circular table	2–3in (50–75mm)

DOLLS (height)	Gentleman	3in (75mm)
	Lady	$2^3/_4$in (70mm)
	Toddler	$1^1/_8$in (30mm)
	Baby	$^3/_4$in (20mm)

▲ Chippendale produced many variations of the interlacing on the pierced central splat of his chairs, and the miniaturist's skill is tested to the full with this complicated arrangement, shown above in both 1/12 and 1/24 scales.

▼ Four-poster beds again show the size differential between the two scales. Astonishingly, the 1/24 hangings are of hand-knitted lace.

▼ The 1/24 chest of drawers is made from fine-grained mahogany while the 1/12 is made from yew. Both bowls are porcelain, which a skilled maker can produce in 1/24.

Advantages and disadvantages of 1/24

One major bonus for most of us is that 1/24 dolls' houses are, in general, less expensive than 1/12. Working in small scale is economical, because there are many low-cost materials which can be utilized for decoration (see pages 281–283).

Another advantage is the lack of weight with 1/24 scale pieces. You can pop your entire 1/24 house or room box into a holdall or shopping bag and take it to a dolls' house club meeting to share with your friends and fellow hobbyists.

There are some disadvantages, too, however, but all potential problems have their solutions and I hope that I have checked out most of them. Here are a few things which may occur to you if you are starting on your first small-scale project.

Q *Will it be difficult to reach into rooms with such low ceiling heights when decorating or arranging furniture?*

A Most makers are aware of this and are ingenious in incorporating a number of openings and removable fittings.

▲ A set of shelves to hang on a wall is supplied assembled, ready for staining or polishing. The saucers are made of pewter and can be painted.

Q *I have never tackled carpentry. Will I need to put in fiddly wooden fixtures and fittings?*

A Fixtures and fittings can be simplified; in tiny rooms too much detail will not show to advantage. Thin stripwood, which can be cut with scissors, can be used to make, for example, a fireplace.

Q *Where can I find ornaments and accessories which are small enough?*

A Accessories in 1/24 scale are available at miniatures fairs and by mail order. Many items too small to be made in wood are cast in metal, ready to be painted.

Q *Where can I find kits, furniture, fixtures and fittings?*

A In the United States, the majority of dolls' house outlets supply fixtures and fittings in both scales. This is not yet the case in Britain, although more and more shops have some space devoted to 1/24. If you are not within easy reach of a retail stockist, the answer is mail order. Dolls' house magazines carry advertisements by both makers and suppliers, whose catalogues offer everything from dolls' house kits to the smallest miniature. Many of these suppliers also exhibit at miniatures fairs, details of which are advertised in dolls' house magazines and elsewhere, so you will be able to look before you buy. Makers will sometimes make to order something which is not in their standard range – it is always worth asking if you have a special request.

IMPROVISATION

The dolls' house hobby gives plenty of scope for lateral thinking. Finding new uses for leftovers is both economical and rewarding.

■ Spare 1/12 picture-frame mouldings can be used as cornice (see page 281).

■ Sections of wallpaper borders make good friezes.

■ Scraps of velvet or suede can be used as carpets (see page 298).

■ Textured art papers simulate plastered walls (this is much less messy than doing the plastering yourself), and marbled card makes beautiful floors (see pages 281–284).

■ A short length of wooden moulding will make a shelf.

■ A plastic bottle top can be transformed into a table when painted, or it can even become a pottery kiln (see page 269).

▼ Items in 1/12 scale are often suitable. For example, the smaller sizes of cooking pans intended for 1/12 are just right on a 1/24 range. A Chinese vase can be included as a floor-standing ornament in a 1/24 room, rather than placing it on a table.

▼ An example of a 1/12 scale ornament which can be used in a 1/24 room (see page 297).

Where to shop

Try using modelling materials from craft shops to make floors and food, and search for tiny beads to use as vases. Jewellery 'bits and pieces' can also be transformed into vases and light fittings.

Railway modelling materials are essential for miniature gardens. Buy inexpensive stripwood to make plain skirting boards, door frames and shelves, and ask for a shade card showing the range of model enamels and varnishes.

Check out the range of adhesives at a stationer's and choose the correct type to suit the material you plan to use. Stock up on Blu-tack, Gripwax and similar products. Look out also for unusual textured papers and cards for decorating walls and floors. Postcards can be useful to adapt for trompe l'oeil effects and wall coverings.

Foamboard (from art suppliers) is ideal for making the bases and liners of room boxes. Note that art shop masking tape is available in a choice of widths and is more suitable for miniaturists than decorator's masking tape.

CHAPTER 23

CHOOSING YOUR HOUSE

Even if you are new to the doll's house hobby, you will probably have an idea of what kind of dolls' house you want. Town or country, formal or informal, period or modern – there is plenty of choice.

In this chapter there are some examples of different 1/24 scale houses to consider; you may find something here which will link up with your own initial ideas or even set you off in a new direction. Visit some miniatures fairs and dolls' house shops before you buy, look at specialist dolls' house magazines and send for makers' illustrated catalogues to look through.

A ready-made house

The cheapest ready-made dolls' house will be a basic, unpainted 'shell', leaving you to decorate inside and out. Most such houses are made of strong plywood, or MDF (medium density fibreboard), which will look equally good with a simple painted finish or with realistic cladding added. Internal features such as chimney breasts and fireplaces may be provided.

Other options

Not everyone wants to take on the entire decoration themselves, and more expensive houses may be offered with the exterior finished, leaving you to concentrate on the inside. This type of house is a good choice if you want, for example, a thatched cottage, or a town house with elaborate architectural detail, which you might prefer the maker to provide.

More expensively, you can commission a house from a craftsman who will provide everything you specify. You will be able to ask for the type of finish you want, and decide exactly how much decoration will be included. Such a house will be an heirloom to pass on to your family and will give unending pleasure.

◀ An American Colonial-style house with interesting windows, veranda and porch. The elaborate fretwork roof ridging is hand-carved and gilded.

Room boxes and vignettes

The 1/24 hobby is not only about complete dolls' houses. It is also concerned with single-room settings, arranged in open-fronted room boxes. These individual scenes are delightful projects to tackle and allow the hobbyist more freedom to explore different styles and periods than a whole dolls' house, where everything needs to be in keeping. A series of room sets take up very little space.

Room boxes are practical, because they can be moved easily if your only work surface is a table which will be needed for other purposes during the day. They can be a complete project or a try-out for decorating and furnishing a dolls' house. With a room box, you can experiment to see whether a particular style really appeals to you.

If, like me, you are fascinated by modern architecture and design, which is way ahead of current styles in ready-made dolls' houses, room boxes offer an opportunity to complete an unusual room and incorporate features which appeal to you most from the pick of modern styles. Exhibitions and articles in books and magazines can spark off many ideas for such projects.

Individual period and modern rooms are pictured and discussed in detail on pages 292–303, with ideas on alternative schemes and things to make for inclusion.

Wooden room boxes can be purchased with a sliding or lift-out front to keep the contents free from dust, and are available ready-made or as a kit. A foamboard box is rigid and reasonably strong and you can make your own open-fronted box very easily.

A vignette, which can be hung on the wall, is another space saver. The box should be only 2–3in (50–75mm) deep, the front surrounded by a picture frame. There is enough depth for a scene which will give the illusion of a three-dimensional room yet take up no more wall surface than a small picture.

▼ A realistic scene arranged in a room box assembled from a kit. The furniture, by the same maker, is available separately either with distressed paint finish or plain. Accessories, dolls and food can be added to personalize the setting.

▲ The Fairfield is an American version of a Victorian-style house. The completed house measures 15in (380mm) wide, 16in (405mm) deep and 20in (500mm) high.

▲ This mill house is country style with an extra touch of imagination. It has half-timbered walls, a neatly chamfered chimney and two opening doors. It is supplied undecorated. See pages 261–265 for some ideas for decorating the mill house.

Assembling a house from a kit

This option will appeal to many hobbyists. Most kit houses in 1/24 scale are American, and are available through British stockists as well as in the United States. Assembly requires no carpentry skills and is usually achieved by means of slot-together sections.

If you have assembled a dolls' house kit before, you will have a good idea of how long it may take to complete the project. American kits are often fanciful creations and are likely to have plenty of interest in the form of porches, balconies and intriguingly shaped roofs with turrets. The basic structure will be of thin wood, as it is intended to be covered with surface decoration; siding and shingles may be provided with the kit, or available as optional extras. Most British dolls' house makers prefer to provide an assembled wooden house ready for decoration, but there are exceptions. Plans are also available from some British makers. Assembly may be more challenging than an American kit, but should be within the capabilities of anyone who enjoys woodwork, and detailed instructions are provided.

A kit house has other advantages apart from being economical. Decoration will be easier because it is possible to paint window frames and small trims before they are fixed in place permanently. In addition, a real feeling of satisfaction can be gained from assembling your own dolls' house.

▲ This cottage ornée is a limited-edition kit, which is also available completed and decorated. It is based on Vine Cottage, designed by John Nash and built 1810–11 for a unique village, Blaise Hamlet, near Bristol, England.

◄ A pair of shops built from a set of plans. The roof is covered with tile sheeting. The windows and doors are of white plastic, which can be painted if a colour is preferred.

HINTS ON MAKING UP A KIT HOUSE

■ Check first that all the parts are included. Lay them out and familiarize yourself with them.

■ Read the instructions provided, check the parts mentioned at each stage of assembly and make sure that you understand how they fit together.

■ Sand each piece with fine glasspaper, grade 000.

■ Check that any pre-cut slots or grooves are the right size to take slot-in parts. You may need to make minute adjustments by sanding to ensure a perfect fit.

■ Assemble each stage 'dry' and check that all is correct before you use wood glue. Once the glue has set it will be impossible to undo.

■ While the glue is setting, it is best to hold the pieces firmly together with masking tape, because it will take several hours until full strength is achieved.

■ Ensure that the walls and floors are at right angles, or you could end up with a leaning house. Check the angles with a set square. It is advisable to make a jig to support the structure while the glue dries. If you do not have an appropriately equipped workshop, make a jig by using blocks of wood with perfectly squared corners, or improvise by using piles of books.

■ It can be useful to paint structures and other internal features before fixing them in place. Check whether some of the room decoration might be done more easily before assembly.

■ Allow plenty of time. It will take longer than you anticipate.

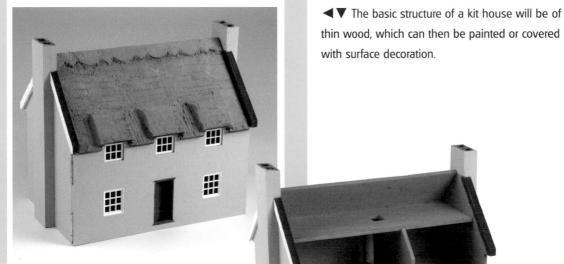

◄▼ The basic structure of a kit house will be of thin wood, which can then be painted or covered with surface decoration.

Period style options

Once you have decided whether to assemble a kit or buy one ready-made, you can choose an architectural style. Unless you plan an updated, modern interior, your decorative schemes, patterns and furnishings will all follow through from the period of the house itself.

▼ A splendid dolls' house version of a Tudor house with medieval origins, complete with carving copied from existing examples.

Tudor

There are many variations on Tudor style, from a house with medieval origins to a tall town mansion. The exterior of a Tudor house can be more tricky to decorate than a plain, classical facade, but will be worth the effort. Tudor houses have existed for over 400 years, and many real houses are still lived in very comfortably today.

The English cottage

The miniature cottage is always pretty, and most dolls' cottage exteriors are fully finished by the maker, so that only interior decoration is needed. In reality, such buildings are undoubtedly picturesque, but originally they were cramped and often damp. The dolls' house version will be enchanting, if somewhat romanticized by the omission of these flaws.

▼ Prentice Cottage is a copy of a cottage in Suffolk, and was commissioned by the Puppenhaus Yoshima Museum in Japan as an example of a typical small English home.

▶ An accurate Victorian facade which conceals an unusual interior. It was commissioned as a cabinet in which to keep private papers, and four rooms inside are designed to be used as storage space.

▲ A linked pair of fishermen's cottages. Decorating the interiors in contrasting styles would make an interesting project.

The seaside cottage

Cottages are not confined to the depths of the country. Attractively painted, simple cottages, originally dwellings for fishermen, have now become holiday homes in many seaside towns. For the miniaturist, a 1/24 cottage of this type can be great fun to decorate and furnish, with fishy items included to show its original purpose, or even updated to modern use. A twentieth-century beach chalet or beach hut is the ideal smaller seaside project, complete with whiffs of nostalgia for childhood holidays (see page 312–313).

Georgian

Georgian style is a perennial favourite and in 1/24 it is possible to have a complete mansion which takes up very little space. A house similar to the one illustrated on page 290 will be a long-term project, as there is as much to keep a hobbyist occupied as when dealing with a 1/12 house of grand proportions.

Victorian

Victorian houses have plenty of detail on the facade, and the rooms can be filled to overflowing with miniatures, as ornament and decoration is the essence of this style. A Victorian house is a good choice for someone who wants to create a lived-in look. The kitchen, in particular, is the favourite room for many (see page 291).

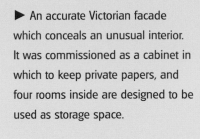

▲ A medieval house with a later, Jacobean extension. Interior decoration and furnishing might reflect the lapse of time between the date of the original aisled hall and the later timber-framed addition. The dolls' house is made from papier-mâché as infill for the timber framing, by the artist maker, who enjoys working with this unusual technique. She uses her painting skills to reproduce the colours of worn stone.

Twentieth-century styles

Charles Rennie Mackintosh has had a continuing influence on modern design, and his colour schemes and furniture have enjoyed a huge revival. He was the first truly modern architect and designer, the forerunner of Bauhaus style and Art Deco, both of which followed his lead in using white with strong colour accents (see page 294). His distinctive style is equally impressive when miniaturized and has become popular with hobbyists who relish the challenge of modern design.

Mackintosh was influenced by traditional Japanese style, and his cool, sparsely furnished interiors were in deliberate contrast to the overfilled rooms in vogue when he began his career.

▲ The simplicity and originality of Charles Rennie Mackintosh's Janitor's House for Scotland Street School in Glasgow has been copied faithfully in this 1/24 dolls' house version.

▼ Single rooms are preferred by Japanese hobbyists rather than a complete dolls' house. Lack of clutter and a calm atmosphere are valued, and in this miniature every detail has been considered carefully.

In the early years of the twentieth century, grand houses built by Sir Edwin Lutyens incorporated many elements of Tudor style. His houses fitted well into the English landscape, and inside the emphasis was on comfort.

The smaller Edwardian house, a mass-produced version of the revamped Tudor style, influenced suburban house building for years to come. Inside, the fashion for oak furniture was almost obligatory.

The Tudor revival continued until the outbreak of the Second World War, when house building in Britain virtually ceased. Rows of identical, suburban houses all had gable ends and mock beams. These houses were well built and comfortable. For many people living in this type of house today, a 1/24 version would provide a delightful project. The rooms could be furnished in Art Deco or modern style.

▶ A typical Edwardian suburban home, which, when built, appeared ultra-modern after the over elaboration of late Victorian style.

▲ White paintwork, stained glass panels in the front door and square bay windows were the hallmark of Edwardian style.

▶ This type of house was so popular in the 1930s that such homes still form the bulk of domestic housing in towns and cities across Britain today. Attention to detail by the dolls' house maker includes stained glass embellishments to porch windows.

CHAPTER 24

CREATING A HOME

As with any house, it is the careful addition of the finishing touches and the presence of people to appreciate it, that make it feel like a home.

Furnishing a dolls' house room requires balanced judgement. The secret of successful real-life interior decoration is to know when to stop and the same applies in miniature rooms. The ardent collector may be tempted to accumulate more and more miniatures, but it is a good idea to pause and take a critical look at intervals while you furnish a room. It may be perfect with one or two items removed rather than with another added.

This applies especially to 1/24 scale; the rooms are so tiny that they do not need a great deal of furniture to create a good impression. Leave some space between the miniatures you display, so that they can be seen and appreciated.

There are exceptions to this rule. Kitchens and nurseries, and in particular late Victorian rooms, seem able to accommodate a huge number of gadgets, ornaments, food or toys before they look overfilled. The classical Georgian room, on the other hand, was sparsely furnished, with most of the pieces arranged neatly against the walls. Tudor and Jacobean houses had very little furniture, and what there was, was essential – to sit on, to lie on, or to eat off.

◄ A gorgeous Venetian Palace is the perfect setting for Louis XIV furniture. This remarkable miniature Hall of Mirrors represents months of work.

▼ A cosy corner in a 1/24 scale Victorian kitchen.

A QUICK-REFERENCE FURNITURE STYLE GUIDE

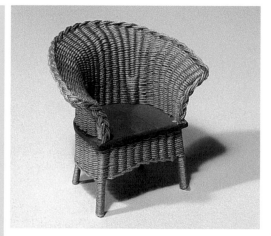

▲ **Georgian** A plain mahogany table was the epitome of good taste in the early Georgian period.

▶ **Victorian** The Victorian prie-dieu chair was designed for prayer and often richly upholstered. This miniature version is beautifully finished and would make a decorative addition to the bedroom or drawing room.

▲ **1920s/30s** An instantly recognizable design classic, the Lloyd Loom chair was first made in Britain in 1922 and during the 1930s there was generally at least one in every middle-class home. Here, the miniaturist has scaled down the original materials used commercially – brown paper-covered wire – and uses fine wire and crochet thread to make this exact reproduction.

The cost of furnishing

Simple furniture will be inexpensive, but not all 1/24 miniatures are cheaper than their 1/12 counterparts. I have come across dismayed makers of exquisite 1/24 pieces who have been told that their prices should be half the cost of a similar item in 1/12 scale.

There is certainly a small saving on materials which can be passed on to the customer, but very often,

if the piece is elaborate, it will have taken as long or even longer to make than the larger equivalent. If it is finely carved or gilded, the time taken in making will be reflected in the price. Tiny needlework, too, can take much longer to make and finish properly than when worked on a coarser fabric.

However, in general, furnishing in 1/24 is economical compared with

1/12. Outlay on materials for home-made items will be small – soft furnishings will need little fabric, card can sometimes be used instead of wood. Plain, well-made furniture is inexpensive, and can be varnished or painted in your choice of finish. For modern interiors, 1/24 scale plastic kits of television sets or audio equipment are easy to assemble and paint, and look realistic.

Dolls are not obligatory in today's hobby. It depends on whether your priority is interior decoration and furnishing or to have fun with a house that looks lived in. Your decision whether or not to include dolls may also be influenced by the views of other members of your family, particularly if you have children or grandchildren.

Buying dolls for the 1/24 scale house

Professional miniaturists make costumed dolls to suit any period style, from exquisitely dressed Tudor ladies and gentlemen to casual modern-style people. Kits are also available to make and dress your own dolls, even in this small scale. Heads are usually of porcelain, with soft bodies and wired arms and legs so that the dolls can be posed.

▲ Men's dress in the time of Charles II was extraordinarily elaborate. The cavalier is dressed in lace-trimmed velvet in exquisite detail, and carries a matching hat with feathers.

▶ A fairy-like creature made from papier-mâché as one of the dancers in a ballroom scene. She is a miniaturist's fantasy from the top of her elaborate wig to the tip of her dainty sandal.

▲ (Top picture) Tudor gentlefolk and their retainers.

◀ A Regency couple dressed in the height of fashion. The lady's high-waisted striped silk dress is covered by a matching lace-trimmed coat, while the gentleman wears buckskin trousers, a waisted coat and an elaborate cravat.

▲ A Victorian mother and two delightful children. Tiny, beautifully dressed dolls which can be posed in a really lifelike manner, make a homely scene in even the smallest dolls' house room.

◀ This doll was dressed by the maker, but is also available as a kit to assemble and dress to suit any dolls' house setting.

Lighting

Electric lighting creates a magical effect in any dolls' house, and 1/24 is no exception, but it is even more fiddly to get just right. If you plan to light your house, it is best to work out a detailed lighting plan at the start; miniature lighting suppliers can provide a booklet with detailed instructions or a kit tailored to your needs.

The copper tape system is the most popular – the flat conductors can be concealed under the floor covering or below ceilings and taken through to the lighting points. You will need an adaptor, which can be purchased from a lighting supplier, railway modeller shop or electrical shop stocking television and radio equipment. It may have switches for different voltages, so that it can be used with either 6 or 12 volt bulbs.

For low, atmospheric lighting, which is particularly suitable for very tiny buildings or two-room cottages, use 6 volt bulbs – screw-in bulbs and holders with two solder wires to be attached to the wiring can be obtained from stockists as above. Screw-in bulbs (also available in 9 and 12 volt) can be changed easily when necessary.

For stronger lighting, 12 volt is needed, and for this, 12 volt grain-of-wheat bulbs are standard. These are, however, more difficult to replace if they burn out. Check out procedures in your lighting instructions booklet before you choose.

Hobbyists will find stands specializing in lighting at most major miniatures shows. An expert will be available to give explanations and advice on the best system for your project.

▼ Period lighting installed in a cottage gives a welcoming impression.

◄ A well-lit interior makes it possible to see every detail of the woodwork in this period home.

CHAPTER 25

THE TUDOR HOUSE

On the following pages, the decoration of a typical Tudor building, inside and out, is discussed stage-by-stage. Instructions are given to explain the simplest and most economical ways to achieve effects, with further suggestions on how to tackle more elaborate schemes that you might care to try out.

Tudor-style dolls' houses are available in all shapes and sizes, many based to some extent on real houses, although a few craftspeople produce the most engaging imagined homes.

The Wealden house

One typical Tudor style is the Wealden house, instantly recognizable with a central hall and a bay at either end. Originally, the hall would have had an open fire, an external chimney breast, fireplace and hearth were added later. Wealden houses are popular with makers, and there is plenty of choice for hobbyists. Pictured here are two versions of the Wealden house, by different makers.

▲ This version of a Wealden house demonstrates additions made in the later Tudor period to include brick facing on the original hall. Like the brick additions, the close-studded timbers at either end show later work. This dolls' house was made by a hobbyist in three separate sections. Although wood has been used to provide the timbering, the walls and roof are made of foamboard and sheet cladding has been added.

► This view of a house under construction shows the amount of timber used in the traditional method of building a Wealden house. It is copied from an actual building now at the Weald and Downland Open Air Museum in Sussex, England.

A CHECKLIST OF TUDOR FEATURES

Tudor houses vary a great deal in both size and status, although they all have one thing in common – timber framing. The suggestions for decoration and furnishing in this section should help you to decide what would suit your house best, and how much to include. Here is a quick-reference list of features common to all Tudor houses:

- Timber framing,

- Plastered walls,

- Oak or stone floors,

- Inglenook fireplace with log fire,

- Painted or stencilled decoration and/or tapestries,

- Oak furniture.

▼ This house is Tudor, although like many such buildings that survive the timbers have been plastered over. Its origins are instantly recognizable by the jettied front and massive chimney.

▲ An extended version of the small mill on page 263. Real brick and stone cladding have been added. The roof features real slates and even the mill yard is stone clad.

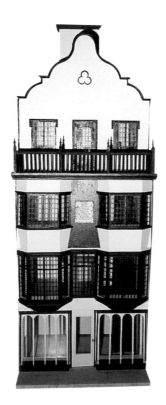

◀ An exact replica of a remarkable house in the cathedral close at Exeter, England. It has a distinct maritime feeling, appropriate to its situation in a once thriving port. The miniature was produced as one of a limited-edition kit.

Tudor exterior decoration

Exterior walls can be treated in a variety of ways. Deal with the half-timbering first, because although you can paint over stain if necessary, you cannot stain or varnish over paint.

One version of the Tudor house seen today has blackened timbers and white infill. To decorate a house in this way, use a very dark woodstain (if necessary applying two coats) and an off-white rather than pure white for the infill (see below).

On a tiny house, the 'infill' (the spaces between the wooden timbers) can be very small and almost impossible to paint without smudging on to the wood. The best method is to make a paper pattern of each space, using a thin paper which can be creased along the beam edges initially, then transfer the shape to a firmer paper to use as a template. Adjust the template so that it fits exactly.

Paint a sheet of thin textured card with emulsion paint in your chosen colour: cream, any shade of ochre or pink are most suitable. When dry, cut out the shapes using the templates and glue the textured paper in place. This method needs patience, but it works well and the plaster-look finish will be perfect.

Brick infill is another variation, and you may choose to add at least

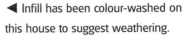

◀ Infill has been colour-washed on this house to suggest weathering.

▲ Textured, painted stone represents the colour variations of natural stone after 400 years of exposure to the elements. The undulating roof is a pleasure to look at.

some brick facing to the exterior, provided that the spaces between the timbers are square or rectangular (see page 259). The quickest method is to use sheets of brick cladding, which can be cut to fit the spaces between timbers as above. For complete realism, use brick slips. This is time-consuming but well worth the effort. Easy-to-follow instructions are provided by the supplier, who will also provide a cement-based adhesive, or you can use tile grout.

Stone cladding is also an option, using sheet cladding or making individual stone slabs and painting.

The roof

Roofing slate is also available both as sheet cladding or individual slates. If using real slate, start at the bottom and work up to the top of the roof, overlapping each row to cover about a third of the slate underneath. Stagger the slates, as on a real roof, using a half-slate at the ends of rows where necessary.

◀ Brick slips have been added below the ground floor windows on this sturdy yeoman's house. When completed, the russet-coloured slate roof will add to the realistic effect.

▲ An atmospheric Tudor interior.

Tudor interior decoration

Basic decoration is a simple matter in a Tudor house, and if internal timbers and ceiling beams are provided, there is little you need to do initially beyond the application of a coat of off-white emulsion. It may be helpful to use the card method suggested for the exterior walls.

Many makers omit interior timbers, leaving you to add beams if you wish after decoration; use stripwood, stained before gluing in place. Cut the lengths slightly crooked for realism. In at least some of the rooms, walls can be assumed to have been plastered over, and in a tiny house, some plain walls will make it appear more spacious. Colour-wash in pale yellow ochre or pale pink, with perhaps one wall or a ceiling in a deeper Suffolk pink.

If your house has many rooms, you might like to add wooden panelling somewhere.

Stain the panelling with woodstain and finish with a coat of satin or matt varnish, depending on the degree of shine you prefer.

◀ Wood and tile floors in an unfinished Tudor house. The maker is building up the tiled floor to show the effects of wear and age.

Flooring

Simulate a stone floor in card, which can look very realistic on a small floor area. Cut out a paper pattern first from stiff paper (used photocopying paper or stiff brown paper is economical). Check the fit carefully and make any adjustments before you cut the actual floor. Colour the front edge of the card to match the surface with a felt-tip pen to avoid a white line showing up later. Cover the reverse side of the card with general-purpose glue, making sure that there is plenty around the edges. Wait until the glue is tacky before pressing the card into place, to avoid any seepage onto the top surface.

Stone floors are suitable in many other situations besides Tudor houses. Country cottages and Georgian and Victorian houses may all have stone floors.

Providing you can find a good pictured representation of stone on card, this is the simplest option to take (see below right), but there are other ways to simulate stone. Make use of leftover materials from full-size decoration for realism.

IDEAS FOR RE-CREATING A STONE EFFECT

The following methods can be used to make stone floors, or to provide stone facing for cottages, or garden paths.

- Plasticized sheets of stone cladding can be used in the same way as brick and slate.

- Modelling clay makes good stone slabs. Roll out thinly, score and paint as above. Glue in place with PVA wood glue.

- Paint the floor with textured paint (from craft and decorating shops).

- Tile adhesive is a good off-white/grey colour and does not need painting. Spread over the floor, score with a knife or a metal spatula to mark out stone slabs and leave to dry.

- Car body filler can be used similarly, then painted in random colours.

A Tudor flour mill

The mill was a very important building in Tudor times, when bread was a staple part of the diet. Without it, people would have starved.

The plain decoration of this 1/24 scale traditional mill is simple but effective.

An updated version of the same building is pictured on page 268.

▶ The basic Tudor mill model. It can be adapted to make an individual building.

▶ Inside, the plastered walls of the mill house are of rough textured handmade paper in a greyish-white, to suit a working building. The 'stone' floor is made of card. A few flour sacks help to create atmosphere (see page 265 for how to make these).

How to make a mill 'race'

The Tudor mill has a mill wheel which can be turned round. A mill race (running water effect) is fun to make and adds realism. This method can also be adapted to make a small stream or a flat pond for a garden setting.

1 Cut a card base to fit the shape required – in this case, under the planking and around the wheel. The wheel is removable, but to make sure that there is enough space left for it to turn, it is best to cut two pieces of card to fit together under the centre of the wheel, the lowest point. Cut two separate pieces, it is easier to try out for size and slip in place when completed.

2 To make a stream, measure the length and width required and cut a length of card with gently curving edges to suit your garden setting. For a gentle, trickling stream, you need only a little white, before the final coat of varnish. Add some tiny slivers of grass or greenish raffia to represent weeds floating in the water. For a garden pond, omit the white flecks.

3 Mix some interior filler with a little water and PVA wood glue and cover the card base, making a raised shape to resemble the flow of the water. When set, paint with a green/brown mix of model enamel, to make a muddy colour.

4 Varnish with three coats of gloss varnish. After the second coat, paint white flecks to resemble foam and spray using gloss white paint. Paint on in a swirling motion, feathering lightly. Then add the final coat of varnish.

▲ The finished 'race' effect below the mill wheel, which can be turned with a fingertip.

▲ After texturing and painting, the card used for the mill race is realistically watery.

Make your own flour sacks

Miniature sacks are essential for a flour mill, but also have many other uses. It is economical to make your own sacks for garden and shop use too. Use any fine, linen-type fabric to reproduce sacking in this scale – an old linen handkerchief is ideal. The flour sacks are off-white, but sacks for shop or garden use should be darker. Stain pale material by dipping in cold, weak tea or coffee before making up.

1 Cut a strip of fabric approximately $1^1/_2$in (40mm) wide by $3^1/_2$in (90mm) high. (Exact size is not crucial.) Turn in $^1/_4$in (6mm) on all edges. Tack turned-in hem in place.

2 Fold in half and crease firmly. Sew sides together neatly, or glue if preferred.

3 Fill sack three-quarters full with couscous or bird seed to give a realistic look and feel.

4 Sew or glue tops together neatly. Pinch together in the top centre, twist firmly at corners and add a stitch or dab of glue to hold the twist together.

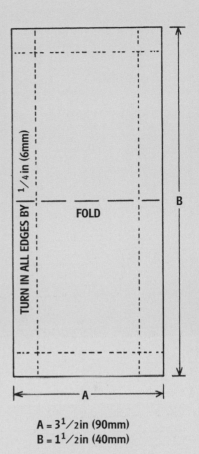

A = $3^1/_2$in (90mm)
B = $1^1/_2$in (40mm)

Make a log fire

If your house boasts an inglenook fireplace provide a good fire. Gather up some small twigs next time you go for a walk, or look round the garden. Keep some spare twigs to make a log pile by the fire.

1 Cut a card base a fraction smaller than the length of the inside of your fireplace and $^1/_4$in (6mm) less than the depth. Cut the front edges unevenly.

2 To build up the fire so that it shows to advantage from the front, cut a thin length of wood strip or card about $^1/_4$in (6mm) wide by $^1/_8$in (3mm) thick to fit along the back of the card base, and glue it in place.

3 To create 'ash', spread a layer of interior filler over the base, making it a bit bumpy. When this is set, paint it with textured paint or ash grey model enamel and add a few flecks of black. Glue the 'logs' on top.

4 Finally, paint part of the logs with ash grey and some black, plus a red/orange mix on the undersides of some of the logs which are in view.

▲ The finished fire before fitting it into the inglenook fireplace.

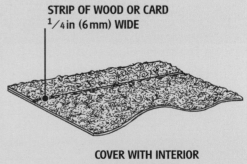

STRIP OF WOOD OR CARD
$^1/_4$in (6mm) WIDE

COVER WITH INTERIOR FILLER AND PAINT

◀ A suit of armour and weapons are the ultimate decorative addition to a Tudor house of grand proportions, as visitors to stately homes of this period will know. Pewter in a plainer guise is used for the tankards and dishes on the table, left unpolished to show use.

Furnishing a Tudor house

Tudor houses had very little furniture. Even grand homes often possessed only one four-poster bed, a chair for the master and a similar, smaller one for his lady. Everyone else had to make do with truckle beds and benches, and servants sat and slept where they could find a space. There might be a chest for storage and a cupboard (known as a hutch) (see pages 283 and 284).

Gleaming pewter candle sconces, plates and mugs, flagons and dishes will make the house look lived in. Tapestries can be hung on the walls to add warmth, and replicas of swords and shields can also decorate walls.

▲ Taken from the French millefleurs design, this tapestry is not stitched but reproduced photographically.

▼ Red, green and gold is a good colour combination to brighten a Tudor house.

Miniature tapestry cushions

You could work your own tapestry, but in such a small scale this may be too much of a challenge. Fake tapestries can look much like the real thing, once hung on a wall.

If you are fond of canvas work embroidery, however, work a piece of Florentine stitch for a cushion to make a stool or settle look more comfortable. Use fine linen or Aida and work upright stitches over two threads in a zig-zag, using enough strands of embroidery cotton to fill the holes.

Alternate rows of stitches should be in a different colour (as shown, left). Once you have worked the first row to set the pattern, follow the same sequence until your work is large enough. Turn in the edges and stitch neatly to a backing of thicker fabric.

▲ This carved bed is based on an early design where wood was used rather than fabric to keep out draughts.

▶ Exquisite hand-embroidered hangings taken from a Tudor design complete this plain oak bed.

Furnish a four-poster bed

Most people like to include a four-poster bed in a Tudor dolls' house. For the hangings, the usual features are a canopy at the top and a valance at the base. Curtains at the corners can be looped back with cords (made from gilt giftwrap string or plaited embroidery silk) to display the coverlet.

A canopy:

1 A strip of braid or fabric with the top edges sewn neatly together, to form a canopy, can be attached in one piece or in separate sections to leave carved posts exposed. Fix on with double-sided adhesive tape.

2 Hangings and a coverlet can be made from thin velvet, embroidered or plain linen. Red striped 'worsted' was also a popular choice and can be simulated in striped cotton. The coverlet should overhang the valance to cover the top edges.

To make a valance:

1 Measure the height of the bed base (not the height of the frame). Cut a length of fabric twice this measurement plus $3/4$in (20mm) for the turnings and long enough to fit along the sides and foot of the bed with $1^1/2$in (40mm) turnings at the ends. Fold in half lengthwise and press.

2 Turn in and stitch the top edges and ends neatly. Attach double-sided adhesive tape to the sides of the bed base and press the valance in place.

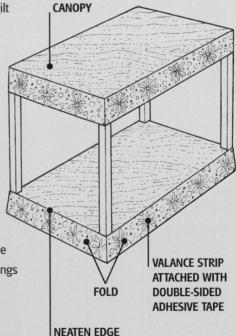

CANOPY

VALANCE STRIP ATTACHED WITH DOUBLE-SIDED ADHESIVE TAPE

FOLD

NEATEN EDGE

The updated Tudor mill

Once you have completed your mill house, you might like to update it. Many Tudor houses are still in use today, adapted as comfortable modern homes. Although the exterior will have changed little, this arrangement is a chance to explore sympathetic updating, with some original features still in evidence. Some modern furniture will add interest to a Tudor interior.

Decorating the little mill house was discussed in detail in the preceding section, and apart from the flooring in the upper part of the building, the interior decoration has not changed for its new use. It is still a working building, as the ground floor is now used as a country potter's workshop, while the upstairs features a colourful, modern sitting room/kitchen and a galleried bedroom.

In the upstairs sitting room the television is mounted on a round table so that it can be swivelled for family viewing. A large modern sofa is essential. Make one from balsa wood and cover with fabric in a bold colour.

▲ The completed interior of the mill house in its updated mode. Any small Tudor house can be treated in an individual way while keeping the period features.

▼ In the simple country kitchen the Aga provides both warmth and cooking facilities. Plain wooden chairs and tables have been limed in modern style by wiping over with cream-coloured emulsion to give a streaky effect.

A potter's workshop

Combining a traditional Tudor building with a modern interior provides many opportunities to make interesting furniture and fittings. The ground level of my modern Tudor home has been converted into a potter's workshop. It is not tidy, in fact the accessories are fairly heavily spattered with clay.

Completing the pottery

Shelves to stack unfinished pots, a potter's wheel and a small kiln, tables, and shelves made from any odd pieces of wood which come to hand, are essential. A small sink is needed too and a few jugs and bowls.

Accessories

For a potter's wheel, use a button, preferably with grooves in concentric circles, and mount it on a small bead. The wooden base can be triangular or rectangular in shape. Cut the pieces from balsa or stripwood, glue together, and mount on a small table. Sponge on a watered-down mix of grey/white emulsion.

Paint a plastic bottle cap to make a kiln, using two coats of metallic paint such as Metalcote, then burnish it.

Add some mounds of prepared 'clay'. Mix some interior filler to a stiff paste. Add a drop of paint for terracotta clay. Shape into small mounds; these can be kept ready for work on a table or shelf topped with a slate slab. A lidded doughbox is useful for storage. Paint a ready-made box with a watered down mix of grey/white emulsion.

▲ The artfully clay-spattered pottery in this picture is based on some real-life examples. The miniature potter specializes in making plant pots, and the finished wares are displayed at the front of his workshop to attract passing trade.

CHAPTER 26

THE COUNTRY COTTAGE

Being small and pretty, cottages lend themselves well to 1/24 scale. Delightful results can be achieved by applying traditional methods, such as thatching and stone cladding. Many makers have been inspired by the quirky designs of real cottages, some examples of which you will see on the following pages.

Cottages were built of humble but durable materials – a surprising number of sixteenth-century cottages still in use today have walls of wattle and daub construction – a framework made of branches lashed together, infilled with twigs and rubble and plastered over. In areas of the countryside where stone was available, cottages were roughly built from local rubble stone.

There are a huge number of styles of cottage to choose from, and dolls' house makers working in 1/24 seem to provide all the variations. In this chapter you will find examples of different types of cottage to inspire you.

Cottage exterior decoration

All the cottages shown here are ready decorated, and it is obvious that the makers have enjoyed their work. To finish an undecorated cottage yourself, stone cladding can be added (see page 263).

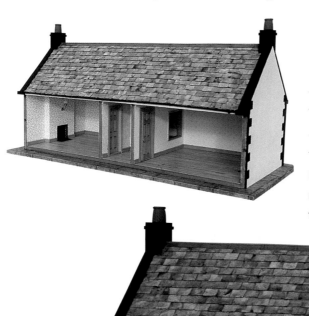

◀▼ A Scottish crofter's two-room cottage, known as a 'but and ben', is neat and appealing. The black paintwork contrasts well with the traditional white rendered finish, known as 'harling'. The maker has provided a working letter flap and a rainwater downpipe. Inside, the 'but' is the kitchen, kept warm by a range fitted on the end wall. The typically Scottish feature of a box bed built into the inside wall takes advantage of the warmth from the range. Planked flooring updates the original earth floor, and a tiled fireplace is fitted in the 'ben'.

▲ A neat, pretty garden surrounds this charming thatched cottage.

Cottage gardens

The urge to surround a cottage with a garden can be almost irresistible, so much so that some sort of garden is almost an integral part of the dolls' house cottage rather than a separate entity. A token garden can be achieved by attaching climbing plants and a small border to the walls (see page 272).

Frame a cottage garden

If you plan a small garden around the cottage, one easy method of deciding how much you can fit into it is to make a few card frames (draw round picture frames or books as a guide) and try them round the cottage. It is much easier to work out what you can fit into a given space if you can see a mock-up in front of you rather than a scaled-down plan on paper.

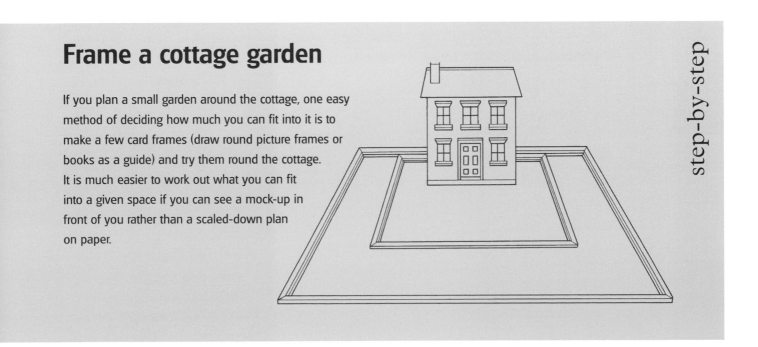

step-by-step

Ideas for thatched cottages

Thatch is a basic form of roofing that has been used for centuries and in many different countries. Today, for many people, the ideal home is still a thatched country cottage. There are a number of different ways of reproducing thatch, although all of them are time-consuming, so here are some hints.

Hints on thatching

Coconut fibre, raffia and broom bristles are all suitable materials. The chosen material should be cut into short lengths, made up into bundles 1in (25mm) wide, and carefully flattened. Everyone evolves their own method, but one which works well is to glue each bundle onto a thin strip of card or wood, ready to apply, so that it does not scatter around.

Thin staves of narrow stripwood should be glued across the roof at intervals and the bundles (known as 'yealms') should be glued on in rows, starting at the bottom of the roof, each row overlapping the one underneath in the same way as rows of slates. Note that the first row should overhang the edge of the roof.

► Complete with thatched roof and roses around its door, this is everyone's idea of the perfect country cottage.

◄ This is a regional variation on a stone cottage. Stone walls with brick surrounds like this beautifully detailed one are peculiar to an area of Oxfordshire, England.

▶ Brick infill and a shaggy thatch give this cottage a rural appearance.

▶ This style of thatch is unusual but based on a real cottage, and must have caused problems in wet weather.

◀ A Devonshire stone cottage, with a local variation on ridging to thatch. Based on a cottage at Berry Pomeroy in Devon, England, this stone cottage shows a different style of thatch with a narrow ridging.

◀ This Japanese thatched roof illustrates the different style used in the East, with a singular form of ridge and a great deal of mossy growth. This miniature was made in Japan.

Windows and porches

Dormer windows and porches need to be covered separately, and it is best to do this before starting on the main roof. The ridge which tops the thatch can be added in a variety of regional styles and the pattern stitched using a strong needle and carpet thread.

▼ In the eighteenth century, the fashion for a weekend home began with the introduction of the 'cottage ornée', a vision of life in the countryside dreamed up by eccentric town dwellers. This cottage is based on 'Circular Cottage', designed by John Nash.

▲ Essentially a cottage, but with a distinctive difference, this eighteenth-century toll house has a unique charm. Round or octagonal toll houses, often with pretty Gothic windows, can still be found. This attractive miniature is based on one at Chew Magna, Somerset, England.

Inside the cottage

Interior decoration is best kept simple – white or off-white emulsion paint looks good, and a touch of pink or ochre will give some variation. A small stencilled design can be added, perhaps used round a window or fireplace.

The original floors might well have been of beaten mud, but later residents soon altered that. Most will have been replaced by quarry tiles, brick or planking.

Furniture will depend largely on whether the cottage is intended for traditional or modern living. Many old cottages today are used as weekend homes, and the rooms can be furnished with modern furniture and colourful textiles.

To arrange plates on a dresser, attach the plate to the vertical surface of the wood, not to the shelf underneath, using Blu-tack or Gripwax.

▲ An attractive cottage interior with pink-washed walls and a dog-leg staircase. Originally such a cottage would have had only a ladder up to the attic room; the staircase would be a later addition.

▶ A dresser is the ideal way to show off a selection of rustic pottery.

▼ A cottage living room can be much more cluttered, with brass and copper ornaments and the cosy atmosphere created by a glowing fire. This homely scene is set in a room box, complete with inglenook fireplace and oak plate rack.

CHAPTER 27

THE GEORGIAN HOUSE

The perfect proportions of classical Georgian houses look as good in a small scale as they do in reality, and for the collector, this is the perfect showcase for miniature furniture. The style appeals to many talented professional miniaturists, so there is a good choice of beautifully finished pieces to fill the rooms.

Classical Georgian houses are based on the Palladian style taken up with enthusiasm by those rich enough to build new and impressive homes in the eighteenth century. In complete contrast to the Tudor buildings featured earlier, a Georgian house, with its plain facade and well-proportioned rooms is an equally interesting decorative project.

▲◄ This classical Georgian house is supplied undecorated. There are six well-proportioned rooms, a hall, staircase and two landings.

Exterior decoration

Stone-coloured paint is effective on a classical facade. There are a whole range of stone colours, from cool to warm, so even with the basic decision made, there is an element of choice. It can be helpful to make a shade card to try out sample colours which will be next to each other on the house, to see how they will look together. Do not forget that colours may look a little different on wood. As well as keeping the sample card for reference, try out the shade on a spare piece of wood before making your final choice.

Before painting the exterior, remove the front door and put hinges and screws in a container with a secure lid (a plastic film container is ideal). Also remove the fastening hook and screws and keep them safe to put back on after decoration is completed.

The front opening of a dolls' house is often a very neat fit, and a layer of paint on the edges may make it too tight to close properly. Check after undercoating and if necessary, sand off a little from these edges – wrap the glasspaper round a block of wood to make sure you keep the edges straight. Apply only one top coat of paint.

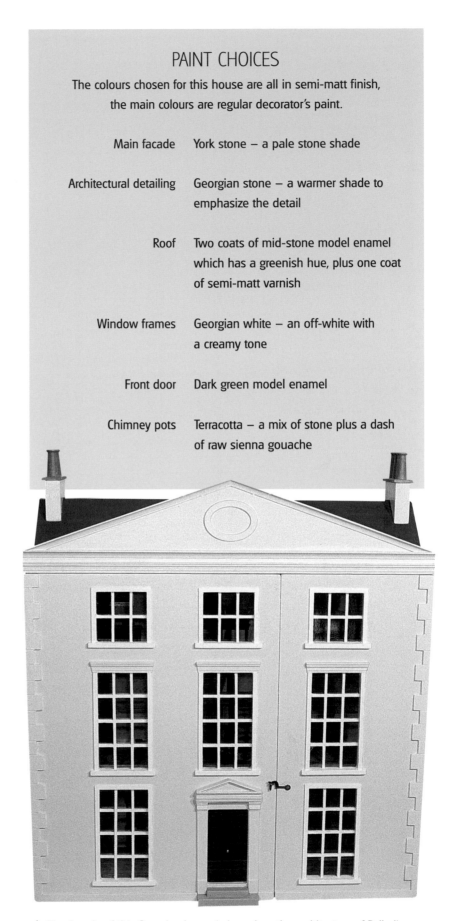

PAINT CHOICES

The colours chosen for this house are all in semi-matt finish, the main colours are regular decorator's paint.

Main facade	York stone – a pale stone shade
Architectural detailing	Georgian stone – a warmer shade to emphasize the detail
Roof	Two coats of mid-stone model enamel which has a greenish hue, plus one coat of semi-matt varnish
Window frames	Georgian white – an off-white with a creamy tone
Front door	Dark green model enamel
Chimney pots	Terracotta – a mix of stone plus a dash of raw sienna gouache

▲ The facade of this Georgian house is based on the architecture of Palladio, and following Italian precedent, would be built of stone. In 1/24 scale, paint is the best option for the exterior finish.

▲ A lift-off roof can be placed on wooden supports for painting; this will allow the lower edges to dry cleanly.

Roof and chimneys

Paint the chimneys first, wipe off any drips of paint and allow to dry thoroughly before starting on the roof. When painting a sloping roof, check immediately after painting and again a few minutes later, to make sure there are no paint runs to spoil the surface.

Window frames

Some houses are supplied with plastic window frames which do not need painting. Most period-style houses have wooden frames, and of these, sash windows are particularly tedious to paint because of the many sections.

Whatever type of window frame you are painting, sand gently first to make sure the wood is smooth – an emery board (designed for nail care) is ideal for this purpose.

Use emulsion paint instead of regular undercoat – this will avoid a thick build up of paint. Sand again and apply top coat.

Note that sanding will generate a fine dust which needs to be removed before each coat of paint. A suction cleaner is the most effective way to deal with dust.

When painting sash windows, follow the same sequence with each window to avoid missing out any parts of the glazing bars – undersides, sides and then top and bottom of each. Don't neglect the inside. You will fit the glazing against the bars inside so it is important that they are really smooth.

◄ This house has eight (non-opening) 'sash' windows, making a total of seventy-eight individual panes to decorate. A perfect finish can be achieved with care and patience.

The front door

Paint the front door in your chosen colour. Undercoat is unnecessary if you use model enamel. Paint one side of the door, the side and top edges and leave to dry laid on a small piece of wood before painting the second side. Do not paint the bottom edge or the door may not fit over the step or floor. Add any door furniture and refit the hinges.

▶ The perfect Georgian entrance. This miniature front door has all the detail of the original house's pediment and pilasters. The railings and steps indicate that this is a town rather than a country house (see page 288 for more of the house).

Internal doors and frames

Fitting an internal door yourself in a 1/24 house may cause problems because of the exceptionally small size of hinges and screws, if they are to scale. Use impact glue to fix hinges on to the door and the inside of the door frame, and pin on with brass pins rather than screws.

In a formal, classical house, an appropriate door frame is essential. The frame should be fitted after the walls have been painted or papered (see page 280).

Cut two pieces of stripwood or moulding to the height of the doorway and one piece that fits neatly over the top. Mitre the joins at the outer top edges of the doorway, so that they create a neat, clean finish.

Fitting an internal door frame

step-by-step

The style of door frame shown here – based on many in Italian villas – has a piece of plain stripwood on either side, as above, but without the mitred join at the top, where a piece of heavier moulding is added straight across to form an impressive pediment. The top of the moulding fits flush with the front but the inner edge is cut at an angle to show off the detailed moulding. This idea can also be used to emphasize a doorway in the middle of a wall, in this case both ends of the top moulding should be angled.

When cutting the ends of the moulding to use over a doorway in this way, the wood should be placed in the mitre box with the plain back of the moulding upright.

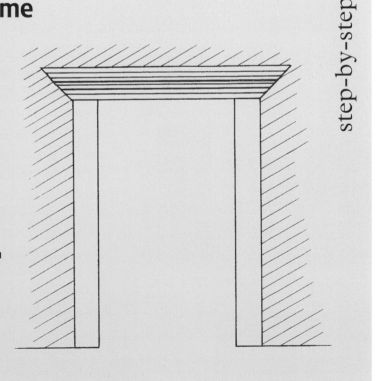

Internal window frames

Window frames can be glued in place after painting or papering internal walls. One simple idea is to glue on narrow braid; it is neat, will look attractive, and is a good option if you do not want to have curtained windows. For a more realistic look, make wooden window frames.

◀ As a decorative, unified effect, the inside front of the house is papered with giftwrap which reproduces an old manuscript. Curtains or braid would detract from this; instead, wooden window frames with mitred corners are fitted.

Alternatively, added curtains or blinds will cover the top and side edges of the window and a thin strip of wood, glued on as a windowsill, will be all that is necessary.

Always check before fixing any added frame or curtain that it will not brush against the front edge of the floors inside the house and prevent the front closing. If this is the case, a paper border, which is thinner than braid or wood, is the only option. Cut and fix a length from wallpaper border in an appropriate colour or design.

▲ The grand effect of the staircase is emphasized by the addition of green and gold ribbon used as carpet. Small prints of 'painted' scenes over the doorways provide additional decoration on the walls.

Entrance hall and staircase

Most staircases can be removed for decoration. If however the staircase is fixed, it can be difficult to see when painting balusters. Prop up a piece of white card behind the stairs if you are using dark-coloured paint, or black card if you have selected a pale shade, so that the detail stands out.

Georgian paintwork was often in rich, warm colours such as deep red, brown or green. Rooms in 1/24 can look small and cramped if the paintwork is too dark, but the staircase is a good place to use an authentic shade. The balusters and handrail in this house are painted in bronze-green, which shows up well against the pale walls. The sides of the stair treads are painted to resemble stone.

Skirting board and cornice

Georgian houses need the formality of skirting boards and cornice to look their best. The simplest method is to use plain stripwood and butt the ends together in the corners. Reproduction 1/24 wooden period mouldings are superior and will give an authentic effect. To fit these, mitred corners are again essential to ensure that the grooves in the mouldings fit together neatly.

In 1/24, any gap at a join, however tiny, will show up badly. It is essential to fill the joins between mitred corners after fitting, because even if they fit perfectly, the join line will be noticeable. A little interior filler can be wiped over the join, using a wooden cocktail stick, sanded gently when dry, then painted over.

INTERIOR FEATURES CHECKLIST

Here is a quick checklist of Georgian interior features for reference:

- Cornice and skirting board, optional dado rail.

- Ceiling roundel or painted centrepiece (see page 289).

- Unpolished, wooden planked floors; simulated marble or stone.

- Fireplace: early Georgian can be plain and of wood, late Georgian were of marble and much more elaborate (1/24 miniature versions are available in cast resin).

- Chinese-style wallpaper.

- Door frames, sometimes surmounted by a pediment (see page 279).

Trompe l'oeil effects

Trompe l'oeil works especially well in 1/24. A painting with a classical subject will suit a Georgian house, and if it covers a whole wall (see below) it need not be framed. Place it immediately below the cornice and above a dado rail, which will form convenient borders.

▼ The painting on the landing wall is a reproduction of a genuine trompe l'oeil painting by Rex Whistler, which is in the dining room of Plas Newydd on the Isle of Anglesey. Used at the back of the stairs, it appears truly three-dimensional.

Georgian interior decoration

A classical house can conform to conventional decorative schemes and look stunning. Authentic eighteenth-century paint colours, wallpapers with a dash of Chinoiserie, paintings and sculpture and a formal arrangement of furniture all set the style. Stone or marble fireplaces (mimicked in cast resin) and decorative cornices will enhance the rooms.

Try some colour co-ordination with samples of paper and flooring materials and sort out some pictures to use for trompe l'oeil effects. Plan the decorations so that adjacent rooms do not have clashing colours. Before wallpapering, remove any fastening hooks inside and mark the holes with a pin or small tack for easy relocation.

Decorative ideas

The decoration of this house is partly standard Georgian and partly idiosyncratic. The main reception rooms are typically Georgian, but other rooms show a strong Italian classical influence with the use of fake marble and 'fresco' paintings. These ideas were taken up by many gentlemen in the eighteenth century, on their return from the grand tour. I hope these ideas will be a starting-point to adapt for use in your own house.

▲ The salon is much too grand to be termed a sitting room. The decorations and furniture are elegant and delicate. The spinet, with its charming floral decoration, is a reminder that long before the advent of television, music was a regular after-dinner entertainment.

Room arrangements

The principal rooms in this house are formal and impressive, just as they would have been in the eighteenth century. The salon and dining room are on the first floor, with a bedroom and study/library above, while there are two kitchens below in contrasting styles. English and Italian influences are combined to make an attractive and pleasing interior with a few surprises.

The salon

Chinese-style wallpaper is appropriate for an eighteenth-century room and can be simulated in card. Postcard-size designs are often the correct scale to suit 1/24, and although it is a little more trouble to glue on separate cards rather than one sheet of wallpaper, the effect works well. Remember to use general-purpose glue to make sure that the cards do not curl up at the corners.

Below the dado rail, a pink-tinged rough-textured paper is used to reproduce a plaster effect, so that the room is not swamped with pattern.

▶ The centrepiece of the marble floor is a reproduction of a classical painting, which is echoed on the ceiling above. The paintings on the walls reinforce the Italianate feeling. The pyramid mineral sample is introduced as an object for scientific study, and is independent of dolls' house scale.

The library/study

It always enhances an otherwise conventional interior to include an unusual room which will develop an idea which appeals to you. It can be designed to suit a particular story-line. As an example, this library/study is tailored to fit the personality of the imagined patrician owner.

Naturally, there should be plenty of books in such a room. Remember when making books to suit this scale that you will need to reduce the number of pages as well as the page size, as the finished book will look clumsy otherwise. The fake bookcase towards the back of the room is a magazine cutting. Look through old magazines until you find a pictured example which is of a suitable size and clearly printed. Glue to the wall and fit a wooden surround of thin stripwood to give the 'bookcase' some depth. Library steps and a few real books in front will add to the realistic effect.

▶ The repainted bust is now a convincing replica of a bronze casting.

▼ The completed trompe l'oeil 'bookcase'.

◀ The dining room is simply and beautifully furnished with 'antique' oak furniture. Like the salon, the ceiling is painted in a pale pink-tinged white enlivened by a gilded centrepiece to add an air of grandeur and formality.

The dining room

Like the other formal rooms, the dining room is floored with 'marble', an idea copied from Palladian villas in Italy. With the exception of the ground floor, this would be unacceptable in reality owing to the weight, but is fine in a dolls' house. The floors are of marble-patterned card – the colours are subtle and the size of the marbling is in the correct scale.

▼ The border round the bedroom is made of thin silk braided roses, which is also used as tiebacks for the knitted lace bed hangings. Golden stars are cut and fitted in a random arrangement over the ceiling and there is a small shower of stars on the wall behind the bed. The exquisite painted chest adds emphasis. Although there is little furniture, all the essentials are there.

The bedroom

Pretty decorations are important in a bedroom and can be more feminine and frivolous than in other rooms. First decide on a colour scheme and then search out accessories which will emphasize and accent it, for example, a painting to hang on the wall. The starting point for the pretty colour scheme in the Georgian bedroom is a patterned floor with blue-green as the dominant colour – a new use for an unusual greeting card.

An updated kitchen

A modern kitchen is another surprise in this setting, updating the house for an owner who may have inherited the antique furniture featured in the other rooms. This is an upmarket kitchen and an Aga is essential. In a 1/12 kitchen it is usual to set an Aga or a range into a recess, but in 1/24 a tiled panel works well and creates much the same effect without taking up valuable space. Surround the panel with a frame made from three thin pieces of stripwood to provide a neat edge. (Mitre the corners in the same way as for a picture frame).

The right type of food is tremendously important in a kitchen. The examples displayed here were professionally made and include some extremely realistic salami, especially to suit the English/Italian theme. Fruit, such as apples and oranges, is the easiest to model yourself, with one of the modelling clays which can then be painted.

▲ The kitchen gains an added dimension from the fake doorway at the back of the room. This bit of trompe l'oeil is part of a greeting card, showing a drawing done by John Ruskin during a visit to Italy.

▶ The replica tiling is extended to form a hearth under and in front of the Aga.

Paint effects for 1/24 sculpture

Sculpture is almost obligatory in a grand house, whether it is of plaster or bronze (as shown, left). To provide a realistic bronze classical bust, such as the one in the Georgian library/study on page 283, repaint an inexpensive pewter miniature with a metallic finish.

You can use this technique for other settings too – try a greenish-brown model enamel and a gold top coat for a convincing effect on an Art Nouveau or Art Deco statuette.

▲ A stylish modern figure which could be included in a variety of settings. It looks magnificent as a large work in a 1/24 hallway (see page 301), but could equally be used as a desktop figure in 1/12. The scultpure was hand-modelled then cast in bronze resin by the maker.

1 Paint the sculpture with one coat of dark brown model enamel. This will dry very quickly on metal or resin.

2 Top coat with bronze metallic model enamel, rubbing off here and there with tissue or rag before it dries to reveal the duller brown.

▲ Work in progress on the Georgian house. The fireplace here is of cast resin. The marble hearth and surround will be glued to the wall and floor before the fireplace is fitted.

Fireplaces

Chimneypiece is the original term for a fireplace surround, which we now refer to simply as a fireplace. In the early eighteenth century, fireplaces were plain and simple, without even a mantelshelf, and were usually painted to match any surrounding wooden panelling.

A chimney breast can be made from a $\frac{1}{4}$in (6mm) thick piece of balsa wood, long enough to reach from the floor to the ceiling. Mark the centre, measure carefully and cut out a rectangle for the grate aperture. In a 1/24 room it will save space if you dispense with a chimney breast and fit the fireplace flush to the wall.

A typical height for a 1/24 Georgian fireplace including mantelshelf is $2\frac{1}{4}$in (55mm). Width varies from (50mm) to $2\frac{1}{2}$in (65mm) to suit the chosen style and the size of the room.

During the latter part of the Georgian period, fireplaces became very elaborate and were made of marble, or of wood with added mouldings of 'composition', painted to simulate marble. A decorative fireplace in cast resin, similar to those used in the Georgian house featured on pages 276–284 will also suit the grander town house.

Two styles of fireplace for the Georgian home

To make a plain fireplace:

A plain fireplace is suitable for the early Georgian house. All you need is three pieces of thin stripwood to outline the space for the grate, which can be backed with black card (see diagram). There is no need to mitre the corners, as this was a later refinement. A further addition dating from slightly later in the Georgian period, is to add a piece of thin picture frame moulding to the inner edge of the plain stripwood. Here, the corners can be mitred (see diagram below).

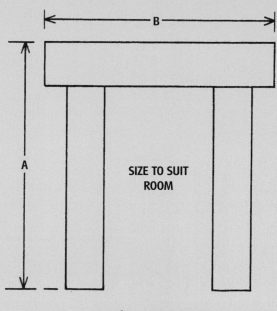

SIZE TO SUIT ROOM

A = 2^1/$_4$in (55mm)
B = 2-2^1/$_2$in (50–64mm)

A fireplace with a mantelshelf:

It is useful to have a mantelshelf to display ornaments or candlesticks. Here is a design for a fireplace with a little more detail from the mid-eighteenth century. A separate mantelshelf is fitted above the fireplace, a common arrangement at this time. The outer corners of the mantelshelf should be cut at an angle in the same way as the pediment over a door frame (see page 279).

In 1/12 scale it would be necessary to add a side section to fill the gap, but in 1/24 this is not needed as the gap is so tiny.

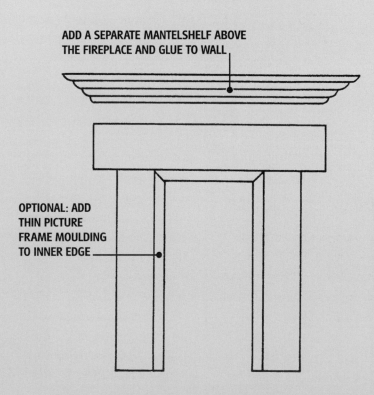

ADD A SEPARATE MANTELSHELF ABOVE THE FIREPLACE AND GLUE TO WALL

OPTIONAL: ADD THIN PICTURE FRAME MOULDING TO INNER EDGE

▲ For the more confident hobbyist, brick slips and real slates will be realistic.

◄ Slates are available in a range of colours based on regional variations.

▲ A splendid town house which shows Georgian brickwork at its best. It is based on a real house which was refaced in the eighteenth century and the miniaturist has included the unusual original feature of a sundial on the facade. The bricks were made and painted by the dolls' house maker. The detail achieved in 1/24 is astounding.

A Georgian town house

Georgian town houses were frequently built in brick, and many older houses were refronted in brick during the eighteenth century to give a more modern appearance. Georgian brickwork is a delight, and the dolls' house enthusiast with a plain house to complete has a number of options for producing a beautiful brick façade.

The easiest method is to cut and glue on Georgian-style brick cladding supplied in a sheet. Such cladding is realistic, a far cry from the 'brick paper' sometimes used on Victorian dolls' houses, which tore easily and soon looked shabby. Roofing tiles are another option supplied in sheet form.

Another, more time-consuming method is to use real brick slips and roof tiles. They are available in a variety of colours so that you can choose a regional variation to suit the imagined location of your house.

Weatherboard (siding) immediately brings Shaker houses to mind, as well as modern homes in many parts of the United States.

However, weatherboarding has been a feature of houses in some parts of England since the eighteenth century. Like brick facing, siding can be added either in individual lengths or in one piece; either looks realistic. Sheet siding in simulated wood is ready coloured, whereas real wood can be painted or stained as you wish.

The town house interior

The interior of a Georgian town house can be simple or grand, according to taste and to suit the exterior. For the traditional English look, the walls can be painted with Adam green or blue emulsion. Pearl (a lovely pale shade of green) which is now available in historic colour paint ranges, was also much favoured for the best rooms. Off-white semi-matt paintwork is also appropriate.

Floors

Stone, rather than marble floors were usual on the ground floor, and card offers a simple way to provide such flooring. For the Georgian house, try to find pictured flagstones or a better class of stone than that used in a Tudor house (compare to page 263). Iron-on floorboards in oak, pine or mahogany are also suitable. Georgian floorboards were left unpolished, but a coat of matt varnish will give a good finish without being too shiny.

Another authentic finish for unpolished floorboards in a Georgian house is to wash them over with a coat of pale grey emulsion paint. Mix a very small amount of grey model enamel with some white emulsion and thin with water to make a wash. Rub this over the floorboards using a rag rather than a brush, and rub off most of the paint with a dry rag. Georgian floorboards were kept clean by sprinkling them with sand and sweeping daily, which gave a greyish tint to the wood.

Ceiling decoration

Plaster roundels and painted centrepieces were a feature of the better-class Georgian town house. Painted decoration is easily reproduced by gluing on an appropriate painting and you can also provide a good facsimile of elaborate plasterwork without too much effort.

Use a doily to make a ceiling decoration

Paper doilies in cutwork designs and a range of sizes are available from good stationers and can be used to create any size of ceiling design from a small central medallion to all over coverage. Paper gives a raised effect which is exactly right in this scale.

1 Measure the size of the ceiling and decide on the best size for the centrepiece.

2 Carefully cut out the central part of the design to suit, using sharp scissors.

3 Apply one coat of emulsion to the ceiling and, when the paint is dry, mark the centrepoint.

4 Glue on the doily design, matching the centrepoints, using general-purpose adhesive. Press on carefully but firmly to avoid tears in the delicate paper.

5 Apply a second coat of emulsion over the whole doily and ceiling.

▲ Sections of doilies cut to illustrate possible designs which could be used as ceiling centrepieces. White paper doilies can be painted over to match the ceiling colour. Occasionally, gold or silver can look impressive in a grand room, but cannot be painted over successfully.

step-by-step

CHAPTER 28

VICTORIAN & EDWARDIAN STYLE

Victorian and Edwardian interiors are great fun to decorate and furnish, and it is worth considering this style if you plan a large house. One with many rooms would be a never-ending source of pleasure to fill, either for the collector or in order to make many of the contents yourself.

A Victorian house could be furnished as though additions had been made over generations, in an easy, comfortable style which would happily include a mixture of periods to show the passage of time.

A large house offers further pleasure for the miniaturist in arranging the servants' quarters in a different way from the family rooms, with simple furniture and bare floors. A conservatory can be filled with flowers and fruit, and garden furniture too, with perhaps a table set out with food and a tea service all ready for afternoon tea, just as it would have been in the house's heyday.

On a more homely scale, a small villa might be a more manageable project. The late Victorian and Edwardian periods provide the first opportunity to include a bathroom, and a miniature suite of fittings based on original designs will be an attractive addition. A clawfoot bathtub or even a hip bath would be suitable additions, as well as the newly invented flushing water closet.

▲▶ Georgian and early Victorian styles overlapped by at least twenty years, particularly in the provinces, where builders took longer to adapt to new fashions in architecture. This miniature was commissioned as a replica of the owner's home, a former vicarage. Even in 1/24, it is about 28 in (710 mm) square and has twelve rooms plus the conservatory.

◀ A grey stone villa with red roof tiles and bright paintwork. Victorian house exteriors were more colourful than in previous eras. Stained glass was also incorporated where possible, and the miniaturists have provided a window in the side wall over the staircase.

▼ The mangle and sink in this spick-and-span kitchen are evidence of the weekly wash, which was generally done in an adjacent scullery or even outside in the yard. Both the realistic mangle and the range shown below are fridge magnets. The grandfather clock in the corner and a tobacco jar on the mantelpiece are as authentic as the tiny mouse on the floor.

The kitchen

Whatever its size, the hub of the Victorian home was the kitchen. Brick or stone floors were usual as often the kitchen was in a basement. Pottery and porcelain in 1/24 are plentiful and even the smallest gadgets are reproduced in pewter, which can be painted, or in etched nickel silver.

A range will be the centrepiece of the kitchen, whether with glowing coals if the house is electrified, or painted. An inexpensive fridge magnet was used in the kitchen below. The other essential is a dresser filled with a matching set of plates or a variety of pottery. Add food to taste!

CHAPTER 29

TWENTIETH-CENTURY ROOM BOXES

Most of the single rooms featured in this chapter have been designed and completed as individual settings in open-fronted room boxes made from foamboard. The section ends with two versions of a vignette – an even smaller setting which can be personalized as an enchanting gift to a friend or relative.

The settings in this chapter will demonstrate that it is possible to achieve a professional finish by using inexpensive and recycled materials which are a little

▼ An evocative 'lounge' from the 1930s–40s, arranged in a room box made from a kit which includes the then fashionable 'brick' fireplace.

different from the standard ranges of wallpaper and flooring made specifically for the scale.

Such rooms are simple to complete; wall coverings and floorings can be glued in place or attached with double-sided adhesive tape. They range from a Charles Rennie Mackintosh room through the styles of

decoration of the 1920s and 30s and lastly, the epitome of aspirational present-day living, a loft. In most cases, inexpensive furniture is modified or transformed with paint and full instructions for achieving these effects are given and illustrated. In some settings, professionally made miniatures are featured which will appeal to the collector.

Make your own room box

It is easy to make a simple three-sided room box from foamboard to try out initial ideas, and then transfer the contents to a more permanent, wooden structure. Most of the boxes featured were made open ended, in order to give the camera a better view – I added the end wall after the photographs were taken.

To make a room box that is suitable for experimental settings, use 3.5mm (approx $^3/_{16}$in) foamboard, which is easy to cut with a craft knife and raised-edge metal ruler.

1 Cut walls and floor, using the lines on a cutting mat as a guide to make sure that the edges are straight and the corners square. A ceiling is optional and can be added later. The front can be left open (see diagram).

2 Cut off part of a thick cardboard shoe box (see diagram). This will provide temporary support while glue sets – very thin cardboard will not provide sufficient support as it may warp out of true.

3 Glue the foamboard walls together and onto the base. Place the box structure inside the shoe box shell and tape at the back with masking tape.

4 After the glue has set firmly, remove the shoe box support.

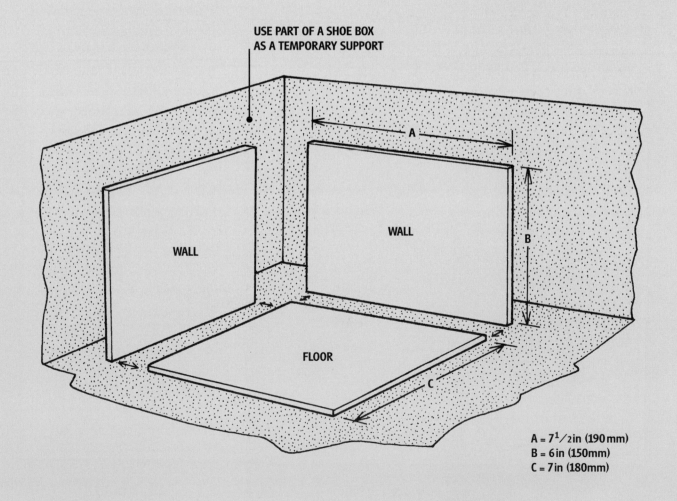

USE PART OF A SHOE BOX
AS A TEMPORARY SUPPORT

WALL

WALL

FLOOR

A

B

C

A = 7$^1/_2$in (190mm)
B = 6in (150mm)
C = 7in (180mm)

Mackintosh and modernism

Twentieth-century house design began with Charles Rennie Mackintosh, the innovator. His austere style has now become so popular in that many miniaturists are drawn to recreate rooms which include Mackintosh decorations and furniture.

Mackintosh enjoyed the contrast of a very dark room next to one which was almost entirely white, to offer a change of mood.

Set the scene in an almost-white room by using postcards to make a distinctive wall covering. Black lines on the walls are complemented by the chairs

▲ The only colour accents in this room are the green on the walls, the pink of the roses, and the gleam of the beaten metal floor.

▼ In an almost all-white room, one or two colour accents make a considerable impact. The black glass bottle is Tudor in style, here transformed into an art object.

and tables, and Mackintosh's rose 'signature' – in this case, two flowers in simple glass vases. The floor panel is a flight of fancy, a beaten metal design, again taken from a greetings card. The main floor covering is a shimmering multi-coloured paper in pale pinks, green and white.

There are so many postcard and greetings card reproductions of Mackintosh designs and those by his wife, Margaret, that any number of similar schemes could be devised to include different elements of his style. Pink and purple were other colours which he favoured to use as accents.

An all-white room has been tried from time to time by modern designers. To create an all-white, modernist room, start with a floor of foamboard; the shiny surface is perfect to simulate a polished, modern flooring material. For the walls, white card covered with translucent white paper will create a light and airy effect.

Furniture should be minimal – small Perspex boxes make excellent tables. All that is needed to complete such a room is a couple of modern paintings – choose your own from a magazine or art gallery catalogue. They will look best unframed, glued on to thin white card as a mount and attached to the wall with Blu-tack or Gripwax.

▼ Painted furniture, well-placed flowers and a blue-and-white rug encapsulate the Swedish style.

▲ The essence of Swedish style is colour and light. The basis for this look is brightly painted or white furniture, blue-and-white fabrics in fine stripes or small checks, and plenty of flowers. The final touch is to add blue-and-white striped floor rugs – those shown here are of cotton, the fringed edges made by carefully pulling out threads to the desired length.

The Swedish room

Almost contemporary with Mackintosh, Swedish style first became accepted through the work of the artists Carl and Karin Larsson in the early 1900s. They, too, were innovators, trying out colour effects on their often home-made furniture, and they were quite prepared to repaint period furniture in bright colours.

Swedish-style decoration and furnishings have become an accepted part of modern living, and the Larssons' influence has filtered through to become an international style. Many furnishing stores today stock designs that the Larssons would recognize.

The walls of a modern Swedish room can be painted a strong pink or green. Planked floors are usually a cool blue-grey (see page 289). You can use almost any simple modern-looking furniture, painted white, with perhaps one or two pieces in bright blue or pink. Make cushions from blue and white checked ribbon, and use ribbon with a flowered trim to make borders on walls. The dining table should be covered with an embroidered cloth; the one shown in the picture is cut from an old handkerchief.

Make a fake window. For this, a good-sized window is essential. In a room box, a fake window works well (see above). Reproduce lattice with nylon mesh, glued onto a piece of blue-green paper to give the effect of cool, northern light. To avoid smears use a wooden orange stick to apply the minimum amount of general-purpose glue around the edge of the card only, and leave it to become tacky before pressing into place.

Flowers and plants are always included in a Swedish room, and a row of potted plants on the window sill will add further colour. Packs of ivy, made from brass, which are ready for painting, are inexpensive and available in most dolls' house shops. The leafy stems are flexible so that the ivy can be bent into realistic curves to trail around a window.

Make a Swedish stove

A huge tiled stove was the dominant feature in any Scandinavian room from the eighteenth century to the early 1900s. Such a stove will be beautifully decorated, and can be either cylindrical or square. A bought stove can be painted white and gilded, using a gold writing pen (see picture on page 295), or you can make your own square or rectangular version.

To make a stove similar to the one shown here, you need two blocks of wood to form the upper and lower parts. The height of each piece of wood is not crucial, as either the lower or upper part of the stove can be the taller, but the completed stove should reach the ceiling of the room. You will also need some pictured tiling – mine came from a greetings card.

▲ The stove is based on one in the home of Swedish artist/designers Carl and Karin Larsson. The tiles are not the more usual blue and white, but a colourful flowered design.

1 Glue the top and bottom pieces of wood together.

2 Measure and cut the card to the same height as each block of wood and wide enough to fold round the sides. Glue in place and trim to fit. Glue another piece of 'tiling' across the top of the lower part of the stove to form a shelf.

3 To make the doors, cut a rectangle of card, size approximately $3/4$in (20mm) wide x $1/2$in (13mm) deep and paint with Metalcote 'burnished steel' model enamel. When dry, rub with a cloth to bring up the shine. Glue in place (see diagram for position).

If you prefer to fix miniature ceramic tiles on to the stove individually, you will need to work out the measurements accurately and cut the wood so that the tiles will fit the height and width of the two sections and also the depth of the shelf formed above the lower part.

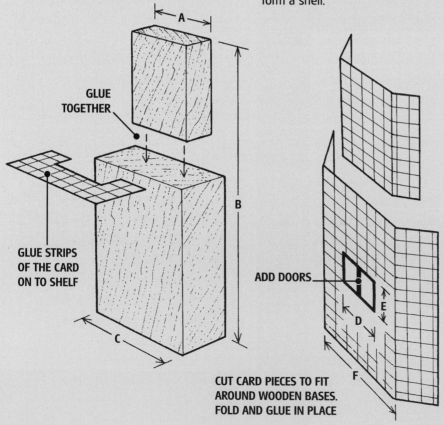

GLUE TOGETHER

GLUE STRIPS OF THE CARD ON TO SHELF

ADD DOORS

CUT CARD PIECES TO FIT AROUND WOODEN BASES. FOLD AND GLUE IN PLACE

A = $1^1/2$in (40mm)
B = Total height to reach ceiling (probably $5^1/2$–6 in (140 –150mm)
C = $2^1/2$in (65mm)
D = $3/4$in (20 mm)
E = $1/2$in (12mm)
F = $2^1/2$in (65mm)

A 1920s oriental room

Oriental furniture and ornaments intrigue Europeans and Americans alike. This was particularly so in the 1920s, when some bizarre schemes were created by those rich enough to indulge their whims. Rooms were decorated in deep, rich colours, lighting was subdued, and frequently both Chinese and Japanese art treasures were included. I am sure that their owners enjoyed these exotic rooms a great deal, and it is just as much fun to make a miniature version.

Finding the perfect carpet for such a room setting may take time. Try using a paper one cut from an advertisement in a decoration magazine.

▲ The starting point for this room is the purple and gold wallpaper, found in an exhibition catalogue. It makes a splendid background for the pair of black and gold panels, made from museum postcards. An essential element in this room style is a large oriental vase, or preferably a pair. Vases in 1/12 scale can be used as floorstanding ornaments.

Adapt a table to an oriental style

Imported oriental-style tables in 1/12 are widely available and can be adapted to suit 1/24. The low, black 'lacquer' table shown here was inexpensive and heavily varnished. It was cut down from a taller size and treated, as follows, to give it a more oriental look.

1 Strip off the varnish. Use a proprietary paint stripper, wear rubber gloves and follow the instructions on the can. Protect the work surface with layers of newspaper.

2 Sand smooth with fine glasspaper and wipe over with white spirit (mineral spirits) to provide a clean surface for repainting.

3 Cut off the curving feet, then cut the legs down to about half length. (It is easy to do this accurately if you support the table top on a lump of Blu-tack in a mitre box to keep it level while cutting.) Sand smooth, then reglue the feet with impact adhesive.

4 Paint the table with black satin-finish model enamel.

step-by-step

▲ A distinctive set of Art Deco
dining table and chairs. The maker
prefers to use a close-grained wood
when working in 1/24, but in this
instance the colours of sycamore and
rosewood are essential for the style.
Extra care is needed when selecting
wood to avoid knots or blemishes
which might spoil the clean effect.

▲ A strikingly original Art Deco room, which includes a cocktail cabinet and
coffee table, both newly invented items of furniture, and a radio, known then as
a 'wireless' which would have been made of Bakelite, one of the first plastics.
The lampshades are made from Nepalese tissue paper stretched over a brass
frame, with rosewood inserts – when wired up the light shines through very
effectively. The Clarice Cliff pottery is reproduced in hand-painted porcelain.

An Art Deco dining room

An Art Deco interior is easily
recognizable. Bold furniture
with unusual combinations of
wood in pale and dark
veneers, arranged in segmental
patterns, is complemented by
the vivid colours of pottery
designed by Clarice Cliff, who
for many epitomizes this style.

It is now possible to find
1/24 copies of original Art
Deco furniture and ornaments
to complete any room in a
typical 1930s period home.

It is essential to get the
background right to set the
scene. Pale, painted walls, or
boldly patterned wallpapers,
and polished wooden floors
simulated with 1/24 planking
or more simply, in woodgrain
paper, are the beginning.
Add skirting boards, painted

white or cream, and a carpet
square; a leather sample,
suede side up, will give a
feeling of luxury. Charts are
available to work a boldly
patterned rug or small carpet
in Art Deco designs.

Like everything else in this
newly invented decorative
style, fireplaces were original.
Buy a simple tiled fireplace,
or make a more unusual
version from foamboard or
balsa wood echoing the
curves and ridges on some of
the elegant furniture of the
time. Fit a hearth to simulate
polished metal – a piece of
not too shiny silver card will
be suitable. A fan of metal or
paper in the grate completes
the effect.

Paint a statuette

Statuettes where the figure is poised for the next movement, such as a dancer or an athlete, were made in bronze and ivory as well as pottery, and needed a high degree of skill from the craftsman. Cake decorations in the smallest sizes can be adapted as statuettes. Suitable figures can be found but you may have to search to find one small enough. A ballerina will give the idea of movement so important in Art Deco style. Undercoat the figure and then paint to simulate bronze and ivory with model enamel.

▲ The completed statuette of a dancer, painted in bronze and ivory and the 'golfing trophy', painted in silver, are cake decorations. These are too large to suit 1/24 as table decorations, but would look impressive in a hallway or a niche.

A 1930s bedroom

In this 1930s bedroom, the pale wood-look paper flooring has a greenish tint which complements the wallpaper, while the floor rug is part of an embroidered silk panel from a greetings card, with an added fringe.

Walnut furniture was admired in the early 1930s. Stain simple furniture with walnut woodstain to give the right impression. Make a bed, using a small block of wood or a rigid box – once made up, this economical base will not be seen. The bed should have a headboard, which again, can be stained, or alternatively painted cream. For a painted version, the edges can be gilded with a gold pen.

▲ The wallpaper in this room, from a specialist paper supplier, is a bold wavy design which gives the right period impression. The little dog – a dachshund – was a popular breed in the early 1930s, when many wealthy ladies had a small dog as a pet. A Tiffany glass vase adds an extra touch of glamour used as a floorstanding sculpture. Use a 1/12 scale ornament if it reinforces a period impression.

▲ The bed is of walnut and the exotic coverlet is made from leopard print ribbon.

It is not difficult to create a modern minimalist room setting which might be recognizable to the young professional living in Tokyo, London's Docklands or New York. Cosiness is not, of course, the idea here; living in a bustling city area suits the architect or the film director, who can relax while gazing at wonderful views of waterside and townscape.

The Japanese approach

The Japanese rooms on this page follow traditional style, but are treated in the modern manner now taken up by many younger Japanese people. A floor of tatami matting is obligatory, as is a low shelf to display a doll or flower. Colour accents are provided by a lacquer chest, a screen, or a painting on the wall – in real life, not always Japanese, as western art is now highly regarded. A Japanese bedroom is very empty by western standards. Personal belongings are all stored away in cupboards, which in a full-size room, would have sliding doors and no door furniture.

A courtyard

However small the space available, a courtyard of some kind is essential to the modern Japanese home, even if it is arranged in a narrow passageway. The courtyard is not intended to be used, but to be looked at, for contemplation and spiritual refreshment. The fake bamboo doorway in the tea ceremony room (above right) gives a tantalizing glimpse of a small courtyard inspired by pictures of modern Japanese garden designs.

A small flat wooden box can be used for the courtyard – the sort which contain guest soaps or cigars, are ideal, with sides about $1^1/2$in (40mm) high. Stain the sides both inside and out and on top, to make a surround. Line the box with textured paper in grey or stone colour. (Non-clogging finishing paper, a type of glasspaper with a grey fine-textured finish can be used.) Choose the objects in the courtyard with care to provide a minimum of detail.

▼ The courtyard measures only 6 x 5^1/2 x 1^1/2in (155 x 140 x 40mm) high, and yet contains the essential features of a Japanese garden courtyard. The iris and goldfish are in a tiny pond which measures ^{3}/4in (20mm) in diameter. The pebbles (which came from a Japanese garden in Kyoto) are carefully arranged in groups of three, avoiding the unlucky number four.

▶ The Japanese bedroom walls are covered with a white-on-white patterned Japanese paper. A strip of bright orange provides a strong colour accent. A touch of orange is favoured as a contrast to the mainly neutral colours. See page 302 for details of how to make the futon.

◀ In the tea ceremony room, a teapot and two tea bowls are laid out ready for the tea ceremony on a low shelf. The black lacquer writing desk was made in Japan. On the wall, a pictured three-panel screen is used as a painting, and stands out against the black background.

A tea ceremony room

Contrasting textures are important in a mainly monochromatic room where grey, white and black provide elements of light and shade. Try covering one wall with thin black card, another with pale fine voile. Make a low shelf from stripwood approximately $3/4$in (20mm) deep by $1/2$in (12mm) high. This can be painted black or grey, or fine wood veneer can be glued, as shown.

Loft living

The huge, wide open spaces of a loft which has been converted to modern living need a no-expense-spared minimalist decor to look good.

A larger size of room box is necessary to reproduce a loft: 12in (300mm) long by 7in (180mm) deep by 7in (180mm) high gives an equivalent ceiling height of 14ft (4.3m) and the right impression of space. A room box of this size is large enough to be divided into two spaces. A partition wall of foamboard with a doorway cut out close to the back of the room can be glued in to allow for a hall or a bedroom next to the main room. Create a perspective effect with a suitable picture glued to the back wall of the narrower room, as shown.

▶ It is easy to imagine that this modern loft apartment is the home of someone working in film or television. The modern sculpture was intended for 1/12 scale (see page 286). Yellow and orange were the trendy colours in home furnishings in the late-1990s. Add some unframed modern paintings or black and white photographs. A floor cushion or large modern sofa and audiovisual equipment made from plastic kits will complete the setting.

How to make a non-opening cupboard

This cupboard can be seen in the Japanese bedroom on page 300.

1 You will need a piece of balsa wood approximately $^1/_2$in (13mm) deep, 2in (50mm) wide and the height of the room.

2 Draw a line down the centre. Cut and glue on finely corrugated card in contrasting colours – one half can be black or dark grey, the other dark blue or light grey. The lines on the card should run vertically on one half and horizontally on the other.

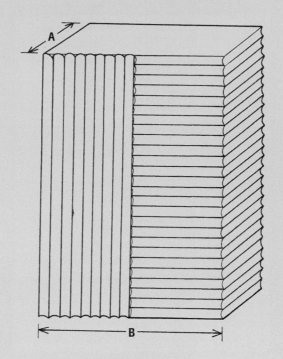

A = $^1/_2$in (12mm)
B = 2in (50mm)

◄ Space is at a premium in modern Japan, where houses are much smaller than in the west. The futon would be stored away during the daytime so that the room could be used for other purposes.

How to make a futon

The futon for the centre of the Japanese room should measure approximately 3in (75mm) long by 1$^3/_4$in (45mm) wide.

1 For the base, use something fairly stiff, as this should not look soft like a western mattress. Plasticized card from gift box packing is suitable and can be cut with scissors. Alternatively, use balsa wood.

2 Cover the base with a scrap of flower-patterned silk and arrange an additional layer of almost transparent paper over it and fold neatly at the corners. (The thinnest dressmakers' interfacing is a good alternative to paper.)

Two vignettes

The dictionary definition of a vignette is 'an ornamental or decorative design of relatively small size'. Although not exact, the miniaturist's term for one of the boxed scenes set in a picture frame is now generally understood.

◄ All the essentials are included in this pretty setting to welcome a new baby. 'Mother' is a lavender bag doll; the stork attached to the wall is a painted cake decoration.

▲ Celebrate a child's birthday with plenty of tiny toys.

Make a vignette box

step-by-step

A ready-made 'picture box' will not be expensive, but if you have a small picture frame you can make one from foamboard. The inside measurements of the frame used for the vignettes shown are $6^1/_2$in (165mm) wide by $4^1/_2$in (115mm) high and 2in (50mm) deep, which gives ample room to make a pretty scene.

1 Measure the frame carefully and cut foamboard to fit into the back of the frame behind the glass. Use the backing card or wood of the frame as a guide to cut the back of the box exactly to size, and glue the sides, top and bottom pieces as shown (see diagram).

2 Line the box with a pretty paper and arrange the scene. It is best to glue tiny objects into place, or fix with double-sided adhesive tape if preferred.

3 Push the box firmly into place, adding a dab of glue at the corners.

4 Finally, paper the back and sides of the box to tone with the frame. Hang with picture cord from the hooks on the frame, cutting a long length so that it can be taken across the back of the box and tied firmly before making a loop to hang.

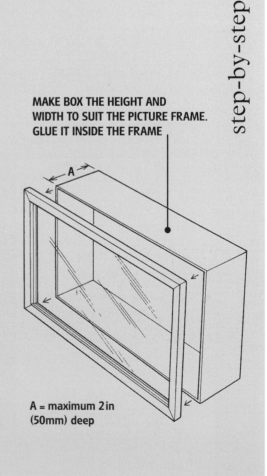

MAKE BOX THE HEIGHT AND WIDTH TO SUIT THE PICTURE FRAME. GLUE IT INSIDE THE FRAME

A

A = maximum 2in (50mm) deep

CHAPTER 30

GARDEN & SEASIDE SETTINGS

Creating an outdoor scene offers the opportunity to design and make anything you wish, whether it is a replica of your own garden, a period garden to complement the style of you dolls' house, or a favourite beach setting 'souvenir' of a happy holiday by the sea.

Even those who do not enjoy full-scale gardening seem to like creating a miniature garden, either as an addition to their dolls' house or to stand on its own.

The miniature garden is, in effect, a room, and can be arranged in a two- or three-sided room box. The walls can be clad in brick or stone or provide a base for hedges, trailing plants and foliage.

Before you begin, it is worth browsing through garden books to find details to suit the chosen period and style. I have provided plenty of ideas as a starting point for your own variations.

▼ A pretty garden with plenty of interest, planned as an addition at the side of a house. A paved path continues behind the house, and the view through the arbour gains an added dimension with a scenic backdrop (cut from a magazine), the edges disguised with added foliage.

IDEAS FOR PERIOD GARDENS

■ **Tudor** Tudor gardens were herb or 'knot' gardens. Draw out a design and make neat, geometric beds surrounded by low hedges of box.

■ Try using green pan-cleaning pads, trimmed to size, for the hedges.

▶ Add a dovecote, either freestanding or fixed to the house wall.

■ **Georgian** Georgian gardens too, were very formal. Neat beds, planted with rows of flowers and often with a taller, standard plant in the centre of each bed, were separated by gravel paths. An arbour was provided in which to sit and admire the garden features.

■ To make gravel paths, use textured stencil paint, or cut out from fine sandpaper.

■ **Victorian and Edwardian** Victorian and Edwardian gardens relied heavily on bedding plants, and a miniature conservatory or greenhouse would be a great asset (see page 290). Espaliered fruit trees were trained up against brick walls. Metal leaf sprays (see also page 295) in several varieties can be painted and twisted into shape for this purpose. Use tiny wooden or plastic beads, painted as fruit, and fix in place with thin wire threaded through the holes and twisted around the stems.

■ **1930s** A rockery was a feature of the 1930s garden. A small pond was also included if space permitted. Polystyrene packing, crumbled into suitable size pieces, will make lightweight 'rocks'. Paint to resemble stone before fixing into a base of Plasticine moulded into a small mound. There is no need for glue, as Plasticine will fit snugly around the rocks. Provide ground cover with foliage and flowers.

■ Make a pond from fake mirror glass, or by using the method described on page 264. Or buy one, made from cast resin – these may also include water plants and goldfish (see page 300).

■ **Modern gardens** The essential feature of a modern garden is a lawn.

■ Simulate with self-adhesive green baize, or railway modeller's grass strip; cut to size and fix in place in one piece.

■ Make paved paths from brick or stone-cladding or use real ceramic flagstones or brick slips. These materials can also be used to construct a complete terrace.

▼ A potting shed will provide useful storage for tools, plant pots or trays of seedlings. The little model below can be assembled from a kit.

A romantic garden

There is nothing more romantic than an old garden with a neglected Gothic folly and plenty of white flowers. This is the sort of garden you sometimes come across in the grounds of an old manor house, a little unkempt but the stuff of fairy-stories.

To achieve the colour of faded eighteenth-century paint which might originally have been a deeper blue or green, first paint with a white base coat of emulsion. Next, paint with two paint mixes, the first in a light and the second in a darker turquoise blue, using the same method as for the Roman folly (see opposite). A few drops of acrylic or model paint in mid- or deep-blue, stirred into a little pale blue emulsion paint, will make up suitable shades. Finish as before, with a coat of matt varnish.

Brick sheet is again used as a background for this garden, with herringbone bricks laid as a path at the side. The trees and shrubs are railway modelling foliage, which is very suitable for 1/24, while the mossy grass is flock powder in two distinct shades of green, applied over a bumpy base of Plasticine. The path stones are real.

To add to the effect, use a mixture of artificial and real leaves and flowers. Long-lasting gypsophila is a perfect size for the white flowers, and can be supplemented by some fresh rockery flowers in white or mauve, which will need changing regularly.

▲ This little wooden building, with its charming castellations, was copied from an illustration in a magazine. The distressed finish mimics faded original paint.

Build a romantic folly

A very grand old country house is usually surrounded by parkland extending outside the formal garden, and there will be follies or 'eye-catchers' to impress visitors. In the eighteenth century, Roman temples were popular as follies, and there are still a few remaining to be enjoyed today. The 1/24 Roman temple used as an example here is made of wood, painted with a mix of emulsion and artist's gouache to resemble stone.

1 Apply a base coat of magnolia emulsion.

2 Add a dash of yellow ochre to the emulsion to make a pale yellow. Apply over the base coat and rub off here and there with a damp rag to give a patchy effect.

3 For the second coat, add a little raw sienna to the paint mix, again paint on quickly, rubbing off as you paint to expose some of the paler shade beneath. To simulate natural weathering, the darker shade should be left under the eaves of the roof and near the base.

4 Finish with a coat of matt varnish.

5 To fit an imagined placing of this folly in the English Cotswolds, the roof is tiled with fibre roofing tiles in a grey-green shade, to represent Cotswold stone. They are cut and distressed by nicking and clipping the edges with tile cutters to simulate weathering. The courses are smaller towards the top of the roof, following local style.

6 A mosaic floor can be made from museum postcards, cut to fit and glued in place.

▲ Alongside this folly, a wooden jigsaw puzzle of a Roman mosaic provides an extension which adds to the effect. This is appropriate, as Roman pavements have been disinterred and preserved in the Cotswolds area, the imagined siting of this folly.

▲ A well makes an interesting feature, especially suited to a cottage garden. This brick-built, slate-roofed example, complete with bucket and chain, can be built from a kit.

Make your own garden feature

A well or modern barbecue corner, depending on the style of your garden, will add interest and also be enjoyable to construct yourself. Kits with straightforward instructions are available to build such a feature in real brick slips to add realism.

Arbours, statues and fountains will enhance your tiny plot, while you can have as much fun decorating a gazebo or summerhouse as a larger project.

The formal garden

A brick or stone-built gazebo can be the centrepiece of a small area of formal garden. In large grounds, a raised, grassy terrace is usually approached by a path and stone steps, so that a view of the surrounding garden can be viewed from the building.

Surround the setting with tall hedges of clipped yew (see page 305). Brick cladding can be glued on to a background wall.

◄ A gazebo based on a real example at Hidcote, a beautiful hillside garden in the English Cotswolds. The maker has reproduced the old brick in wood, painted in subtle colours. The path is made from roof tiles. The gazebo measures only about 3in (75mm) square below the curving roof, but is large enough to provide useful storage for plant pots. The walls are lined with thin card depicting mosaic tiles, which are to scale.

A Japanese tea garden

To make a Japanese-style garden like this one, you will need to practise painting skills. The greens of the moss are softer than English grass, and although railway modelling materials can be used successfully, it is necessary to tone down the colours with many washes of muted green, brown and grey acrylic paints, well watered down, to achieve the soft effect.

Stones can be made from modelling compound and painted with brown and green diluted acrylic paint. Make trees from fine wire (used to make artificial flowers) twisted together to make the trunk, then the strands twisted out to make first branches and finally twigs. Paint the completed tree with a modelling gel, mixed with paint to add texture.

This is a time-consuming process, and not for the faint-hearted, but if you enjoy modelling and admire Japanese gardens, it will be worth the time and trouble.

▲ A Japanese tea garden has many things in common with an English garden, but the ground cover is moss, not grass, and has a much softer effect. The trees are distinctive Japanese varieties. The professional maker of this garden also provided the buildings, and the stone lantern, water basin and flume also come from Japan.

ORNAMENTS FOR THE JAPANESE GARDEN

■ The smallest sizes of pottery buildings sold for use in fish tanks can be adapted to provide a Japanese lantern, repainted as stone.

■ Make a water basin from modelling clay, and add a bamboo flume cut from a thin piece of bamboo taken from a rattan table mat. Lash the flume to a bamboo support with strands of raffia.

A Persian garden

A Persian garden brings thoughts of shady spaces, hot sun and turquoise-coloured ceramic tiles. In modern Iran, sunken courtyards surrounded by low walls are still designed to complement modern buildings, with small shrubs in containers which can be moved around to change the scene.

The floor of the courtyard can be reproduced with card painted with textured paint, in a light sandy colour, or as shown, by using handmade paper of a suitable texture and colour. To make a raised edge which can be tiled, use woodstrip and cover it with an Iznik-patterned paper or card – museum postcards of Iznik ceramics are ideal.

▲ The Persian garden is an imagined setting, turned into a miniature scene. To be successful, it helps to include things which might be present in reality; in this case Iznik tiles seemed essential.

Use blue-and-white miniature ceramic tiles if you feel a little more extravagant. Take care to cut the wood-strip to the exact size needed so that the tiles will fit neatly along the top and side edges.

Bronze-patinaed garden ornaments look good in this scheme. To transform metal castings with a verdigris paint finish, first paint with a base coat of pale blue emulsion and follow with a coat of bronze model paint, using the rub-on and rub-off method described earlier. Using the same method, add two further coats of paint mix, one of light blue-green and one of a darker blue-green, rubbing off to expose some of the bronze underneath.

A Chinese pavilion

An exotic Chinese pavilion would be a suitable addition to many garden settings. The pagoda in Kew Gardens, London, still delights visitors today, and there are many other examples of oriental-style follies in the gardens of stately homes.

► The maker has paid great attention to detail on this tiny Chinese pavilion. The gently curving, tiled roof is masterly and the gilded pinnacle and oriental finials add to the exotic style.

A Mediterranean courtyard

In hot climates, gardening is often restricted to a courtyard, with shade provided by high walls. This type of inner courtyard provides an oasis of tranquillity in many Mediterranean countries and is used for al fresco lunches and afternoon siestas.

Inspiration for the courtyard shown came from the magazine pictures which provide the background. The idea of sunshine and shade is crucial to this setting, and the backdrop is arranged to provide one sunny wall while the other is in shade and is painted stone colour. The flagstones are also made of painted card.

▼ You can almost feel the heat in this sunny courtyard. The setting is complete with a table and a bottle of wine. The pictured flight of stone steps is an effective piece of trompe l'oeil. An orange tree is placed to echo the shadows on the walls, and plants in pots can be moved around.

A beach chalet in a seaside setting

The dolls' house hobby gives scope for exploring new ideas and developing ways to use them in miniaturized form, and the smaller size of 1/24 scale offers many opportunities to try out skills without taking up too much space or over-spending. This beach chalet with its seaside setting, combines everything in one tiny space – the fun of mixing paint to achieve just the right colour and degree of weathering, childhood memories, and the joys of a seaside holiday.

▼ The buckets and spades are made of metal recycled from baked bean cans and the design is handpainted.

Decoration

First choose the colour scheme. This is one dolls' house project where you can use bright colours to advantage. Blue, green, purple or yellow are all colours traditionally used for beach huts to make a rainbow effect on holiday resort beaches. Add some white for contrast.

The weathered look

Alternatively, you might decide to go for a weathered, slightly shabby look. This is achieved by sponging on a thin acrylic paint mix (add a little water and a small amount of emulsion paint to give it body). Wipe some of the paint off before it dries, leaving some bare wood showing. Add highlights with a slightly different, brighter shade.

▶ Deckchairs are necessities for a beach scene, and these examples can be folded and taken inside for storage. Choice of materials for such delicate pieces is crucial if they are to fold properly. In this case, canvas is represented by Nepalese tissue paper, striped by hand with a watercolour pencil.

◀ Shells, sand – and a delicious picnic – the perfect setting for a happy day on the beach.

The beach background

Fine sandpaper simulates a beach. Add some small pebbles and larger stones as 'rocks' to make the background cliffs. Use tiny shells brought home from the seaside, or buy packs from gift shops. Add striped blinds or an awning – cut a zig-zag edge with pinking shears rather than hemming. Make sandcastles from miniature plant pots, turned upside down, with flags of cut paper.

Accessories

A party stick 'parasol' can be used as a beach umbrella. Provide picnic food – sandwiches and ice-cream wafers. (The food in the setting shown was professionally made.) And for the British beach chalet, at least, cups and saucers for tea are essential.

Makers and suppliers

Anglesey Dolls' Houses panelled room box 100, 101, garden setting 121, Gothic gatehouse top of back cover

Angus Puffins Arts & Crafts billiard room 66, 67, Georgian Adam-style library 98, corner of modern room 215

Avon Miniatures rose-pattern plates 75

Marie-France Beglan Edwardian dolls 150

Jill Bennett dolls 257 (centre right)

Carol Black Miniatures (mail@carolblack.co.uk) hexagonal patchwork quilt 202, Michelin man figure 231

Christiane Berridge room box 97

David Booth chaise longue 53, carver and side chair 54, Chippendale chairs 243, double-ended sofa 282

Borcraft Miniatures fireplaces 162, 163, 195, bedroom 192 (top), 195, shelves 244, 247, 'Grannie's Cottage' interior 275 (bottom), lounge 292

Box Clever Miniatures Art Nouveau packaging 139

Barry Brettell Voysey-style table and benches 69

Gill Brookes (of Honeychurch Toys Ltd) French kitchen 39, French bedroom 59, French interior 60

Brooklea Crafts Tudor chest and chair 283, Tudor 'hutch' cupboard 284

Neil Carter sculptures 85, 87, 126, 151, 286

Wendy Chalkley (Dolls of Distinction) Charles II doll 256, Regency dolls 257 (top)

David Chitson black and white timbered house 260 (bottom left), Chinese pavilion 311 (top)

Derek Clift dining room suite 161, two tables 169 (top)

Colbert Designs Art Deco house 153, Art Deco bathroom 156

Jeremy Collins (Gable End Designs) houses 184, 189 (bottom), 203, 290, Aga cookers 201, 285

Sue Cook plaster frieze 89, Buddha figure 90

Glenda Cunningham cottages 262 (top), 275, 272 (centre)

Matthew Damper chair 66, 1950s furniture 70, Art Deco furniture 298

John Davenport 54, 92, 93 (bottom left)

Delph Miniatures skip (dumpster) 184, home office 206 (top)

The Dolls House Emporium front and back covers, 8, 9, fireplace 139, Mackintosh-style interior 141, fireplace (adapted) 142, 145 (bottom), houses 152, 157, 158

Judith Dunger japanned chair 48, japanned chest of drawers and low table 196, nursery play furniture 171, cabinet and screen 202

Edwardian Elegance furniture 148, 149, eiderdown 148

Elf Bathroom Fittings 202, 207, 215, bedroom furniture 170, 192, kitchens 191, 206

Frances England (England's Magic) porch and entrance hall 33, houses 145 (top), Victorian house 251 (top)

Farthingale fireplace 18 (bottom), Georgian rotunda 126 (bottom)

Alison Fleming fancy dress shop 209 (top)

Phillip Freemantle oak refectory table 255

Bryan Frost 261 (bottom) (brick by Richard Stacey), mill houses 260 (brick by Richard Stacey), 263, 268, 269

Lesley Goodall pet shop 209 (bottom)

Grandad's Playroom 37 (bottom), 42 (bottom)

Greenleaf kit house 248 (top)

The Heritage Doll Company dolls from kits 136

Barry Hipwell chest 44, table 49, cabinets 93 (top left and top right)

John Hodgson 14, 35, 36, 38 (top), 43 (bottom)

Ian Holoran Mackintosh-inspired furniture 143, 144

Honeychurch Toys Ltd Georgian dolls' house 276–278

Murial Hopwood porcelain plates and platters 36

Charlotte Hunt Miniatures 17 (bottom), Swedish stove 18

David Hurley cupboard 95, chest 96, bed 267 (top left)

Icon Art icon paintings 106, 107

Jackson's Miniatures shops from plans 248

Japanalia Japanese food 27, display 31 (bottom right), rice steamer 39, traditional room box 252

Tony Knott candlestick 45, picture frame and candlesticks 68, armour 77, 255, jug 138, pewter tableware 266

Lenham Pottery Models bathroom suites 41, 149

Lincolns of Harrogate cheeses 26, ham 28, partridges 45

The Linen Press quilt 163, bed hangings 267 (top right)

Carol Lodder tulip vase 49, Kakiemonware porcelain 75

The Luggage Lady leather luggage 235

Coleen & Valentine Lyons Tudor dolls 256 (top)

Photographic acknowledgements

Jean Nisbett and the Guild of Master Craftsman Publications gratefully acknowledge the following people and agencies for granting permission to reproduce their photographs in this book.

Angus Puffins 67, 98, 215 (top)

Marie-France Beglan 150

David Booth 54, 243

Alan Borwell (of Borcraft Miniatures) 192 (top), 247, 275, 292

Gil Brookes (of Honeychurch Toys Ltd) 39, 59, 60

J C Brown (of Edwardian Elegance) 148, 149

Neil Carter 85, 126, 151

Wendy Chalkley (of Dolls of Distinction) 256 (left), 257 (top)

David Chitson 260 (bottom left)

Derek Clift 161, 169 (top)

Jeremy Collins (of Gable End Designs: www.gable-end-designs.co.uk) 189 (bottom), 201, 203, 285, 290

Glenda Cunningham 262 (top), 272 (top) 275

Matthew Damper 66, 70, 298

John Davenport 54, 92, 93 (bottom left)

Robert Dawson (of The Modelroom) 34, 101

The Dolls House Emporium (www.dollshouse.com) 8, 9, 139, 141, 145, 152, 157, 158 (and front and back cover, main picture)

Judith Dunger (photographs by Trevor Dunger) 48, 202

Frances England (of England's Magic) 33, 145 (top), 251 (top)

Bryan Frost 260 (centre), 261 (bottom)

A G Funnell (of Lenham Pottery Models) 41, 149

Grandad's Playroom 37, 42

Greenleaf 248 (top)

James Hemsley (of Trigger Pond Dolls Houses) 210

Hever Castle Ltd (www.hever-castle.co.uk) 14, 35, 36, 38, 43, 62

Barry Hipwell 44, 49, 93 (top two pictures)

Ian Holoran (photographs by Colin Brown) 143, 144

Charlotte Hunt 17, 18

David Hurley 95, 96, 267 (top left)

Jackson's Miniatures 248

Carol Lodder 49, 75

Alan McKirdy 52, 79, 95 (top and centre)

Mike Marsden (of Yesteryear Homes) 242

Peter Mattinson 17, 32, 37, 48, 250

Catherine Munière 170

Brian Nickolls 76

George Parker (of Elphin Dolls Houses) 151, 159, 253

Pat Pinnell 256 (photograph of Tudor dolls by Coleen and Valentine Lyons), 259

Patrick Puttock 41

Kenneth and Kay Rawding (photograph by Kenneth Rawding) 159 (top)

Gill Rawling (of Petite Fleur) 59

Chris and Joan Rouch (of Toptoise Design) 140, 141, 143, 189, 252, 253 (top), 291 (top)

Rowen Dolls' House 258 (bottom)

Brian Rumble 270 (bottom)

Harry Saunders 34, 358, 272

Richard Stacey 288 (top right), 308 (top)

Charlotte Stokoe (photographs by Giles Stokoe) 153 (Art Deco house by Henry J Colbert), 172 (Egg chair by Kim Selwood), 170, 192 (bedroom furniture by ELF), 191, 210 (top left), 211 (kitchens by ELF)

Penny Thomson 251 (centre right), 256 (bottom right), 261, 273 (top)

Keith Thorne 247, 248, 251 (left), 273 (centre), 274 (centre and bottom)

Ivan Turner 93 (centre right and bottom right)

Pat Venning 156, 165, 168

Michael Walton 96 (top and centre)

Trevor Webster 49, 259 (bottom)

June and Albert Wells 271, 274

Paul Wells (photographs by Paul Dane) 33, 50, 250, 254 (left), 279, 288 (top)

Geoffrey Wonnacott 94

About the author

Jean Nisbett began to take notice of period houses, their decoration and furniture, before she was ten years old, and they have been a major interest ever since. While bringing up a family, she began working in miniature scale and has since developed an equal enthusiasm for reproducing modern architecture and design small scale. Her work has been shown on BBC Television, Channel 4, UK Style and TFI France. She began writing while working in the London offices of an American advertising agency, and is well known as the leading British writer on dolls' houses and miniatures. Her articles have appeared in specialist dolls' house magazines since 1985, and regularly in GMC's The Dolls' House Magazine since the first issue in 1998. This is Jean's eighth book for GMC Publications.

Acknowledgements

I would like to thank the publishing team at Guild of Master Craftsman Publications for producing this omnibus edition, and in particular Gerrie Purcell for her continued support and Clare Miller for all her work and skills in amalgamating three books into one.

This book includes a huge number of photographs of my work and that of others taken by my husband, Alec, and represents many hours of his time and expertise; as always, I am grateful.

Special thanks are due to all the miniaturists and suppliers who provided examples of their work for us to photograph or loaned their own photographs of remarkable dolls' houses and miniatures. In this Big Book, there are too many to name individually, but their help is very much appreciated.

Index

To request a full catalogue of Guild of Master Craftsman titles, please contact:
GMC Publications, Castle Place, 166 High Street, Lewes, East Sussex BN7 1XU, United Kingdom
Tel: 01273 488005 Fax: 01273 402866
www.gmcbooks.com